NATIONAL

REAL ESTATE

LICENSE EXAM PREP

Your Complete Study Solution with In-Depth Knowledge, 500 Expertly Explained Questions, Flashcards, and Proven Test Strategies

PROPERTY PRO ACADEMY

Introduction

Thank you for choosing the National Real Estate License Exam Prep. We know that preparing for the real estate licensing exam can be daunting, and we're honored to be a part of your journey toward success.

Our Commitment to Your Success. We've poured countless hours into summarizing the most critical information you need to pass your exam. Our goal is to provide you with a streamlined and efficient study guide that makes your preparation as effective and straightforward as possible. The theory presented in this book is not just dry content but a powerful tool to help you understand the intricacies of real estate.

The Power of Practice. While understanding the theory is essential, true mastery comes from applying that knowledge. That's why we've equipped you with over 500 carefully crafted practice questions. These questions are designed to mirror the format and complexity of the actual exam, giving you the confidence and competence to tackle any question that comes your way.

Your Ultimate Study Companion. This book is more than just a collection of information and practice questions; it's your ultimate study companion. From detailed explanations to real-life examples, each section is crafted to build your knowledge and boost your confidence. Our proven methods have helped hundreds of candidates transform their apprehensions into success stories, and we are excited to help you do the same.

Preparing Smarter, Not Harder. We believe that efficient study sessions are the key to success. By condensing vast amounts of information into digestible parts, this guide ensures that you focus only on what truly matters. There's no filler here—just the crucial information you need to ace your exam with ease.

A Resource for Your Career. Beyond exam preparation, this guide will continue to be a valuable resource throughout your real estate career. Whenever you need a quick refresher or an update on the latest trends and regulations, this book will be there to support you.

Study Recommendations

To maximize your chances of success, we recommend the following study strategies:

1. Go Over the Theory Multiple Times: Repetition is key to retention. Make sure you review each section thoroughly and revisit the material several times to solidify your understanding.

2. Tackle the Practice Questions in Stages: Start with the initial set of 300 practice questions. These will help you get a strong grasp of the fundamental concepts and identify any areas where you need further review.

3. Simulate Exam Conditions: Once you feel confident with the practice questions, attempt the two full-length mock exams included in this guide. Try to replicate the conditions of the real exam as closely as possible. This means timing yourself strictly and minimizing distractions. This practice will help you manage your time effectively and reduce exam-day anxiety.

4. Review Your Answers: After completing the mock exams, take the time to go over each question and understand the rationale behind the correct answers. This will help reinforce your knowledge and highlight any remaining areas that need improvement.

Let's Get Started. Ready to embark on this transformative journey? Dive into the following sections with confidence, knowing that each page brings you closer to your goal. With dedication, practice, and the right tools, passing your real estate licensing exam is within reach. Let's set the stage for your success in the real estate industry!

Unlock Your Real Estate Exam Success

We're committed to helping you pass your exam and excel in your real estate career. To further enhance your study experience, we've created an exclusive online resource for you.

Practice with Our 300 Essential Flashcards

Scan the QR code below to access our collection of 300 flashcards, designed to reinforce your knowledge and boost your confidence. These flashcards cover key concepts and terminology you need to master for the exam.

Why Use Our Flashcards?

- **Comprehensive Coverage:** Each flashcard targets critical topics and terms to ensure you're well-prepared.
- **Convenient Learning:** Study on-the-go with our mobile-friendly flashcards, making it easy to review anytime, anywhere.
- **Effective Reinforcement:** Repetition and active recall are proven methods to enhance memory and retention.

Visit Us Online

Simply scan the QR code or visit real-estate-exam-prep.webflow.io to start practicing now. Turn your study sessions into a powerful tool for success with our expertly crafted flashcards.

Good luck on your journey to becoming a licensed real estate professional!

Chapter 1: Property Ownership

Overview

This chapter is designed to cover essential aspects of property ownership, an area accounting for approximately 8% of the Salesperson Exam, translating to at least six questions. By the end of this chapter, students should have a clear understanding of different types of property, the characteristics and legal descriptions of real estate, as well as the forms and structures of property ownership.

Definitions and Concepts

Real Property vs. Personal Property

- **Real Property**: This encompasses real estate along with the interests, benefits, and rights inherent in real estate ownership. Real property is transferred from one party to another via a deed.
- **Real Estate**: This includes the land itself and all things permanently affixed to it, either naturally or through human intervention.
    - **Land**: Refers to the earth's surface, extending downward to the center of the earth and upward to the limitless sky, inclusive of permanently attached natural objects.
    - **Improvements**: These are artificial attachments to land, such as buildings, fences, and other structures.
- **Personal Property**: Also known as chattel, this includes all items not classified as real property and is transferred using a bill of sale or receipt.
    - **Example**: A freestanding washing machine is considered personal property because it can be easily moved and is not permanently fixed to the home's plumbing system. On the other hand, an integrated dishwasher, which is built into the kitchen cabinetry and connected permanently to the plumbing, is considered real property.

Bundle of Rights (Ownership Rights)

Ownership of property extends a bundle of rights to the property owner, related to the physical components of land. These rights may include but are not limited to:

- **Possession**: The right of the owner to occupy the property.

- **Control**: The owner's authority to determine uses of the property.
- **Exclusion**: The ability of the owner to decide who can and cannot enter the property.
- **Enjoyment**: The owner's right to use the property in any lawful manner.
- **Disposition**: The right of the owner to sell, lease, or otherwise convey the property.

Real Life Application

Consider a scenario where a property owner leases out a portion of their land for agricultural purposes. By doing this, the owner relinquishes certain rights, like exclusive possession, but retains others, such as disposition and control. This demonstrates the divisible nature of property rights, where specific rights like air, mineral, or water rights can be sold or leased separately.

The MARIA Tests

The acronym MARIA provides a helpful framework to determine whether an item is considered real or personal property based on five tests.

1. **Method of Annexation**: This test examines how an item is attached to the property. Items permanently attached, such as built-in appliances or custom cabinetry, are generally considered real property. The permanence of the attachment plays a critical role; more permanent attachments suggest the item is real property.
2. **Adaptability for Use**: This test considers how an item is adapted to the property. If the removal of the item would significantly alter or impair the use of the property, it is likely to be considered real property. For example, removing built-in furniture that is integral to the functionality of a home office could qualify it as real property.
3. **Relationship of the Parties**: Courts often look at the relationship of the parties involved to determine the status of an item. Generally, the interpretation favors tenants over landlords and buyers over sellers, reflecting the assumed intentions and agreements of these parties.
4. **Intention in Placing**: The initial intention when placing the item on the property is also a factor. Items intended as temporary fixtures or personal decorations are usually considered personal property.
5. **Agreement of the Parties**: Often the clearest determinant, any agreement between parties about whether an item should remain or be removed will generally be upheld, provided it is in writing. This ensures clarity and prevents disputes over what is included in the sale of the property.

Fixture vs. Trade Fixture

- **Fixture**: An item that becomes real property by virtue of its permanent attachment to the land or buildings. Examples include lighting fixtures or HVAC systems. If there is any ambiguity, it should be explicitly addressed in the sales contract to specify whether such fixtures are included in the sale.
- **Trade Fixture**: These are fixtures used in the course of business and attached to a leased space. They are generally considered personal property, and tenants can remove them at the end of a lease term. However, tenants are responsible for any damage caused by the removal of trade fixtures.

Practical Application

Consider a ceiling fan installed in a rental property. The ceiling fan becomes real property through annexation as it is physically integrated into the home. However, if specified in a lease agreement, such a fixture might be treated as a trade fixture, allowing a tenant to remove it at the end of the lease period, provided they repair any resultant damages.

Emblements

- **Definition and Treatment**: Emblements, or crops produced by a tenant's labor on leased land, are considered personal property. This allows the tenant to return and harvest their crops even after the lease has expired or the property has been sold.

Characteristics of Land and Legal Descriptions

Here, we explore the essential characteristics of land and delve into the specifics of legal land descriptions, which are fundamental in real estate transactions and property rights.

Physical and Economic Characteristics of Land

Physical Characteristics

1. **Immobility**: Land's geographic location is permanent. Unlike other assets, its position cannot be altered.
2. Uniqueness (Nonhomogeneity): Each parcel of land is unique, differing from all others in at least one or more aspects.
3. **Indestructibility**: Land itself does not deteriorate over time, although any improvements on it might.

Economic Characteristics

1. **Scarcity**: The finite nature of land implies a fixed supply, which is a critical factor in its value determination.
2. **Situs (Location)**: The location of a property plays a crucial role in its market value and appeal, illustrating the real estate maxim "location, location, location."
3. **Improvements**: The value of land can be significantly influenced by improvements such as buildings, roads, and other structures; these can either enhance or detract from its value.
4. **Permanence of Investment**: Investments in land and its improvements are typically long-term, with the potential for sustained value over time.

Legal Descriptions of Land

Legal descriptions are critical tools used by surveyors to precisely locate and define specific parcels of property. Understanding these descriptions is essential for real estate professionals, as they provide the legal framework for property boundaries and ownership. There are three primary types of legal descriptions:

1. Metes and Bounds
2. Rectangular Government Survey System (RGSS)
3. Lot-and-Block System

Metes and Bounds

Metes-and-bounds legal descriptions are one of the oldest and most complex methods for defining property boundaries. This system is characterized by its detailed, narrative style, and includes the following key elements:

- **Point of Beginning (POB)**: This is the starting and ending point of the description. It is a precise location identified by coordinates or a specific landmark.
- **Metes**: These refer to the direction and distance between points that outline the property. For instance, a metes description might state "north 100 feet."
- **Bounds**: These are the physical features that define the property boundaries, such as roads, rivers, or neighboring properties. For example, "bounded by Conservation Drive on the west."
- **Monuments**: These are permanent markers used to identify key points along the boundary. They can be natural (like trees or rocks) or man-made (such as stakes or iron pins). Monuments are crucial for indicating where the boundary changes direction or to mark significant boundary points.

Metes-and-bounds descriptions require precision and often rely heavily on the physical landscape and man-made markers, making them unique to each parcel.

Example of Metes-and-bounds legal description

Starting at a point on the northside of Jones Creek, one mile west of Stone Bridge, proceed northeast for 400 yards to reach Spring Hill. From there, head northwest to the large oak tree. Then, move southwest to the rock located on the north edge of Jackson Creek. Follow the north bank of the creek back to the original starting point.

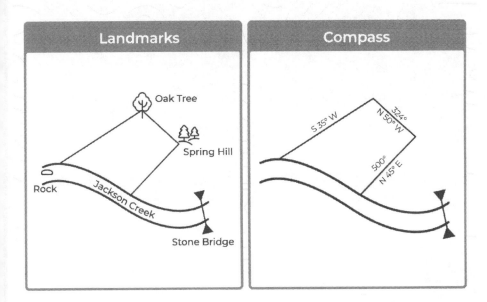

Rectangular Government Survey System (RGSS)

The Rectangular Government Survey System (RGSS), also known as the Public Land Survey System (PLSS), is used to survey and divide land primarily in the western and southern United States. Managed by the U.S. Department of the Interior, Bureau of Land Management, this system is essential for real estate professionals.

Structure of the RGSS

Principal Components

- **Principal Meridian**: A north-south reference line for surveying. There are 37 principal meridians in the U.S., each identified by a specific name or number.

- **Base Line**: An east-west reference line for land measurements. Together with the principal meridian, it forms a central reference point.

Subdivisions

- **Range Lines**: Vertical lines running north-south, spaced 6 miles apart.
- **Township Lines**: Horizontal lines running east-west, spaced 6 miles apart. Together, these lines create a grid dividing the land into townships.

Township and Section

- **Township**: A 6-mile square area, encompassing 36 square miles or 23,040 acres, divided into 36 sections.
- **Section**: Each section is a square mile, comprising 640 acres, numbered in a zigzag pattern from the northeast corner.

Example Description

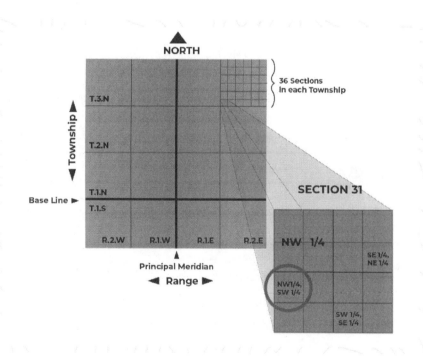

In the provided diagram, the land circled in red is described as:

- **NW 1/4 of SW 1/4 of Section 31, Township 1 North, Range 1 East**

This means the land is located in the Northwest quarter of the Southwest quarter of Section 31 within Township 1 North and Range 1 East.

Detailed Breakdown:

1. **Section 31**: The land is in Section 31.
2. **SW 1/4 of Section 31**: The land is in the Southwest quarter of Section 31.
3. **NW 1/4 of SW 1/4 of Section 31**: Finally, the land is in the Northwest quarter of the Southwest quarter of Section 31.

Full Legal Description:

The land is described as:
NW 1/4 of SW 1/4, S31, T3N, R2E

Or in full words:
The Northwest quarter of the Southwest quarter of Section 31, Township 3 North, Range 2 East.

Lot-and-Block System

The Lot-and-Block system is another method used to describe property locations within a subdivision. This system is typically used after an area is initially surveyed using either metes and bounds or RGSS, providing a detailed breakdown into lots and blocks for urban development.

Key Features:

- **Plat**: A map detailing divisions of land into lots, blocks, and streets, which is then recorded in official land records.
- **Description Example**: "Lot 4 of Block B of the Lotus Cove Subdivision, as recorded in Map Book 23, Page 12 at the Recorder of Deeds."

This system is critical for identifying property boundaries in residential neighborhoods and commercial areas where precise lot identification facilitates legal clarity and property management.

Example of a legal description of Lot-and-Block System

Lot 4, Block B, Rolling Acres Subdivision, Pinellas County, Florida.

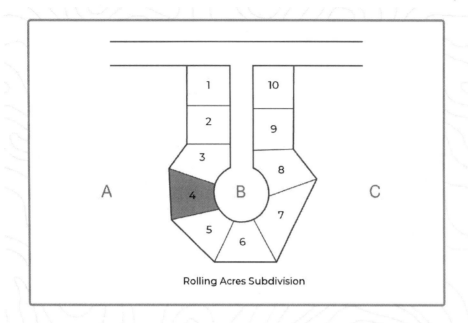

Rolling Acres Subdivision

Air Lots and Survey Datums

Air Lots

- **Definition:** Air lots are parcels of airspace above land parcels. These are often defined and regulated in urban areas for the development of airspace and the construction of structures like skyscrapers.
- **Measurement:** The boundaries are typically based on the perimeter of the land parcel below, with heights determined by local government regulations.

Datums and Benchmarks

- **Datum:** A horizontal plane from which heights and depths are measured. In surveying, it serves as a point of reference for measuring land elevations.
- **Benchmark:** A physical marker that indicates a known elevation point. These markers are often metal plates fixed at certain locations, providing a reliable reference for elevation measurements throughout the surveying process.

Mineral, Air, and Water Rights in Real Estate

Mineral Rights

Mineral rights, or subsurface rights, are the entitlements to extract minerals—such as oil, gas, and coal—from beneath the surface of a property. These rights can be sold or leased independently from the land itself, creating potential income streams for the landowner or rights holder.

Air Rights

Air rights pertain to the use of the space above the physical surface of the land. This can include constructing buildings or other structures above the land, and these rights can be particularly valuable in densely populated or urban areas.

Water Rights

1. **Riparian Rights**
   - Applicable to properties adjacent to flowing bodies of water like rivers and streams.
   - Navigable Waters: Property owners own the land up to the water's edge.
   - Non-navigable Waters: Owners possess the land extending to the midpoint of the waterway.
2. **Littoral Rights**
   - Pertinent to properties abutting static bodies of water such as lakes and seas.
   - Owners can use the water but cannot alter its natural state, such as by diverting or containing it.
3. **Prior Appropriation**
   - Often the rule in drier regions, this doctrine grants water rights to the first person to take water from a source for "beneficial use" (e.g., irrigation, industrial use).
   - Rights are maintained through continued use and are not dependent on land ownership.

Natural Processes Affecting Water Rights

- **Alluvion**: The new land gained from accretion, which legally becomes part of the property to which it is added.
- **Erosion**: The gradual wearing away of land by water, wind, or other natural forces, which can diminish property boundaries.

- **Accretion**: The natural process by which a water body deposits sediment that gradually builds up, extending a property's boundary.
- **Avulsion**: A rapid and noticeable loss of land due to sudden changes in water flow, such as during a flood.
- **Reliction**: The increase in land area when water recedes permanently, uncovering new land that becomes part of the adjoining property.

Encumbrances and Their Impact on Property Ownership

Encumbrances are legal liabilities attached to property that can limit the owner's ability to use or transfer the property and potentially affect its value.

Types of Encumbrances

Common Encumbrances

- **Liens**: A lien is a legal right or interest that a creditor has in another's property, lasting until a debt or duty that it secures is satisfied.
- **Easements**: The right of one property owner to use another's land for a specific, limited purpose.
- **Encroachments**: When part of a structure or improvement intrudes into neighboring land without permission.
- **Licenses**: Permission that can be revoked to use the land of another without possessing any estate in the land.

Lien Classifications

1. **Voluntary Liens**
   - Typically, these are created with the property owner's consent.
   - Example: Mortgages are voluntary liens where the homeowner chooses to borrow money, securing the loan against their home.
2. **Involuntary Liens**
   - Imposed without the property owner's consent.
   - Example: Property tax liens or judgment liens where a court grants a creditor an interest in the debtor's property.

Specific vs. General Liens

- **General Liens**: These liens can affect both real and personal property and may include judgment liens, federal and state tax liens, and debts of decedents.
- **Specific Liens**: These are attached only to specific real property. Examples include:
    - **Mortgage Liens**: Security for the loan that finances the property.
    - **Property Tax Liens**: Arise from unpaid property taxes.
    - **Mechanic's Liens**: For nonpayment for work performed on the property.
    - **Special Assessment Liens**: For public projects that benefit the property.
    - **HOA Liens**: Arise from unpaid homeowners association dues.

Lien Priority and Effects on Property

Priority of Liens

The principle of "first in time, first in right" typically governs lien priority, but exceptions exist. For instance, certain types of liens may supersede others regardless of the order of recording:

1. **Property Tax Liens**: Generally have the highest priority.
2. **Mechanic's Liens**: May supersede other liens if work commenced prior to other liens being recorded.
3. **First Mortgage Liens**: Typically follow property tax and certain mechanic's liens.
4. **Other Liens**: Prioritized according to the date they are recorded in public records.

Super Lien Status

- Some states provide HOA liens with a "super lien" status, allowing them to take precedence over almost all other liens, including first mortgages in some cases. This reflects the importance of ensuring the financial stability and maintenance of common properties within an association.

Understanding Easements

An easement is a non-possessory right to use another party's land for a specific purpose. It is typically established via a written agreement and remains a significant factor in property valuation and utility.

Types of Easements

1. **Easement Appurtenant:**

- Characteristics: Tied to the land, not the owner. It transfers with the property when sold.
- Dominant Estate: Benefits from the easement.
- Servient Estate: Bears the burden of the easement.

2. **Easement in Gross:**
   - Characteristics: Assigned to an individual or entity rather than the property. This type does not transfer with property ownership and is commonly used for utility and access purposes.

Termination of Easements

Easements can end through various means:

- **Express Agreement**: Both parties agree in writing to terminate the easement.
- **Abandonment**: The holder of the dominant estate shows clear intent to relinquish the easement, typically through non-use.
- **Merger**: Occurs when the same party acquires ownership of both the servient and dominant estates, thus nullifying the easement.
- **Necessity Ends**: If an easement was created out of necessity and that necessity no longer exists, the easement can be terminated.

Types of Easements

Easement by Necessity

- **Purpose**: Created specifically for ingress and egress (entry and exit).
- **Requirement**: Generally arises when a parcel of land has no access to a public road and is landlocked.

Easement by Prescription

- **Characteristics**: Arises from the continued, uninterrupted, and adverse use of a portion of another's property without permission.
- **Legality**: This form of easement can become legal if it meets specific statutory requirements over a defined period, typically 10 to 20 years.

Right-of-Way

- **Function**: Allows passage through another's property but does not permit other uses of the land.
- **Utility**: Often pertains to paths or roads that enable access to landlocked parcels.

Encroachments

An encroachment occurs when a structure or object extends onto a neighboring property without the owner's permission. Encroachments are considered illegal and can lead to disputes requiring legal action to resolve.

Identification

- **Land Surveys**: Essential for establishing property boundaries and identifying any encroachments that may exist. Proper surveys ensure that all parties are aware of the true extents of the property.

Licenses

A license grants temporary permission to use land for a specific purpose without conveying property interest.

Characteristics

- **Revocability**: Can be revoked at any time by the property owner.
- **Non-transferable**: Cannot be assigned or inherited, emphasizing its temporary nature.

Other Potential Encumbrances

Deed Restrictions and CC&Rs

- **Impact**: These are conditions placed on the property that restrict usage in certain ways, often used in planned communities to maintain aesthetics or functionality.

Leases

- **Property Sales**: Leases typically "run with the land," meaning they remain effective through changes in property ownership.
- **Renewal Rights**: If a lease includes renewal options, the new property owner must honor these terms.

Financing Instruments

- **Non-Disturbance Clauses**: In mortgaged properties with tenants, a non-disturbance clause protects tenants from eviction due to foreclosure, provided they are currently on their rent.

Types of Ownership in Real Estate

Understanding different types of property ownership is crucial for navigating the complexities of real estate transactions and estate planning. This section explains the distinctions between leasehold and freehold estates, the various forms these can take, and the rights and responsibilities associated with each.

Leasehold Estates

Types of Leasehold Estates

1. **Estate for Years**: A lease with a fixed duration that ends on a specified date. Renewal requires mutual agreement.
2. **Periodic Estate**: A lease that automatically renews at the end of each period, such as month-to-month.
3. **Estate at Will**: A flexible arrangement without a fixed term that can be terminated by either party at any time.
4. **Estate at Sufferance**: Occurs when a tenant remains in possession of the property without the landlord's consent after the lease has expired.

Freehold Estates

Freehold estates represent complete ownership as opposed to the possessory interest of leaseholds. There are several types of freehold estates, each offering different levels of control and ownership stipulations.

Types of Freehold Estates

1. **Fee Simple Absolute:**
   - The most extensive form of property ownership.
   - Includes rights to the surface, subsurface, and air above the property, unless these have been separately conveyed.
   - Inheritable and sellable, but subject to probate.
2. **Fee Simple Defeasible:**
   - Ownership with conditions that can cause the estate to be revoked.
   - Fee Simple Determinable: Ownership lasts as long as a specified condition is met.
   - Fee Simple Subject to a Condition Subsequent: Ownership that can be terminated if a specified event occurs.
3. **Life Estate:**

- Ownership limited to the duration of a specific person's life.
- Ordinary Life Estate: Based on the life of the property holder.
- Pur Autre Vie: Based on the life of a person other than the holder.
- Important considerations include the prohibition of acts of waste by the life tenant.

Future Interests

- **Remainder:** The property passes to a named remainderman upon the end of a life estate.
- **Reversion:** Property reverts back to the original owner or their heirs after the life estate ends.

Responsibilities and Implications of Ownership Types

Responsibilities

- **Leasehold**: Tenants must adhere to the terms of the lease and avoid actions that would infringe on the landlord's rights.
- **Freehold**: Owners must maintain the property and comply with all legal stipulations, including zoning laws and restrictive covenants.

Legal Implications

- **Estate at Will and at Sufferance**: These estates provide less security for the tenant and can lead to sudden changes in living or business conditions.
- **Life Estates**: Holders need to manage the property carefully to avoid legal actions for waste and ensure the property retains its value for future holders.

Types of Tenancies

Tenancy in Severalty

- **Definition**: Ownership by one individual without any joint interest from others.
- **Legal Implications**: Upon the owner's death, the property passes according to the will or state laws if no will exists.

Tenancy in Common

- **Characteristics**: Each co-owner has an equal right to possess the whole property, but individual shares can be inherited independently.

- **Termination**: Can be converted to tenancy in severalty, sold, or partitioned, where the property is physically divided among owners.

Joint Tenancy

- **Features**: Requires unity of time, title, interest, and possession among owners. Includes a right of survivorship, meaning upon one owner's death, their share automatically transfers to surviving joint tenants.
- **Sale of Interest**: If a joint tenant sells their interest, the buyer becomes a tenant in common with the remaining owners, disrupting the joint tenancy unity.

Tenancy by the Entirety

- **Participants**: Exclusively between married couples, offering equal possession and the right of survivorship.
- **Protection**: Often provides protection from individual creditors of one spouse.

Common-Interest Ownership

Common-interest ownership structures such as condominiums, cooperatives, and timeshares offer unique approaches to property rights and responsibilities. These models typically require detailed documentation and clear disclosures to ensure transparency regarding what each owner possesses and their responsibilities towards shared spaces and property management.

Condominium Ownership

Characteristics

- **Individual Ownership**: Owners hold title to individual units within a building, but do not own the land or the structure itself.
- **Common Areas**: Ownership includes a shared interest in common areas such as lobbies, gyms, and other amenities.
- **Management**: Governed by a condominium association or homeowners association (HOA) that manages common property and collects fees for maintenance and repairs.
- **Financial Obligations**: Owners are responsible for paying HOA fees which contribute to the upkeep of shared spaces and structures.

Cooperative (Co-op) Ownership

Structure

- **Share Ownership**: Instead of owning real property directly, each co-op member owns shares in a corporation that owns the property.
- **Proprietary Lease**: The right to occupy a unit is granted via a lease derived from the share ownership.
- **Financial Aspects**: The co-op corporation typically pays the overall property tax, while individual shareholders contribute through their monthly maintenance fees.

Legal and Financial Considerations

- **Approval Requirements**: Potential buyers usually must be approved by the co-op board, which can consider financial qualifications and other factors.
- **Resale Restrictions**: Selling co-op shares can be more complex compared to conventional real estate due to the approval process and potential buyer limitations.

Timeshare Ownership

Formats

- **Timeshare Estate (Fee Simple)**: Offers real property ownership, meaning the timeshare can be sold, inherited, or otherwise transferred like other real estate.
- **Right-to-Use Timeshare**: Provides the right to occupy a property for a specified period each year without conveying property ownership.

Usage and Flexibility

- **Duration of Use**: Typically, ownership or usage rights are divided into weekly increments over a year, commonly resulting in each owner having access for one to several weeks.
- **Exchange Programs**: Many timeshare programs allow owners to trade their weeks or locations, providing flexibility in vacation planning.

Financial Commitments

- **Maintenance Fees**: Owners are responsible for annual fees that maintain the property, regardless of usage.
- **Transferability**: Fee simple timeshares can be sold or passed on, whereas right-to-use timeshares often expire after a set period without inheritance rights.

Common-interest ownership offers alternatives to traditional property ownership, catering to diverse needs and preferences in real estate. Each model presents unique advantages and challenges, from the shared responsibilities in condominiums and co-ops to the flexible vacation options provided by timeshares.

Specialized Forms of Property Ownership

In addition to traditional forms of property ownership, there are specialized types that cater to specific living arrangements and community planning concepts.

Townhomes

Definition and Structure

- **Ownership**: Owners of townhomes hold title to both the interior and exterior of their units, including the land on which the unit sits. This contrasts with condominiums, where owners typically do not own the land directly outside their walls.
- **Physical Layout**: Townhomes are characterized by shared walls between units but separate entrances and often multiple floors, combining elements of single-family homes and condominiums.

Planned Unit Developments (PUDs)

Concept and Composition

- **Mixed Use**: PUDs combine residential, commercial, and sometimes industrial components within a single development. This allows for a diversified and integrated community.
- **Land and Improvements**: Owners in a PUD own their individual units and share ownership of common areas, which may include parks, pools, and other recreational facilities.

Townhomes and Planned Unit Developments represent unique forms of property ownership that offer distinct advantages and responsibilities.

Summary

This chapter serves as a foundational exploration into the nuances of property types and ownership in the real estate realm. It distinguishes between land, real estate, and real property, elaborating on the associated legal rights such as possession, control, exclusion, enjoyment, and disposition that accompany property ownership. The chapter also delves into the physical and economic characteristics that define the land, outlines the primary methods for its legal description (Metes and Bounds, Rectangular Government Survey System, and Lot and Block), and discusses the significance of legal terminologies and encumbrances that can affect property transactions.

Additionally, it covers various ownership structures, from freehold and leasehold estates to common-interest ownerships like condominiums and cooperatives, providing a comprehensive overview essential for understanding and navigating the complex landscape of real estate ownership.

Chapter 2: Land Use Controls and Regulations

Overview

This chapter explores the critical aspects of land use controls and regulations, vital knowledge for any aspiring real estate professional. Land use policies are essential for managing community growth, preserving resources, and ensuring the orderly development of communities. This chapter will help you understand both private and public mechanisms that regulate land use, their enforcement, and the roles of various authorities in shaping local land environments. This chapter accounts approximately 5% of the exam.

Government Rights in Land

Police Power

Police Power represents the authority vested in government at any level—federal, state, or local—to enact and enforce laws aimed at promoting the health, safety, and general welfare of the public. This broad power underpins a range of regulations that directly impact land use and real estate practices:

- **Licensing**: Ensuring that individuals and businesses comply with standards that protect public welfare.
- **Public Services**: Implementation and maintenance of services that enhance community living standards.
- **Zoning**: Designating land for specific uses such as residential, commercial, or industrial to ensure orderly development.
- **Building Codes**: Establishing minimum standards for building construction and maintenance to ensure public safety and welfare.

Taxation as a Land Use Control Tool

Taxation serves as a pivotal mechanism under government police power, facilitating the financing of essential public works and services. This financial tool is crucial for maintaining and enhancing community infrastructure, which directly impacts real estate values and quality of life.

- **Ad Valorem Taxes**: These taxes are levied based on the property's assessed value. Typically, they fund critical public services such as educational institutions, law enforcement, and fire protection agencies. The equitable distribution of this tax burden ensures a stable income source for local governments, maintaining and improving public amenities that benefit all residents.

- **Special Assessment Taxes**: These are levied on properties that directly benefit from specific public improvements. For instance, the installation of a new sewer system or water lines on a particular street will be funded by taxing the benefiting properties. This ensures that the financial burden of such improvements is fairly shouldered by those who will benefit the most. Examples of other enhancements that might be subject to special assessment taxes include the paving of streets, installation of curbs and sidewalks, or the addition of street lighting.

It is important to note that in most states, property tax liens have precedence over all other property liens, highlighting the priority given to municipal financing and funding.

Eminent Domain and Related Concepts

Eminent Domain is a critical governmental power allowing the compulsory acquisition of private property for public use, provided fair compensation is given. This power is essential for executing large-scale public projects that require land currently in private hands.

- **Example**: A utility company needs to build a new power line route that crosses private lands. Using eminent domain, the government can acquire these lands to facilitate this necessary infrastructure project, ensuring compensation for affected landowners.

Condemnation Action is the legal process involved in eminent domain, where the government formally takes title and possession of the private property. This process ensures that the property owner receives just compensation, reflecting the property's market value.

Inverse Condemnation occurs when the government effectively takes private property but does not provide compensation. In such cases, property owners must seek legal recourse to obtain due compensation. Inverse condemnation can be either:

- **Physical**: where the government physically occupies or appropriates the property.
- **Regulatory**: where government regulations significantly impair the property's economic value.

Escheat

Escheat is a state's reversionary power to claim property when an individual dies intestate (without a will), and without heirs or creditors. This mechanism ensures that the property is not left ownerless but instead can be utilized for the public's benefit, typically entering the state's public domain.

Government Controls: Zoning and Master Plans

Zoning is a critical aspect of land use planning, employed under the government's police power. This power allows state, county, city, and town governments to classify land for specific uses, ensuring that the development and growth of communities are organized and rational. Zoning ordinances are the tools through which local governments implement their comprehensive plans. These ordinances dictate everything from the size of lots to the types of buildings that can be constructed and their uses, based on the zoning classification assigned to each parcel of land.

Zoning Ordinances and Compliance

Zoning ordinances are local laws that regulate land use and are usually enforced at the city level. They define permissible uses for land and buildings, including:

- Lot size
- Building height
- Permitted uses for each zone
- Setback requirements

Developers must adhere to these ordinances and typically demonstrate compliance by applying for permits, which are granted only if the proposed developments are not at odds with existing zoning laws. It is crucial that zoning ordinances do not conflict with federal laws, such as the Fair Housing Act, which aims to eliminate discrimination in housing.

Master Plans and Zoning Consistency

Zoning should align with the area's master plan—a comprehensive document that outlines long-term goals for growth and development based on community needs and priorities. This ensures that zoning decisions support broader objectives such as economic development, transportation planning, and resource management.

Zoning Classifications

Zoning classifications dictate the permissible uses of land within specific areas, facilitating organized growth and development:

- **Residential**: Areas designated primarily for housing.
- **Commercial**: Zones where retail, offices, and other businesses are permitted.
- **Industrial**: Areas intended for manufacturing, warehousing, and other industrial uses.
- **Agricultural**: Land used for farming and related activities.
- **Open Space**: Areas preserved for natural landscapes, often untouched by development.
- **Parkland and Recreation Areas**: Land used for public recreation and parks.
- **Mixed-Use**: Zones where a combination of residential, commercial, or other uses are integrated into a single area.

Special Zoning Types

- **Incentive Zoning**: Allows developers to exceed typical zoning restrictions in exchange for providing community benefits, such as public parks or affordable housing units.
- **Bulk Zoning**: Controls the density and mass of buildings by setting limits on building height, lot width, and other spatial dimensions.
- **Aesthetic Zoning**: Ensures that developments conform to a community's architectural standards, preserving visual harmony.
- **Downzoning**: Reduces the density of development allowed in an area, typically changing from a higher-density use (like commercial) to a lower-density use (like residential).
- **Density Zoning**: Regulates the number of units allowed per area, such as the number of houses per acre.
- **Spot Zoning**: Changes the zoning for a specific property to a classification differing from surrounding properties, often controversial due to its potential to disrupt existing plans.

Understanding these zoning types and their applications is essential for real estate professionals, as it directly affects property values and development possibilities.

Zoning Actions: Navigating Exceptions and Restrictions

Zoning actions are specific measures and permissions that can alter how properties are utilized, often deviating from the standard regulations dictated by local zoning ordinances. These actions are crucial for property owners and prospective buyers to understand, as they can significantly impact what can and cannot be done with a property.

Key Zoning Actions

1. **Nonconforming Use:**
   - This refers to a property that does not conform to current zoning classifications but is allowed to exist due to its presence before the new zoning laws were enacted. An example is a residential home that now sits within a commercially zoned area. These are often "grandfathered" in, allowing the use to continue under previous conditions despite zoning changes.

2. **Moratorium:**
   - A temporary suspension of new development or zoning permits to halt construction and development activities. This is usually enacted to provide time for planning changes or to prevent uncontrolled growth during critical planning phases.

3. **Special Use Permit (Conditional Use Permit):**
   - Allows for a land use that is not typically permitted within a zoning category but is considered acceptable under certain conditions. For example, permitting a church or school to operate within a residential zone. These permits often require community input and adherence to specific conditions.

4. **Variance (Use Variance):**
   - A variance is a deviation from the set zoning requirements that can be granted when adherence to zoning laws imposes significant hardship or practical difficulties. This is particularly relevant when the strict application of zoning regulations deprives the property of privileges enjoyed by other properties in the vicinity. Public hearings are a prerequisite for obtaining a variance, ensuring transparency and community involvement.

Regulatory Bodies and Public Involvement

- **Zoning Appeals Board**: This board handles appeals and challenges to zoning decisions. It plays a crucial role for property owners looking to contest or modify zoning restrictions impacting their properties.
- **Planning Board**: Responsible for developing and maintaining the master plan or comprehensive plan of a community, which guides long-term development including budget considerations. The board's decisions can significantly influence zoning actions and land use planning.

- **Public Meetings**: Meetings of planning and zoning boards are generally open to the public, mandated by sunshine laws. These laws ensure transparency and public participation in governmental decisions that affect community development.
- **Sunshine Laws**: At the federal level, public access to agency meetings is governed by the Sunshine Act, part of the Freedom of Information Act (FOIA). States typically have their own versions of these laws, facilitating open government and accountability.

Practical Implications for Property Owners

Prospective property owners should be well-versed in local zoning ordinances and the availability of actions like variances and special use permits. Understanding these elements is essential for assessing the potential and limitations of a property, particularly if intending to use the property in ways that deviate from current zoning.

Zoning Terms

Subdivision

A subdivision refers to an area of land that has been divided into lots for the purpose of development. This process typically involves the partitioning of a larger tract into smaller parcels that can be sold separately and developed independently.

Plat Map

A plat map is a detailed map of a subdivision that outlines a tract of land, showing various essential elements such as the boundaries of individual properties, the location of streets, easements, and other significant details. Developers are required to submit this map to a planning board or zoning commission for approval before development can proceed. This ensures that the proposed subdivision conforms to local zoning and planning regulations.

Building Codes

Building codes are regulatory standards that dictate the requirements for construction projects to ensure the safety and functionality of buildings. These codes are crucial for protecting the well-being of occupants and the general public by specifying how buildings must be constructed, the materials used, and other related safety and sanitary standards.

State and Local Building Codes

- **State Building Codes**: These provide the foundational standards for all residential and commercial buildings within a state. They establish the minimum requirements that must be met for the safety, efficiency, and general welfare of building occupants.
- **Local Building Codes**: Local municipalities may implement additional regulations that complement or exceed state codes. These local codes are tailored to address specific needs and conditions of the local environment, such as climate, geography, and local risks.

Compliance and Enforcement

- **Building Permits**: Before construction begins, builders must obtain building permits from local authorities. These permits are essential for ensuring that the planned construction adheres to both state and local building codes.
- **Building Inspections**: As construction progresses, building inspectors conduct reviews to ensure ongoing compliance with the relevant building codes. This oversight helps to prevent potential safety hazards and ensure that construction standards are met throughout the building process.

Existing Buildings

Most municipalities allow existing buildings to be sold and occupied even if they do not meet current building codes, as long as they complied with the codes at the time of their construction. This provision recognizes the impracticality of continually retrofitting older buildings to meet new code requirements.

Federal Building Codes

In situations where no state or local building codes exist, builders must comply with federal building codes. Although less common, these codes serve as a universal standard in areas not covered by state or local regulations.

Understanding and adhering to building codes is essential for developers, builders, and anyone involved in constructing or renovating buildings, ensuring that all structures provide safe and functional spaces for their intended uses.

Regulation of Special Land Types

Wetlands

Wetlands are ecologically sensitive areas saturated with water either permanently or seasonally. The presence of specific vegetation adapted to these conditions is a key characteristic of wetlands. Given their environmental importance, many states have established regulations to protect these areas, complemented by federal oversight from various government agencies under guidelines such as those outlined in the Clean Water Act.

- **Regulations and Restrictions**: The designation of an area as a wetland can significantly restrict what can be done with the property. For example, construction activities are typically limited to prevent disruption of the natural habitat and ecological balance.
- **Impact on Property Value**: The presence of wetlands on a property can affect its value and should be carefully considered during property appraisal processes. While wetlands can enhance the ecological value of a property, they can also impose limitations that might affect marketability and development potential.

Flood Zones

Flood zones, or floodplains, are areas identified as prone to flooding, especially those near water bodies. Understanding flood zone designations is crucial for homeowners and potential buyers due to the implications for property safety and insurance requirements.

- **Flood Zone Classifications:**
  - **100-Year Floodplain**: Indicates a 1% chance of flooding each year. Properties within this area are considered at high risk.
  - **500-Year Floodplain**: Represents a 0.2% chance of flooding in any given year, indicating a lower risk than the 100-year floodplain but still significant.
- **Insurance Requirements**: Properties located in Special Flood Hazard Areas (SFHAs) require flood insurance if the mortgage is obtained from a federally regulated or insured lender. Traditional homeowners' insurance policies do not typically cover flood damage, necessitating separate flood insurance policies. The National Flood Insurance Program (NFIP) offers support to homeowners in these zones, providing affordable insurance options to mitigate financial risks from flooding.

Other Special Land Types and Regulations

Lands Contaminated with Hazardous Waste

Contaminated lands, especially those that house hazardous waste such as radioactive materials from nuclear facilities or toxic chemicals, are highly regulated due to the risks they pose. These sites are typically:

- Located in remote areas to minimize human exposure.
- Subject to stringent regulatory oversight to prevent the release of harmful substances.
- Often feature sealed "tombs" where particularly dangerous materials are stored deep underground, designed to remain secure for thousands of years.

Protected Habitats

Protected habitats are areas designated to conserve and restore natural environments and prevent the extinction of species living within them. This includes:

- Laws like the Endangered Species Act, which aims to protect threatened and endangered species and their habitats.
- Management by agencies such as the U.S. Fish and Wildlife Service and the National Marine Fisheries Service.
- Both legislative and conservation efforts to mitigate habitat destruction from natural events and human activities.

Conservation Easements

Conservation easements are legal agreements that restrict the use of land to achieve specific conservation objectives. These easements:

- Are applicable to both public and private lands.
- Run with the land, meaning they are permanent and remain active across changes in ownership.
- Are recorded in local land records, becoming a part of the property's legal title.
- Limit development and specific uses of the land to protect its ecological or open-space values.

Municipality

A municipality refers to a city or town that is officially recognized and has its own local government. Municipal governments are typically responsible for local ordinances, including zoning and land use regulations.

Historical Landmarks

Historical landmarks are protected areas designated to preserve the cultural heritage of a location. Regulations concerning these landmarks:

- Are enforced by historic preservation commissions at the state or local level.
- Focus on preserving the character and integrity of historic sites and buildings rather than land use per se.
- May restrict owners from altering, demolishing, or otherwise changing the designated buildings, both externally and internally.
- Involve review processes for any proposed changes that affect the historical aspects of the landmarks.

These special land types and the associated regulations play crucial roles in managing environmental risks, conserving valuable habitats, preserving historical and cultural heritage, and maintaining public health and safety.

Regulation of Environmental Hazards in Real Estate

When dealing with real estate properties, it's crucial to be aware of potential environmental hazards that may affect the health and safety of occupants and the legal obligations of property owners and real estate professionals.

Expert Involvement and Inspections

Real estate professionals should advise clients to engage qualified experts to conduct thorough inspections of properties, especially for:

- **Interior home inspections**: To check for any signs of hazardous materials or conditions within the building.
- **Soil, air, and water tests**: To detect contamination that could pose health risks or affect property value.

- **Environmental audits**: Particularly important for commercial or industrial properties where the risk of hazardous contamination is higher.

Documenting any recommendations for environmental testing and noting any client decisions against such advice is critical for legal protection and professional responsibility.

Common Environmental Hazards

Asbestos

A fibrous mineral once commonly used in building materials for its fire-resistant properties, asbestos is hazardous when airborne fibers are inhaled, potentially causing serious lung diseases, including cancer.

- **Properties**: Asbestos is known for its heat resistance and was widely used in building materials before the 1970s.
- **Risks**: When asbestos deteriorates or is disturbed, it becomes friable, meaning it can easily crumble and release fibers that, when inhaled, can cause serious lung diseases, including cancer.
- **Regulation**: The EPA regulates asbestos use and disposal. While there is no federal mandate for asbestos abatement in residential buildings, handling and removal must be conducted by licensed professionals.

Lead

A toxic metal found in older paint, plumbing, and various household items, lead exposure can cause severe health issues, particularly neurological damage in children.

- **Sources**: Commonly found in paint, plumbing, and even soil, lead contamination is a significant concern, especially in older properties.
- **Health Impact**: Exposure to lead is extremely hazardous, particularly to children, and can lead to neurological damage, developmental delays, and various other severe health issues.
- **Regulation**: The federal Lead Renovation, Repair, and Painting (RRP) Rule mandates that contractors disturbing lead-based paint in pre-1978 homes, child care facilities, and schools be certified and follow strict safety protocols. Some states may also have additional requirements for lead abatement.

Radon

Radon is a naturally occurring radioactive gas that can enter homes through cracks in floors, walls, and foundations, and is considered a leading cause of lung cancer among non-smokers.

- **Detection**: Homeowners can use radon self-test kits to measure levels, with results expressed in picocuries per liter of air. A reading at or above 4 picocuries per liter is typically the threshold for concern.
- **Mitigation**: Recommended mitigation practices include sealing cracks in the foundation and installing ventilation systems to reduce radon levels.
- **Regulation**: While there is no federal mandate for radon mitigation, some states have specific requirements to manage its presence in residential and commercial properties.

Mold

Mold thrives in moist environments and can pose significant health risks, particularly to those with allergies or compromised immune systems.

- **Health Impact**: Mold exposure can lead to allergic reactions, asthma attacks, and other respiratory issues.
- **Regulation**: There are no federal regulations for mold testing or remediation in homes. However, some states have guidelines and laws addressing mold remediation. The EPA advises engaging a professional for mold removal in areas larger than 10 square feet.

Carbon Monoxide (CO)

Carbon monoxide is a colorless, odorless gas produced by burning fuel in vehicles, stoves, lanterns, and grills, as well as heating systems.

- **Risks**: CO poisoning can be fatal, as it interferes with the blood's ability to carry oxygen.
- **Detection**: Although there are no federal regulations mandating the use of carbon monoxide detectors, many states and local jurisdictions require them in residential and commercial buildings to prevent CO poisoning.

Chlorofluorocarbons (CFCs)

CFCs are chemicals that have been historically used in air conditioning, refrigeration, and aerosols, known for their role in ozone layer depletion rather than direct health risks.

- **Environmental Impact**: Though not directly harmful to human health, CFCs contribute significantly to the degradation of the stratospheric ozone layer.
- **Regulation**: The Clean Air Act Amendments of 1990 regulate the production and disposal of CFCs, particularly focusing on substances like Freon® used in older refrigeration and air conditioning systems.

Formaldehyde

Formaldehyde is a volatile organic compound (VOC) that off-gases from various building materials and is considered a probable carcinogen by health authorities.

- **Sources**: Commonly found in pressed wood products, such as plywood and laminate furniture, as well as in carpeting and ceiling tiles.
- **Health Risks**: Known to cause respiratory issues, and irritations to the eyes and skin in a significant portion of the population.
- **Regulation**: Recent EPA regulations have enhanced the safety protocols around the use of formaldehyde, including mandating the use of certified products and requiring proper labeling to minimize exposure.

Polychlorinated Biphenyls (PCBs)

PCBs are man-made chemicals that were widely used in various industrial applications before their ban in 1979.

- **Properties**: Odorless and tasteless, these compounds can remain in the environment, particularly in water systems, long after their use has been discontinued.
- **Health Impact**: Classified as carcinogens, PCBs pose serious health risks. Old electrical and hydraulic equipment, and building materials like caulk, may still contain PCBs.
- **Environmental Concerns**: Contamination from PCBs is particularly concerning in aquatic environments, affecting wildlife and humans due to the accumulation of PCBs in fish.

Groundwater Contamination

Groundwater is a crucial resource located beneath the Earth's surface that can become contaminated from various sources.

- **Sources of Contamination**: Includes mining activities, landfill leakage, underground storage leaks, contaminated stormwater, and agricultural pesticides.
- **Impact**: Contaminants can leach into groundwater, affecting both private and public water supplies.
- **Regulation**: Protected under various federal and state laws, these regulations aim to prevent contamination and preserve water quality for safe consumption.

Waste Disposal Sites

Landfills and waste disposal sites are critical areas where waste management practices must be carefully controlled to prevent environmental damage.

- **Management**: Regulated by federal, state, and local authorities, these sites are designed to minimize leakage and off-gassing of decomposing waste.
- **After-Use**: Inactive landfills are often capped with soil to isolate waste material and are equipped with ventilation systems to manage gases produced by decomposition.
- **Reclamation**: Many capped waste sites are repurposed for public use, such as being developed into golf courses, parks, or residential and commercial complexes.
- **Monitoring**: Test wells are frequently installed at these sites to monitor for any potential groundwater contamination.

Recommendations for Real Estate Professionals

1. **Awareness and Education**: Stay informed about the types of environmental hazards and the implications of these hazards on property use and valuation.
2. **Professional Guidance**: Always recommend that clients use licensed professionals for inspections and abatement.
3. **Documentation**: Keep detailed records of all communications and recommendations related to environmental hazards to mitigate potential liabilities.

Understanding and managing environmental hazards is essential for protecting clients, maintaining property values, and ensuring compliance with regulatory requirements in the real estate industry.

Abatement and Mitigation: Understanding Key Environmental Legislation

Overview of Environmental Cleanup Laws

The Comprehensive Environmental Response, Compensation, and Liability Act (CERCLA), commonly known as Superfund, was enacted to address the cleanup of sites contaminated with hazardous substances. It focuses on remediating closed, abandoned, or uncontrolled hazardous waste sites as well as handling spills of hazardous substances.

The Superfund Amendments and Reauthorization Act (SARA) enhanced CERCLA by introducing additional protections and clarifications, including the "innocent landowner" defense. This defense provides that landowners who can demonstrate they conducted all appropriate inquiries (due diligence) prior to purchasing a property may not be held liable for contamination found later unless they contributed to that contamination.

Types of Liability Under CERCLA

1. **Strict Liability**: Under CERCLA, property owners are responsible for cleaning up their properties regardless of whether they caused the contamination. This means that simply owning a contaminated property can make an individual or entity liable for expensive remediation efforts.
2. **Joint and Several Liability**: This type of liability means that any one of the responsible parties can be held responsible for the entire cost of cleanup, regardless of their individual share of the blame. This is common in scenarios where multiple parties have contributed to the pollution.
3. **Retroactive Liability**: CERCLA imposes liability not only on current property owners but also on previous owners. This aspect of the law ensures that responsibility for environmental cleanup can extend back to any party that owned the site during the period of contamination.

Enforcement and Cleanup Process

If those responsible for the contamination do not undertake cleanup efforts, the Environmental Protection Agency (EPA) has the authority to step in. The EPA can hire contractors to clean up the site and then seek reimbursement from the liable parties. This ensures that hazardous sites are dealt with promptly, even if those responsible are reluctant or unable to perform the necessary work.

Contaminated Property Restrictions and Private Controls

EPA Involvement in Contaminated Sites

When the United States Environmental Protection Agency (EPA) identifies hazardous contamination at a development site, it has the authority to halt construction and initiate remedial actions. This intervention can significantly affect the project's timeline and overall costs. Even independent of EPA action, developers are generally required to undertake cleanup efforts before proceeding with construction if contamination is found. Common contaminants that might trigger such interventions include industrial chemicals, underground storage tanks, or pathogenic agents in groundwater, all of which can impose significant development restrictions.

Brownfields and Revitalization Efforts

Brownfields are properties that were previously used for industrial purposes or certain types of commercial activities and are suspected to contain hazardous waste. The Small Business Liability Relief and Brownfields Revitalization Act of 2002 was designed to facilitate the cleanup and redevelopment of such sites. It provides:

- **Funding**: Financial assistance for assessing and cleaning up brownfields, making these sites more attractive for development.
- **Liability Protection**: Shields new buyers or developers from legal responsibility for contamination that occurred before their ownership, assuming they did not contribute to the pollution.

This legislation is crucial as it not only helps in managing environmental risks but also promotes economic development by making previously unusable lands viable for new projects.

Private Land Use Controls

In addition to public regulations, land use can also be controlled through private means, which include:

- **Easements**: Rights granted to use the property of another for a specific purpose, such as utility lines or access roads.
- **Liens**: Legal claims on properties due to unpaid debts, which must be settled before the property can be sold.
- **Deed Restrictions**: Clauses in a deed that dictate certain terms regarding the use or development of the land.

- **Subdivision Regulations or HOA Rules**: Rules set by homeowners associations (HOAs) or similar bodies that govern various aspects of property appearance and maintenance within the community.

When a property is subject to both public and private restrictions regarding the same issue, the more restrictive rule generally prevails. This ensures that the strictest standards for safety, aesthetics, or environmental protection are upheld.

Deed Restrictions

Deed restrictions, also known as restrictive covenants, are conditions placed directly on the deed of a property by the grantor. These restrictions can dictate various aspects of property use, appearance, or maintenance to ensure certain standards are maintained within a community or area. Key characteristics of deed restrictions include:

- **Permanence**: Deed restrictions may be permanent or have a specific time limit, depending on the terms set by the grantor.
- **Legality**: All deed restrictions must comply with existing laws, including fair housing regulations. Any condition that violates such laws is deemed unenforceable.
- **Binding Nature**: These restrictions "run with the land," meaning they are binding on all subsequent owners of the property, not just the original parties to the deed.

Covenants, Conditions, and Restrictions (CC&Rs)

CC&Rs are commonly used in planned communities and are established by subdivision developers or homeowners associations (HOAs) to govern the properties within a development. They serve to maintain the quality and uniformity of a community. Key aspects of CC&Rs include:

- **Form**: They may be included directly in the property deed or in a separate document that is referenced in the deed and recorded with local land records.
- **Enforcement**: Typically enforced by the homeowners association, which has the power to levy fines for non-compliance.
- **Duration**: Often set to expire after a certain number of years unless renewed or amended by the community.
- **Examples**: Common restrictions include mandates on architectural style, exterior design, setbacks, and landscaping requirements.

Homeowners Association (HOA) Regulations

HOA regulations form an integral part of living in a community governed by an association. These regulations are agreed upon by homeowners and the HOA and can significantly influence the daily life and autonomy of residents. Characteristics of HOA regulations include:

- **Scope**: Regulations can cover aesthetic decisions such as paint colors and roofing materials, as well as landscaping choices including the types and numbers of plants.
- **Financial Obligations**: Homeowners are typically required to pay HOA fees which contribute to the maintenance and management of common areas and facilities.
- **Enforcement**: HOAs hold the authority to enforce compliance through fines and, if necessary, legal action. Individual members can also seek enforcement through civil litigation for any breaches of these regulations.

Summary

This chapter provides an in-depth examination of the mechanisms through which both private and public entities regulate land usage. It discusses governmental powers such as police power, eminent domain, taxation, and the role of different zoning classifications enforced by local authorities to shape urban and rural landscapes. The chapter also delves into specifics of environmental law like the Comprehensive Environmental Response, Compensation, and Liability Act (CERCLA) and the control of hazardous substances, addressing how these influence property development and ownership.

Furthermore, it covers private land use controls including easements, deed restrictions, and homeowners associations (HOAs), explaining how these affect property values and community living. This comprehensive overview equips readers with a crucial understanding of how land use and property development are shaped by various regulatory frameworks and legal obligations, ensuring properties adhere to both aesthetic and safety standards while fostering community development.

Chapter 3: Valuation and Market Analysis

Overview

This chapter covers essential concepts that account for approximately 7% of the Exam, translating to at least five questions that you may encounter.

Appraisals and Their Purpose

An appraisal is a professional and formal evaluation of a property's market value, conducted by a licensed appraiser. This evaluation is based on evidence that is verifiable and relevant as of a specific assessment date, all while adhering to the Uniform Standards of Professional Appraisal Practice (USPAP).

Key Points to Remember:

- **Real Estate Appraisal**: This is utilized primarily by lenders to gauge the current value of a property to ensure the loan amount is appropriate.
- **Real Estate Assessment**: This refers to the valuation of a property for the purpose of determining property taxes.

Role of Appraisers

Appraisers are specialized professionals who can focus on either commercial or residential properties. Their main role is to determine the value of a property before it undergoes significant financial transactions such as sales, securing a mortgage, or taxation.

Valuation in Real Estate Transactions

Valuation, or formal appraisal, is an integral process used by mortgage lenders. It serves to verify that the property's value is adequate to cover the loan amount. While appraisal management companies or lenders often appoint appraisers, it is typically the property buyer who bears the cost. This ensures that the financial interests of both the lender and the buyer are safeguarded by an objective property valuation.

Understanding the Appraisal Process under USPAP

The appraisal process, as outlined by the Uniform Standards of Professional Appraisal Practice (USPAP), is a structured approach that ensures the accuracy and integrity of the appraisal. Appraisers adhere to these guidelines to provide a well-supported evaluation of a property's value. Let's delve into each step of the process.

Step-by-Step Appraisal Process According to USPAP

1. **Problem Identification:**
    -   The first step involves clearly identifying the property in question, the rights associated with it (such as ownership or lease rights), the purpose of the appraisal (such as for a loan, sale, or tax assessment), and the type of value being estimated (market value, replacement value, etc.).

2. **Data Collection and Analysis:**
    -   Appraisers collect a broad spectrum of data ranging from general information about the city and neighborhood, demographic statistics, and specific data pertinent to the property itself. This comprehensive data collection helps in making an informed valuation.

3. **Highest and Best Use Determination:**
    -   This involves evaluating what the most profitable, legally permissible, and physically possible use of the property would be if the land were vacant. This assessment is crucial, especially for commercial properties or residential properties in mixed-use areas, as it significantly influences the property's value.

4. **Estimation of Land Value:**
    -   Here, the value of the land is estimated as if it were vacant. Appraisers use one or more of the following three approaches to determine this value:
        -   **Sales Comparison Approach**: Comparing the property to similar properties that have recently sold.
        -   **Cost Approach**: Estimating the cost to replace the building minus depreciation.
        -   **Income Approach**: Based on the income the property generates.

5. **Reconciliation of Values:**
    -   This step involves synthesizing the various value estimates to arrive at a final appraised value. This is not merely averaging the figures but involves a detailed correlation and adjustment

based on how comparable the other properties are and which valuation method provides the most reliable estimate.

6. **Development and Delivery of the Appraisal Report:**
   - The final step is compiling all the findings into a comprehensive appraisal report that details the analysis and conclusions, which is then delivered to the client.

Illustrative Example

Consider an appraiser assessing a residential property in a suburban neighborhood. They might identify three comparable homes that have sold recently:

- **Comparable 1**: Valued at $535,000
- **Comparable 2**: Valued at $479,000
- **Comparable 3**: Valued at $550,000

In this scenario, if Comparable 3 most closely matches the subject property in terms of size, condition, location, and amenities, the appraiser might give it more weight in the final valuation. This detailed approach ensures that the estimated value is reflective of the most relevant market conditions and property characteristics.

Situations Requiring a Certified Appraiser

Understanding when a certified appraiser is required is crucial for compliance with legal standards and ensuring the integrity of property valuations. This section elaborates on various regulations and guidelines that dictate the use of certified or licensed appraisers in real estate transactions.

Federal Requirements for Appraisals

The Financial Institutions Reform, Recovery, and Enforcement Act (FIRREA) of 1989 mandates that appraisals associated with federally related transactions be conducted by state-certified or licensed appraisers. It's important to note that federally related transactions, as defined by FIRREA, do not include transactions involving FHA insurance, VA guarantees, or those that will be sold to Government Sponsored Enterprises (GSEs) like Fannie Mae or Freddie Mac.

Key Exemptions:

- Residential properties valued at $400,000 or less are exempt from the federal appraisal mandates, simplifying the process for many typical home sales.

Specific Requirements for Different Types of Financing

1. **FHA-Insured Loans:**
   - Properties financed with loans insured by the Federal Housing Administration (FHA) must be appraised by an appraiser who is both state-licensed and approved by the U.S. Department of Housing and Urban Development (HUD).
2. **VA-Guaranteed Loans:**
   - Similar to FHA loans, properties backed by VA loans require appraisals from VA-certified, state-licensed appraisers.

Appraiser Independence Requirements (AIR)

Implemented in 2010 by key mortgage industry stakeholders, including Fannie Mae, Freddie Mac, and the Federal Housing Finance Agency (FHFA), the Appraiser Independence Requirements (AIR) were established to ensure that appraisals reflect accurate and unbiased property values.

Key Provisions of AIR

- Appraisers must be certified or licensed in the state where the property is located.
- They should possess thorough knowledge of the local real estate market.
- They must be qualified to appraise the specific property in question.

AIR also strictly prohibits any attempts by lenders to influence appraisers regarding the property's value. To sell conventional mortgage loans to Fannie Mae, lenders must adhere to AIR, often selecting appraisers from an approved list. To ensure compliance, some lenders engage third-party companies to oversee the appraisal process.

Types of Value in Real Estate Appraisal

In real estate appraisals, appraisers typically estimate the following types of value:

- **Market Value**: The most probable price that a property would bring in a competitive and open market.

- **Insurance Value**: The cost to replace the property in the case of loss, not necessarily equivalent to the market value.
- **Replacement Value**: The cost to construct a replica of the property at current prices, using similar materials and construction standards.

The primary focus for real estate transactions is usually the estimation of market value, which serves as the basis for most buying, selling, and lending decisions.

Estimating Property Value

Understanding the estimation of property value is foundational in real estate practice, as it influences almost every aspect of buying, selling, and managing real estate.

Concepts of Value in Real Estate

1. **Market Value:**
   - Defined as the most likely price a property would fetch in a competitive and open market under conditions that presume both the buyer and seller are acting without undue pressure.
2. **Value versus Price versus Cost:**
   - **Value**: Represents the objective worth of a property, which might not necessarily be its price or cost.
   - **Cost**: Refers to the amount required to construct a replacement of the property with equivalent utility at current prices.
   - **Market Price**: The actual transaction price agreed upon by the buyer and seller.

Critical Factors Influencing Property Value

Location

Location underscores the prime determinant of real estate value. Since real estate is immovable and the land supply is finite, location becomes a pivotal factor. Over time, the characteristics of a location can evolve, influencing property values positively or negatively. Factors such as neighborhood safety, quality of local schools, and accessibility to amenities like restaurants, shopping, and parks play significant roles.

DUST - Four Characteristics of Value

- **Demand**: The desirability or interest in a property or location.
- **Utility**: The usefulness or functional capacity of the property.
- **Scarcity**: The availability of similar properties in the market.
- **Transferability**: The ease with which property rights can be transferred. Issues like deed restrictions or encumbrances can complicate transferability, impacting value.

Other Valuation Concepts

- **Value in Use**: The specific value of a property to an individual user, which might be higher than the market value due to personal preferences or specific uses.
- **Assessed Value**: A valuation placed on a property by a public tax assessor for purposes of taxation.
- **Mortgage Value**: The valuation for mortgage purposes, often considered during foreclosure sales.
- **Insured Value**: The cost to replace or rebuild a property, which is critical for insurance assessments.
- **Investment Value**: The potential return an investment property is expected to generate, which can differ significantly from market value based on the investor's criteria.

Economic Principles of Value in Real Estate

Real estate values are influenced by various economic principles that underpin how properties are valued in different contexts. Here we discuss several key principles that play a significant role in property valuation.

Key Economic Principles Affecting Real Estate Value

1. **Anticipation**: This principle suggests that property values are impacted by the expectation of future benefits. Real estate investment decisions are often made based on the anticipated economic and development changes that could affect a property's value in the future.

Example: Consider undeveloped land adjacent to a thriving urban area. The anticipation of future residential and commercial development can significantly increase the land's value as demand for space in growing areas increases.

2. **Balance**: Balance relates to the optimal allocation of resources—land, labor, capital, and entrepreneurship—to maximize property value. It is crucial that the investment in these elements proportionally enhances the property's worth.

Example: Building a $300,000 home on land worth $800,000 is generally considered disproportionate, as the land value greatly exceeds the value of the structure, leading to suboptimal returns on investment.

3. **Conformity**: According to this principle, a property's value is supported when it conforms to the standards of its surroundings. Similarity in use, appearance, and function typically enhances value.

Example: A commercial building in a predominantly residential neighborhood of single-family homes likely suffers a value decrease due to its non-conformity with the area's primary use.

4. **Contribution**: This principle assesses the value added by any single component of a property. The critical aspect here is that the cost of an improvement does not necessarily equal the value it adds.

Example: Adding amenities such as a privacy fence and a deck to a residential property might cost $30,000 but could enhance the property's market value by $50,000 due to increased appeal to potential buyers.

5. **Highest and Best Use**: This concept identifies the most profitable legal use of a property that is physically possible, appropriately justified, and financially feasible. It determines the use that will most likely lead to the highest value of a property.

Criteria for Determination

- **Physically Possible**: Uses that can be physically implemented on the property.
- **Legally Permitted**: Uses must comply with regulatory requirements including zoning laws.
- **Economically Feasible**: The use must be financially viable.
- **Maximally Productive**: The use should yield the highest return or value.

Additional Economic Principles Impacting Real Estate

1. **Plottage**: Plottage refers to the increase in value that results from consolidating adjacent parcels of land into a single, larger parcel. This concept highlights the potential to enhance the utility and value of land through strategic assemblage.

Example: Imagine three adjacent plots each valued at $50,000 when held separately. If combined into a single parcel, they could facilitate a development that dramatically increases their utility, raising the total value to $250,000, thus realizing an additional $100,000 in value over the aggregate cost of $150,000.

2. **Progression and Regression:**

- **Progression**: This occurs when the value of a property increases due to an uplift in the value of surrounding properties. It is often observed in developing or revitalized areas where general improvements enhance the overall desirability.
- **Regression**: Conversely, regression happens when the value of a property decreases because of a fall in the value of neighboring properties. This can result from negative externalities such as poor maintenance of nearby properties or external changes like zoning modifications or natural disasters.

External Factors: Both progression and regression are influenced by factors like zoning changes, shifts in school district reputations, nearby commercial development, and broader economic conditions such as interest rates.

3. **Substitution**: This principle asserts that a savvy buyer would not pay more for a property than it would cost to acquire another with similar utility. Substitution sets a competitive ceiling on prices within the market.

Example: A buyer is likely to compare the costs of purchasing a home against the costs of building a similar home or buying a comparable existing one. This helps ensure that prices for similar properties remain within a close range.

4. **Supply and Demand**: The fundamental economic principle of supply and demand plays a crucial role in real estate markets. The balance—or imbalance—between available properties and the demand for those properties directly influences real estate values.

Market Dynamics Examples:

- **Buyer's Market**: Characterized by either a high supply of properties or fewer buyers, leading to lower prices and greater negotiation leverage for buyers.
- **Seller's Market**: Marked by a low supply of properties or a high number of buyers, resulting in higher prices and quicker sales.

Understanding these principles provides a framework for making informed decisions in real estate valuation, investment, and development.

Sales / Market Comparison Approach in Real Estate Appraisal

The Sales Comparison Approach is a fundamental method used in the appraisal of real estate, particularly single-family homes. It is grounded in the principle of substitution, which posits that a rational buyer would not pay more for a property than the cost of an equivalent alternative. This section delves into how this approach is implemented, the role of comparable properties (comps), and the detailed process of making adjustments to derive an accurate market value.

The Sales Comparison Approach Explained

1. **Utilization of Comparables**: The process begins by selecting three to five comparable properties that have been recently sold in the same area as the subject property. These comps should be as similar as possible to the subject property to minimize the need for adjustments and to reduce subjectivity in the valuation.

2. **Adjustments for Differences**: Since no two properties are exactly alike, adjustments are necessary to account for differences in features, location, condition, and timing between the subject property and each comparable. Appraisers use analytical methods to quantify the value of these differences.

Example: If the subject property has an additional bedroom compared to a comparable property, and the comparable sold for $400,000, an appraiser might add $30,000 for the extra bedroom, estimating the subject property's value at $430,000, assuming all other factors are equal.

Bracketing in Valuation

Bracketing is a technique used to establish a range of values for a property by comparing it to inferior, similar, and superior properties. This method helps in illustrating how various units of comparison align to support an estimated value after appropriate adjustments are made.

Categories of Comparison

1. **Financing Terms and Cash Equivalency**: Adjustments may be necessary to reflect different financing terms under which comparable sales occurred to achieve a cash equivalent value.

Example: A comparable property sold for $550,000 with the seller paying $20,000 towards the buyer's closing costs would be adjusted to reflect a cash equivalent value of $530,000.

2. **Conditions of Sale**: Consideration of whether the sale was under any duress or if there were any special circumstances that influenced the sale price.

3. **Market Conditions**: Adjustments for changes in market conditions between the time the comparables were sold and the valuation date.

4. **Location**: Adjustments for differences in location desirability, which can significantly impact value.

5. **Physical Characteristics**: Consideration of differences in age, size, layout, condition, and quality of construction.

Importance of Sales Comparison Approach

This approach is widely regarded as the most relatable and understandable method for valuing properties, particularly for residential real estate. It offers a clear, market-based context for valuation, making it an essential tool for appraisers.

Cost Approach to Property Valuation

The Cost Approach is a valuation method used in real estate appraisal, especially pertinent for unique properties that do not generate rental income or lack sufficient comparables. This approach calculates a property's value by adding the land value to the depreciated value of any improvements. It is particularly useful for special-purpose properties such as movie theaters, hospitals, churches, and schools, as well as for newly constructed or high-value homes.

Formula for the Cost Approach

The basic formula used in the cost approach is:

- Replacement or Reproduction Cost – Depreciation + Land Value = Estimated Property Value

Determining Construction Cost

Construction cost under the cost approach includes both direct and indirect costs:

- **Direct Costs**: These are expenses directly related to the construction of the building, such as labor and materials.
- **Indirect Costs**: These costs include expenses not directly tied to the physical construction, like architectural fees, permits, and builder's profit.

Methods of Determining Building Value

1. **Replacement Cost**: This method estimates the cost to build a functionally equivalent building using modern materials and standards, which is the more commonly used method in the cost approach.

2. **Reproduction Cost**: This method calculates the cost to construct an exact replica of the property using the same materials and design, typically reserved for buildings of historical or architectural significance.

Common Techniques for Estimating Construction Costs:

1. **Square Footage Method**: Calculates the building value by multiplying the structure's total square footage by the cost per square foot for that type of building.

Example: If the average cost per square foot is $200 and the building is 1,800 square feet, then the estimated construction cost is: 1,800 × 200 = $360,000.

2. **Unit-in-Place Method**: This method involves calculating the cost of individual components of the building.

Example: For 1,500 square feet of hardwood flooring at $15 per square foot, the replacement cost would be: 1,500 × 15 = $22,500.

3. **Quantity Survey Method**: A detailed method that breaks down the costs of individual materials and labor used in construction, providing a very detailed cost analysis.

4. **Index Method**:Adjusts the original construction cost using a published index to reflect the change in costs over time.

Example: A building constructed 8 years ago at $300,000 when the index was 120. With the current index at 140, the updated construction cost would be: 300,000 × (140 ÷ 120) = $350,000.

Understanding the Cost Approach is vital for real estate professionals, particularly when dealing with properties that are unique in nature or have no direct comparables.

Estimating Depreciation in Real Estate Valuation

Depreciation plays a critical role in the cost approach to real estate valuation, accounting for the loss in value of a property's improvements over time due to various factors.

Causes of Depreciation

Depreciation is categorized into three main types, each affecting the value of property differently:

1. **Economic Obsolescence:**
   - This type of depreciation arises from external factors unrelated to the property itself. Such factors might include changes in the neighborhood or nearby developments that adversely affect the property's desirability or usability. **Example**: The construction of a large industrial plant nearby causing increased pollution could lead to economic obsolescence.

2. **Functional Obsolescence:**
   - This form of depreciation results from design features that are outdated or inadequate. It reflects the loss in value due to the property's features no longer meeting current market expectations or standards. **Example**: A commercial building without modern energy-efficient systems or with inadequate parking might suffer from functional obsolescence.

3. **Physical Deterioration:**
   - Physical wear and tear, damage, or inadequate maintenance can lead to this type of depreciation. It is the most straightforward form of depreciation, often visible and quantifiable. **Example**: A roof with missing shingles and leaks due to prolonged exposure to the elements without timely repairs.

Curable vs. Incurable Depreciation

Depreciation can also be classified as either curable or incurable, depending on the cost-effectiveness of remedying the depreciating factors:

1. **Curable Depreciation:**
   - This exists when the cost to repair or improve the depreciating factor is less than the value it will add to the property once remedied.

Example: Replacing old, worn-out carpeting with new flooring might cost $3,000, but if it increases the property value by $7,000, the depreciation is considered curable. Similarly, updating outdated light fixtures can significantly enhance property value, often exceeding the cost of the upgrades.

2. **Incurable Depreciation:**

- Incurable depreciation occurs when the cost to correct a defect exceeds the additional value that would be added to the property.

  Example: Modifying an outdated floor plan might cost $50,000 but only add $30,000 to the property value. Significant structural issues like foundation repairs can also fall into this category, where the high cost of correction does not justify the potential increase in market value.

Depreciation and Income Analysis in Real Estate Valuation

This section delves into two crucial methods of real estate valuation: the Straight-Line Method for calculating depreciation and the Income Approach for assessing properties that generate rental income.

The Straight-Line Method of Depreciation

The Straight-Line Method is a systematic approach to calculating depreciation by allocating an equal amount of depreciation each year over the economic life of the property.

Calculating Depreciation Using the Straight-Line Method:

1. **Determine the Reproduction/Replacement Cost**: This is the cost to construct a replica or equivalent of the existing property at current prices.
2. **Estimate the Economic Life**: This is the total period during which the property is expected to be economically useful to the average owner.
3. **Assess the Effective Age**: This reflects the age of the property in terms of its economic life used up to the point of appraisal.
4. **Calculate Annual Depreciation**: This is done by dividing the reproduction/replacement cost by the economic life of the property.
5. **Compute Total Depreciation**: Multiply the annual depreciation by the effective age of the property.

Example: A property has a reproduction cost of $400,000 and an estimated economic life of 60 years. If the effective age is 15 years, the annual depreciation would be: Annual Depreciation = $400,000 ÷ 60 years = $6,667 The total depreciation accumulated over 15 years would therefore be: Total Depreciation = 15 years × $6,667 = $100,005

Income Analysis Approach

The Income Approach is vital for valuing investment properties, particularly those generating rental income. It considers the income produced by the property to estimate its fair market value.

Methods of the Income Approach:

1. **Gross Rent Multiplier (GRM):**
   - This method is particularly useful for small residential properties (up to four units). It involves comparing the property to similar properties by using their gross rental incomes.
   - **Formula**: The GRM is calculated by dividing the sales price of a comparable property by its gross monthly income.

   GRM = Gross Monthly Rent ÷ Sales Price

Example: A four-unit property generates $13,000 monthly. Comparables sold for $840,000 with $11,000 income, $1,000,000 with $14,000 income, and $1,170,000 with $15,000 income. The GRM for each would be:

- $840,000 / $11,000 = 76.36
- $1,000,000 / $14,000 = 71.43
- $1,170,000 / $15,000 = 78

If we assume a GRM average of 75 for simplicity, the estimated value of the subject property would be: Estimated Value = GRM × Gross Monthly Income = 75 × $13,000 = $975,000

Gross Income Multiplier (GIM)

Used primarily for properties consisting of five or more units, GIM utilizes annual income data to assess property value, making it suitable for larger residential or commercial properties.

Calculation of GIM:

- Formula: GIM = Sales Price ÷ Gross Annual Income
- Application: The GIM is multiplied by the gross annual income of the subject property to estimate its value.

Example: For a comparable property:

- Sales price: $1,000,000
- Annual income: $200,000
- GIM calculation: 5 (from $1,000,000 ÷ $200,000)

For a nearby similar property generating $250,000 in annual income:

Estimated Value = 5 × $250,000 = $1,250,000

Clarifications and Tips for Real Estate Exams

- **GRM vs. GIM**: It's important to note the context in which these multipliers are used—GRM for monthly and GIM for annual income assessments. Confusion often arises because GRM can also be referenced in annual terms, particularly online where "good" investment ranges are quoted using annual GRM figures.For clarity:
  - Annual GRM figures (often quoted as 4 to 7) need to be understood as equivalent to monthly GRM ranges of 48 to 84, considering GRM × 12 months.

1031 Exchange

As an additional tip for investors, the 1031 exchange under the Internal Revenue Code allows for the deferral of capital gains tax on properties by reinvesting the proceeds from a sale into similar ("like-kind") properties. This strategy can significantly enhance the profitability and sustainability of real estate investments.

Reconciliation - A Final Estimate of Value

Reconciliation is a critical stage in the real estate appraisal process, where the appraiser synthesizes information from multiple valuation approaches to arrive at a final estimate of value for the property.

Overview of Reconciliation in Real Estate Appraisal

During reconciliation, an appraiser evaluates the results from different appraisal approaches and determines which approach provides the most credible and relevant value estimate for the subject property. Importantly, the values derived from these methods are not simply averaged; rather, the appraiser must judiciously weigh each result based on its applicability to the specific property being assessed.

Commonly Used Appraisal Approaches

1. **Sales / Market Comparison Approach:**
   - This approach is primarily used for single-family homes and involves comparing the subject property to similar properties that have recently sold in the area.
2. **Cost Approach:**
   - Typically applied to unique properties such as movie theaters, hospitals, churches, and schools, the cost approach adds the value of the land to the depreciated cost of the building to estimate property value.
3. **Income Analysis Approach:**
   - Used for commercial investment properties and residential rental properties, this method calculates value based on the income generated by the property. It is particularly relevant for properties such as shopping centers, office buildings, and large apartment complexes.

Capitalization Rate (Cap Rate)

The Capitalization Rate, or Cap Rate, is a fundamental concept within the Income Analysis Approach and is used to estimate the value of income-generating properties.

Cap Rate Formula (IRV):
- **I (Income)**: Net Operating Income (NOI) of the property.
- **R (Rate)**: Capitalization rate.
- **V (Value)**: Estimated value of the property.

Using the IRV formula, the appraiser can solve for any one of the three components if the other two are known:

- **I ÷ R = V** - Determines the value based on income and cap rate.

- **I ÷ V = R** - Calculates the cap rate when the income and value are known.
- **R × V = I** - Computes the expected income based on the cap rate and value.

Application of Cap Rates:

- Cap rates typically range from 5% to 10%. A higher cap rate implies a higher risk and potential return, while a lower cap rate suggests lower risk and return.
- Cap rates can vary significantly by location and type of building, reflecting differences in market conditions and investment risks.

Calculating Net Operating Income (NOI) for Reconciliation

In the appraisal process, particularly within the Income Analysis Approach, calculating the Net Operating Income (NOI) is a crucial step toward arriving at a property's value. Understanding this calculation helps appraisers and investors determine the profitability and potential return on investment for income-generating properties. Here's how the NOI is typically computed:

Steps to Calculate Net Operating Income (NOI)

1. **Estimate the Potential Gross Income (PGI):**
   - This is the total possible income from all rentable units if the property were fully occupied and all rents collected for an entire year. It represents the maximum income the property could generate under ideal conditions.
2. **Subtract Vacancy and Collection Losses:**
   - Not all units will be occupied at all times, and not all tenants will pay their rent. Vacancy and collection losses account for this reality and are subtracted from the Potential Gross Income. This figure is often expressed as a percentage of the PGI and varies based on historical data for similar properties in the area.
3. **Add Other Income:**
   - Properties can generate additional income beyond just rent from residential or commercial spaces. This might include income from amenities such as laundry facilities, parking spaces, vending machines, etc. This additional revenue is added to the adjusted PGI to arrive at the Effective Gross Income (EGI).

4. **Estimate Building Expenses:**
   - Expenses associated with maintaining and operating the property are subtracted from the EGI to determine the NOI. These expenses are categorized into three types:
     - **Fixed Expenses**: Costs that do not change regardless of the property's occupancy rate, such as property taxes and insurance.
     - **Variable Expenses**: Costs that can fluctuate with the level of occupancy or usage, such as utilities, management fees, and maintenance costs.
     - **Reserve for Replacement**: Costs for periodic replacements or major repairs, like appliance replacement or significant system repairs, which are not regular but must be anticipated.
5. **Final Calculation of NOI:**
   - The NOI is calculated by subtracting the total estimated building expenses from the Effective Gross Income:
   - **NOI=Effective Gross Income (EGI)–Total Building Expenses**
   - This figure (NOI) is crucial as it forms the basis for applying the Capitalization Rate to estimate the property's value in the market.

Example Calculation:

- Potential Gross Income: $600,000
- Vacancy and Collection Losses: 4% of PGI = $24,000
- Other Income: $15,000
- Effective Gross Income: $600,000 - $24,000 + $15,000 = $591,000
- Total Expenses: $250,000 (including fixed, variable, and reserves)
- Net Operating Income: $591,000 - $250,000 = $341,000

Role of NOI in Reconciliation

In the final stages of the appraisal process, the calculated NOI is critical for applying the capitalization rate to estimate the property's value using the Income Approach. Appraisers reconcile this value estimate with those derived from other approaches (Cost Approach, Sales Comparison Approach) to determine the most plausible final value of the property. This reconciliation process involves careful consideration of which valuation method is most appropriate for the property type and market conditions, ensuring the most accurate and defensible appraisal.

Comparative Market Analysis (CMA)

A Comparative Market Analysis (CMA) is a fundamental tool utilized by real estate agents to help determine the value of a property based on the sales of similar properties in the area. While less formal than an appraisal conducted by a licensed appraiser, a CMA provides valuable insights into setting competitive property prices in the real estate market.

Understanding Comparative Market Analysis

1. **Purpose of CMA:**
   - For Sellers: Helps in setting a realistic selling price that aligns with market trends and comparable property sales.
   - For Buyers: Assists buyers in deciding a fair price to offer for a property.
2. **CMA vs. Appraisal:**
   - A CMA is an informal property valuation provided by real estate agents.
   - A Sales/Market Comparison Approach is a formal appraisal conducted by a licensed appraiser.

Selection of Comparable Properties

Choosing the right comparables is critical to conducting an effective CMA. Comparables, or "comps," should meet the following criteria:

- **Similarity**: Comps should closely match the subject property in size, style, condition, and amenities.
- **Recency**: Ideally, comps should have sold within the last 3-6 months to reflect current market conditions.
- **Proximity**: Comps should be located in the same area as the subject property to ensure they reflect similar market influences.

Tip: Avoid using distressed sales as comps, such as foreclosures or short sales, unless the subject property is similarly distressed. This helps in maintaining the accuracy and relevancy of the analysis.

Understanding Arm's Length Transactions
- **Definition**: An arm's length transaction is one in which the parties involved act independently and have no relationship to each other, ensuring that the agreed-upon price reflects fair market value.

- **Importance**: These transactions are considered the most reliable indicators of market value, influencing not only individual investment decisions but also broader financial implications like taxes and property transfers.

Non-Arm's Length Transactions

These transactions occur when there is a pre-existing relationship between the buyer and seller, potentially influencing the agreed-upon price.

- **Examples include**
  - Sales between family members or friends.
  - Transactions involving employees and their employers.
  - Deals between parent companies and subsidiaries.
  - Transactions between trusts and their beneficiaries.

These types of sales may not always reflect the true market value due to the potential for biased pricing, motivated by relationships rather than market dynamics.

Adjusting Comparable Properties in Real Estate Valuation

Adjusting comparable properties is a key process in accurately determining the fair market value of a subject property using the Sales Comparison Approach. This involves systematic adjustments to the sale prices of comparable properties (comps) to account for differences in attributes between the comps and the subject property.

Process of Making Adjustments

1. **Selection of Comparables:**
   - Choose properties that have recently sold and are similar in size, location, and condition to the subject property. The closer the properties in terms of these characteristics, the fewer adjustments needed.
2. **Adjustment Principles:**
   - **Inferior Attributes**: If a comp has features considered inferior to those of the subject property, the comp's sale price is adjusted upward.
   - **Superior Attributes**: If a comp has features superior to those of the subject property, the comp's sale price is adjusted downward.

Examples of Adjustments

1. Inferior Comp Example:
   - Subject Property: 3 beds, 2 baths, 2-car garage, 2,000 sq ft.
   - Comp Property: 3 beds, 2 baths, 1-car garage, 1,800 sq ft, sold for $400,000.
   - Adjustments:
     - Add $8,000 for the additional garage bay.
     - Add $9,000 for the additional 200 sq ft ($45 per sq ft).
   - Adjusted Value: $417,000.

2. **Superior Comp Example:**
   - Subject Property: 4 beds, 3 baths, 2-car garage, 2,200 sq ft.
   - Comp Property: 4 beds, 3 baths, 2-car garage, 2,500 sq ft, has a pool, sold for $515,000.
   - Adjustments:
     - Subtract $25,000 for the pool (not present in subject property).
     - Subtract $15,000 for the additional 300 sq ft ($50 per sq ft).
   - Adjusted Value: $475,000.

Utilizing Price Per Square Foot

Calculating the price per square foot for each property can help validate the adjustments and ensure the estimated value aligns with market conditions.

- **Formula: Sales Price ÷ Total Livable Square Footage = Price per Square Foot.**
- **Example Calculations**
  - Inferior Comp: $380,000 / 1,800 sq ft = $211 per sq ft.
  - Superior Comp: $480,000 / 2,400 sq ft = $200 per sq ft.
  - Median Area Value: $205 per sq ft.
  - Subject Property Value Estimate: $204-$206 per sq ft based on the adjustments.

Best Practices for Accurate Adjustments

- Use the most recent and local comps possible to reflect the current market conditions accurately.
- Factor in neighborhood-specific nuances; values can vary significantly within small geographic areas.
- Consider all relevant property attributes including but not limited to size, condition, location, and amenities like pools or special landscaping.

NATIONAL REAL ESTATE LICENSE EXAM PREP

Conducting a Comprehensive Comparative Market Analysis (CMA)

A Comparative Market Analysis (CMA) is a vital tool used by real estate professionals to help determine the market value of a property by analyzing similar properties that have recently sold in the same area. Here's a detailed checklist to guide you through conducting an effective CMA:

CMA Checklist for Real Estate Professionals

1. **Gather Data on the Subject Property:**
   - **Location**: Include street, neighborhood, municipality, and county.
   - **Square Footage**: Focus on livable space; exclude unfinished basements or garages.
   - **Bedrooms and Bathrooms**: Number and layout.
   - **Lot Size/Acreage**: Especially relevant for privately owned properties.
   - **Year Built and Condition**: Assess age and current condition.
   - **Current Taxes Paid**: Include tax information as it impacts value.
   - **Previous Sale/Listing Data**: Look at historical sale data.
   - **Renovations/Updates**: Note any major improvements since the last sale.
   - **Notable Features**: Such as upgraded kitchens, swimming pools, decks, etc.

2. **Identify Comparable Properties:**
   - **Recency of Sales**: Ideally, select comps that have sold within the last 3-6 months.
   - **Number of Comps**: Start with at least three; more may be necessary to establish a fair comparison.
   - **Proximity**: Choose homes close to the subject property to ensure relevancy.
   - **Market** Conditions: Broaden the search timeline up to the last 12 months in slower markets.
   - **Transaction Type**: Use arm's length transactions to reflect fair market value.

3. **Adjust for Seller Concessions and Special Conditions:**
   - **Seller Concessions**: Consider closing costs or special financing that may affect the sale price. **Example**: A home selling for $550,000 with $20,000 in seller-paid closing costs should be adjusted to reflect a value of $530,000.

4. **Analyze Under-Contract and Active Listings:**
   - **Under-Contract Properties**: Useful for understanding days on market and pricing strategies, though not final comparables since the sale price is not finalized.
   - **Active Listings**: Provide insight into current market competition and asking prices.

5. **Evaluate Properties That Did Not Sell:**
   - **Expired Listings**: Analyze why these properties did not sell; often, pricing issues are a key factor.

6. **Assess Micro-Market Trends:**
   - **Local Variations**: Even small geographical differences, such as school zoning, can significantly impact property values.

Utilizing the CMA Effectively

- **Interpretation and Context**: Understanding the nuances of each data point and how they collectively impact the property's market value is crucial.
- **Market Fluctuations**: Always consider the broader economic and real estate market conditions that may affect property values.
- **Client Communication**: Clearly explain the factors influencing the estimated value to clients, helping them make informed decisions.

Understanding Real Estate Market Trends

Real estate market trends are crucial indicators of the economic health of the housing market, reflecting the balance between supply and demand. These trends significantly influence property values, the dynamics of buying and selling, and the negotiation process.

Types of Real Estate Markets

1. **Buyer's Market:**
   - **Characteristics**: The supply of homes exceeds the demand. There are more homes for sale than there are buyers.
   - **Implications for Buyers**: More options and less competition mean buyers can negotiate more aggressively. Sellers may offer concessions such as paying closing costs or points on mortgage loans.
   - **Implications for Sellers**: Homes may take longer to sell and often sell for less than the asking price. Sellers may need to make more compromises to attract offers.

2. **Seller's Market:**
   - **Characteristics**: The demand for homes exceeds the supply. There are more buyers than available homes.

- **Implications for Buyers**: Fewer homes available lead to competition, often resulting in bidding wars and offers exceeding asking prices.
- **Implications for Sellers**: Homes sell quickly, often for more than the asking price. Sellers have the upper hand in negotiations and rarely need to make concessions.

3. **Balanced Market:**
   - **Characteristics**: The supply of homes is roughly equal to the demand.
   - **Market Dynamics**: Neither buyers nor sellers have a distinct advantage, leading to a more stable and predictable market environment.

Market Trend Indicators

- **Inventory Levels**: The number of months it takes to sell all current listings at the current sales pace. Less than 4 months of inventory typically indicates a seller's market, while 6 months or more suggests a buyer's market.
- **Median Home Prices**: Tracking the rise or fall of home prices can indicate the overall direction of the market.
- **Time on Market**: Average days on market (DOM) can signal market strength. Shorter DOM suggests a seller's market, whereas longer DOM points to a buyer's market.

Negotiation Tactics by Market Type

Buyer's Market Tactics:

- Buyers can expect more room to negotiate deals and may seek concessions from sellers who are competing for their attention.
- Pre-qualification letters may be sufficient for making an offer.

Seller's Market Tactics:

- Buyers need to act quickly and decisively. Offers should be strong, with pre-approval letters to signify serious intent.
- Sellers might reject contingent offers and look for proof of financial stability from buyers.

Real Estate Professionals' Role

Real estate professionals must accurately read and interpret these market conditions to provide valuable advice to their clients. This involves:

- Educating clients about the current market situation and what it means for their buying or selling strategies.
- Strategizing based on market trends to align clients' expectations with reality, whether it involves setting listing prices or making offers.
- Navigating negotiations effectively to ensure clients achieve their real estate goals in various market conditions.

Factors Influencing Real Estate Market Trends and Buying Power

Understanding the factors that influence market trends and buying power is crucial for real estate professionals, as these elements significantly impact the housing market's dynamics and individual purchasing capabilities. Here, we explore how various factors affect buying power and, consequently, the real estate market.

Factors Influencing Market Trends

1. **Housing Inventory**
   - Defined by the months' supply, which measures how long the current stock of listings would last under current demand without new homes being listed. For example, a three-month supply indicates a seller's market where homes are selling quickly.
2. **Buying Power**
   - Represents the total financial resources homebuyers have for purchasing a home, encompassing down payments and the monthly income available for mortgage payments after essential expenses.

Key Influences on Purchasing Power

1. **Economic Factors**
   - **Mortgage Rates**: Fluctuations in interest rates can significantly impact the amount buyers can afford as they affect monthly loan payments.
   - **Inflation**: Reduces purchasing power as it increases the cost of living, thereby affecting how much money is left for mortgage payments.
   - **Taxes**: Higher taxes can decrease disposable income, reducing the amount available for home buying.

2. **Personal Financial Health:**
    - **Income**: Steady income growth is necessary to keep up with inflation and maintain or increase purchasing power.
    - **Credit Score**: Higher credit scores generally secure better loan terms, enhancing buying power.
    - **Debt-to-Income Ratio**: Lower ratios indicate better financial health, making more income available for home buying.
    - **Savings**: More savings for down payments and closing costs can significantly enhance buying power by reducing the needed loan amount and potentially securing better financing terms.

Strategies to Enhance Purchasing Power

- **Manage Debt**: Reducing debt not only improves the debt-to-income ratio but also potentially raises credit scores.
- **Increase Savings**: Accumulating funds for down payments and closing costs reduces the necessity for higher mortgage amounts, which can mitigate the effects of interest rates and taxes on monthly payments.
- **Improve Credit Scores**: A higher credit score can lead to more favorable mortgage rates, directly increasing how much house one can afford.

Applying the Serenity Concept

The differentiation between controllable and uncontrollable factors is akin to the wisdom offered in the serenity prayer:

- **Accept what cannot be changed**: Market conditions like inflation rates, interest rates, and overall economic conditions are beyond one individual's control.
- **Focus on what can be changed**: Personal financial decisions such as saving more, reducing debts, and improving credit scores are within an individual's control and can substantially impact purchasing power.

This approach not only helps in real estate decisions but can also be a valuable life strategy, promoting financial health and preparedness in the face of varying market conditions.

Navigating a Buyer's Market in Real Estate

A buyer's market presents unique opportunities and challenges for both buyers and sellers. Understanding how to navigate these conditions can help real estate professionals assist their clients in making strategic decisions that align with their goals. Here's how to approach a buyer's market effectively:

Tips for Buyers in a Buyer's Market

1. **Take Your Time:**
    *   The abundance of available properties means less urgency and fewer bidding wars. Buyers can afford to be choosy and deliberate in their decision-making process.
2. **Conduct Thorough Research:**
    *   Explore a wide range of available homes to fully understand what the market has to offer. This broad perspective helps buyers make informed choices about value and fit for their needs.
3. **Analyze Comparable Properties:**
    *   Understanding the pricing of comparable homes is crucial. This knowledge not only aids in making a reasonable offer but also strengthens negotiation positions.
4. **Monitor Days on the Market (DOM):**
    *   Properties that have lingered on the market may have more negotiable sellers. Buyers can leverage this for lower prices, favorable terms, and concessions.

Tips for Sellers in a Buyer's Market

1. **Prioritize Repairs and Improvements:**
    *   Addressing any necessary repairs and making thoughtful improvements can help your property stand out in a crowded market.
2. **Enhance Curb Appeal and First Impressions:**
    *   First impressions are crucial. Ensure the home is clean, clutter-free, and well-presented to make a positive impact on potential buyers. Consider staging the home professionally to showcase its potential.
3. **Adopt Aggressive Marketing Strategies:**
    *   Utilize professional-quality photos, virtual tours, and even drone photography to highlight the home's best features. Effective marketing is critical in attracting attention in a buyer's market.

4. **Competitive Pricing:**
   - Set a realistic price based on a careful analysis of comparable homes currently on the market. Overpricing can lead to extended time on the market, ultimately requiring price reductions to attract interest.

5. **Be Open to Negotiations:**
   - Be prepared to negotiate and possibly make concessions to close the deal. This might include offering to pay for some closing costs or agreeing to certain buyer contingencies.

Strategic Considerations

- **For Buyers**: A buyer's market is an excellent time to get a good deal on a property, but it's important to maintain discipline and not overextend financially just because conditions are favorable.
- **For Sellers**: While selling in a buyer's market can be challenging, focusing on the presentation, pricing correctly, and being flexible in negotiations can lead to a successful sale.

Navigating a Seller's Market in Real Estate

A seller's market is characterized by more buyers than available homes, creating a competitive environment where homes often sell quickly and for prices above the asking price. Both buyers and sellers need to adapt their strategies to effectively navigate this dynamic market.

Tips for Sellers in a Seller's Market

1. **Price Your Home Strategically:**
   - Even in a seller's market, it's important to price the home competitively. This can encourage multiple offers and potentially spark a bidding war, driving the price above the initial asking.

2. **Evaluate Offers Carefully:**
   - Consider all aspects of each offer, not just the price. Evaluate the buyer's financial stability, the size of their down payment, and the number of contingencies attached to their offer, as these can affect the deal's security and timeline.

3. **Insist on Preapproval:**
   - Require that potential buyers are preapproved for a mortgage, which indicates that their financial credentials have been vetted by a lender, increasing the likelihood that they will secure financing.

4. Be Cautious with Contingencies:

- Be mindful of offers with numerous contingencies (such as those related to selling another property, financing, or home inspections), as these can delay or derail the sale.

Tips for Buyers in a Seller's Market

1. Act Quickly:

- Be prepared to move fast when you find a suitable property. Have your financial arrangements in place, including preapproval for a mortgage, to make your offer more attractive and expedite the buying process.

2. Minimize Contingencies:

- To make your offer more appealing to sellers, limit the contingencies you include. Understand that in a competitive market, sellers prefer offers that present the least risk of falling through.

3. Stay Patient and Decisive:

- While it's important to act quickly, don't let the competitive pressure lead you to buy a home that doesn't meet your needs or overextend your financial limits. Maintain your standards and be prepared that you might not win the first home you bid on.

4. Evaluate Your Financial Limits:

- Know your budget and stick to it. In a competitive market, it's easy to get caught up in bidding wars that can push you beyond your financial comfort zone.

Balancing Urgency and Prudence

In a seller's market, the dynamics favor sellers, giving them the upper hand in negotiations and the luxury of choosing from multiple offers. Buyers, on the other hand, face the challenge of having to make quick decisions without compromising on their essential requirements for a new home.

- **For Sellers**: Leveraging the market conditions to maximize the sale price and minimize the sale duration requires a balance of competitive pricing and understanding the buyer's perspectives.
- **For Buyers**: Navigating a seller's market means preparing financially and emotionally to act swiftly but also wisely, ensuring the investment is sound and suits long-term needs.

By adopting these tailored strategies, both buyers and sellers can effectively manage their transactions in a seller's market, achieving their real estate goals while navigating the challenges and opportunities that such a market presents.

Summary

In conclusion, this chapter has provided a comprehensive exploration of valuation and market analysis in real estate, equipping readers with the foundational knowledge necessary to understand and apply various appraisal methods effectively. We have dissected the intricacies of the Sales Comparison Approach, Cost Approach, and Income Analysis Approach, illustrating how each is suited to different types of properties and market conditions.

The chapter also emphasized the importance of accurate Comparative Market Analyses (CMAs) for setting realistic property prices. By analyzing both buyer's and seller's market dynamics, we have offered tailored strategies that stakeholders can utilize to optimize their outcomes in varying market conditions.

Additionally, we have discussed the significant impact of economic factors and personal financial circumstances on market trends and individual purchasing power. This chapter aims to empower real estate professionals and investors with the analytical tools and insights needed to make informed decisions, ensuring they can adeptly navigate the complexities of real estate valuation and market analysis.

Chapter 4: Financing Real Estate

Overview

This chapter focuses on the crucial aspect of financing in real estate transactions, which accounts for 10% of the Salesperson Exam. The section is designed to equip learners with a comprehensive understanding of various financing mechanisms and the regulatory environment influencing real estate transactions.

Financing in Real Estate: Key Concepts and Terminology

Mortgages

A mortgage is fundamentally a loan specifically designed for the purchase or refinancing of real estate. It is a secured loan, where the property itself serves as collateral. Should the borrower fail to fulfill the repayment obligations, the lender is entitled to seize the property to recover the borrowed funds.

Components of a Mortgage Application

When evaluating a mortgage application, lenders primarily focus on two critical aspects:

1. **Borrower's Repayment Ability**: Lenders assess the borrower's financial stability and ability to repay the loan. This evaluation includes examining the borrower's credit score, debt-to-income ratio, stable employment history, and the estimated monthly housing costs, collectively known as Principal, Interest, Taxes, and Insurance (PITI).
2. **Property Value**: The loan-to-value (LTV) ratio plays a pivotal role in the lender's decision-making process. It is calculated based on a certified appraisal of the property. The ratio compares the lower of the sales price or the appraised value against the amount of the loan being requested. This helps the lender gauge the feasibility of recovering the loan amount should the borrower default.

Financing Instruments

When a real estate transaction involves a mortgage, certain legal documents are executed to formalize the loan. The most significant of these include:

- **Promissory Note**: This document outlines the borrower's promise to repay the loan under the agreed terms, including the interest rate and duration of the loan.
- **Security Instrument**: This could be either a mortgage or a deed of trust, depending on state laws. It grants the lender a security interest in the property, providing a legal mechanism to foreclose on the property if the borrower fails to comply with the terms of the promissory note.

Mortgage vs. Deed of Trust

It is crucial to understand the differences between a mortgage and a deed of trust, both of which secure repayment of a loan by using the property as collateral. While a mortgage involves two parties (borrower and lender), a deed of trust involves a third party, the trustee, who holds the property title until the loan is repaid. The specific use of these instruments can vary by state and by the preferences of the financial institutions involved.

Roles and Responsibilities in Mortgage Transactions

In the realm of real estate financing, understanding the distinct roles and responsibilities of the involved parties—specifically the mortgagor and mortgagee—is crucial. This section clarifies these roles to ensure a comprehensive grasp of what each party commits to within a mortgage agreement.

Mortgagor: The Borrower

The mortgagor, commonly referred to as the borrower, plays a pivotal role in a mortgage transaction. Here are the key responsibilities and rights associated with this role:

- **Equitable Title**: The mortgagor holds the equitable title to the property. This means while the mortgage is being repaid, the borrower has the right to benefit from and use the property as if they are the owner, although the legal title is held as security by the lender.
- **Promissory Note**: Upon agreeing to the mortgage terms, the mortgagor signs a promissory note. This document is a formal pledge to repay the borrowed amount under specified conditions, including the interest rate and repayment schedule.
- **Possession Rights**: The right to occupy and use the property is granted as long as the mortgage payments are maintained. This includes living in the property and using it within the terms agreed upon in the mortgage.

- **Ultimate Ownership**: Upon the complete repayment of the loan, the mortgagor receives full legal title to the property. Additionally, the promissory note is returned, marked "paid," signifying that no further obligations remain under the original mortgage terms.

Mortgagee: The Lender

The mortgagee, or lender, also has specific responsibilities and rights that secure their financial interests in the mortgage agreement:

- **Holding the Lien or Deed of Trust**: The lender holds either a lien on the property through a mortgage or a deed of trust. This legal framework provides the lender with security for the repayment of the loan.
- **Security Instrument**: At the commencement of the loan, the mortgagee receives a signed security instrument from the borrower. This document pledges the property as collateral, ensuring that the lender can reclaim the loan amount if necessary.
- **Foreclosure Rights**: If the borrower defaults on their loan repayments, the lender has the right to foreclose on the property. Foreclosure allows the lender to sell the property to recover the owed funds.
- **Loan Satisfaction**: When the borrower fully repays the loan, the lender is responsible for issuing a satisfaction of mortgage or a release of mortgage document. This action officially frees the property from the lien and acknowledges the fulfillment of the borrower's repayment obligations.

Understanding Property Ownership and Title Holding in Real Estate Transactions

Property ownership and the manner in which legal title is held during the term of a mortgage vary significantly across the United States, dictated largely by state law. This section delineates the three primary theories of title holding—Title Theory, Lien Theory, and Intermediate Theory—explaining their operation and identifying which states adhere to each theory.

Title Theory

Under Title Theory, the legal title to the property is held by the lender or a trustee until the mortgage is fully paid off. This arrangement involves three parties:

1. **Trustor (Borrower)**: The individual or entity that borrows funds and grants the deed of trust, holding equitable title and possessory rights to the property.

2. **Beneficiary (Lender)**: The lender who provides the funds for the mortgage and holds the legal title until the loan is satisfied.

3. **Trustee**: An independent third party who holds the legal title on behalf of the beneficiary and is responsible for managing the deed of trust.

When the mortgage is fully repaid, two key documents facilitate the transfer of ownership back to the borrower:

- **Release of Deed of Trust**: Issued by the lender, this document signifies the end of the lender's interest in the property.
- **Deed of Reconveyance**: Issued by the trustee, it transfers full legal title back to the borrower, clearing any claims or interests of the lender.

States Implementing Title Theory: Alaska, Arizona, Missouri, Texas, Nebraska, Utah, Colorado, Nevada, Virginia, Washington D.C., North Carolina, Oregon, Georgia, South Dakota, Idaho, Mississippi, Tennessee, Washington State, West Virginia, and Wyoming.

Lien Theory

Under Lien Theory, the borrower retains both legal and equitable titles to the property throughout the term of the loan, with the lender securing a lien on the property as security for the loan. The lien serves as a legal claim against the property until the mortgage is fully repaid, at which point the lien is removed.

States Implementing Lien Theory: Arkansas, Iowa, California, Kansas, Connecticut, Delaware, Kentucky, Louisiana, Maine, Florida, Illinois, Indiana, New Mexico, New York, North Dakota, Ohio, New Jersey, Pennsylvania, Puerto Rico, South Carolina, and Wisconsin.

Intermediate Theory

Intermediate Theory represents a hybrid between Title and Lien Theories. The borrower holds the title to the property, but the title reverts to the lender if the borrower defaults on the loan.

States Implementing Intermediate Theory: Montana, Alabama, Hawaii, Maryland, Massachusetts, Michigan, New Hampshire, Oklahoma, Rhode Island, Minnesota, and Vermont.

Understanding Pre-Qualification and Pre-Approval in Home Financing

When navigating the home buying process, understanding the differences between pre-qualification and pre-approval can significantly enhance a buyer's negotiating power and streamline their purchasing experience. This section outlines the distinctions between these two stages of the loan approval process, highlighting their importance and the role they play in the home buying journey.

Pre-Qualification: The First Step

Pre-qualification is essentially the initial step in the mortgage process. It provides a rough estimate of how much a potential borrower might be eligible to borrow based on self-reported financial information. Here's what it involves:

- **Informal Assessment**: Borrowers provide basic financial information to a lender, such as income, assets, debts, and credit score.
- **Credit Evaluation**: The lender performs a soft credit check, which does not impact the borrower's credit score, to gauge creditworthiness.
- **Estimate Issuance**: The lender uses this information to estimate the amount the borrower may be able to finance, though this is not a guarantee of loan approval.

The pre-qualification process is quick, often taking just a few days or even hours, and is useful for giving potential buyers an idea of their purchasing power.

Pre-Approval: A Closer Look

Pre-approval is a more in-depth evaluation and a stronger indicator of a buyer's ability to secure financing. It carries more weight than pre-qualification in the home-buying process for several reasons:

- **Formal Application**: The borrower completes an official mortgage application, which requires more detailed information and documentation.
- **Extensive Checks**: The lender conducts thorough checks on the borrower's financial background, including a hard pull on credit, which slightly affects the credit score.
- **Specific Offer**: If pre-approved, the lender will extend a conditional commitment in writing for an exact loan amount and possibly at a specified interest rate, based on the borrower's verified financial and credit information.

Importance of Pre-Approval

Pre-approval is highly recommended for those serious about purchasing a home because:

- **Seller Confidence**: It shows sellers that the buyer is serious and financially capable of purchasing the property, making their offer more attractive compared to those without pre-approval.
- **Efficiency in Closing**: With most financial verifications already completed, the closing process is typically quicker for pre-approved buyers.

Final Steps Towards Loan Commitment

Despite the advantages of pre-approval, final loan approval is contingent upon:

- **Appraisal**: The property must be appraised to confirm its market value meets or exceeds the purchase price.
- **Inspections**: The property must pass all required inspections as per the lender's and buyer's requirements.

Mortgage Underwriting

Mortgage underwriting is a critical component of the loan approval process. This chapter will delve into how lenders assess a borrower's creditworthiness, detailing the steps and criteria involved in making lending decisions. By understanding this process, borrowers can better prepare for successful loan applications, and real estate professionals can provide accurate advice to clients.

The Underwriting Process

The underwriting process is a thorough evaluation that mortgage lenders use to determine the risk involved in lending to a particular borrower. It involves several key steps:

1. **Preapproval**: The initial step where potential borrowers receive a conditional commitment from a lender, signaling preliminary creditworthiness.
2. **Verification of Income and Assets**: Lenders check documentation such as W-2s, bank statements, and investment accounts to verify a borrower's income and financial resources.
3. **Credit and Debt Analysis**: This includes assessing debt-to-income ratios, credit scores, and detailed credit history to evaluate financial behavior and repayment capacity.

4. **Property Appraisal**: An appraisal is conducted to determine the market value of the property, ensuring the loan amount does not exceed the value of the home.

5. **Title Search and Insurance**: This step ensures the property is free of liens or disputes, securing the lender's and borrower's interests.

6. **Lending Decision**: Based on the gathered information, the underwriter decides whether to approve, deny, or ask for additional information (conditional approval).

Three Pillars of Underwriting: Credit, Capacity, and Collateral

Underwriting revolves around evaluating three main factors:

- **Credit**: The borrower's creditworthiness is assessed through their credit scores and credit history, including factors like length of credit history, frequency of late payments, utilization of available credit, and types of credit used. This helps predict the borrower's ability to manage debt responsibly.

- **Capacity**: This refers to the borrower's ability to repay the loan. Underwriters review income stability, employment history, and debt-to-income ratios to determine if the borrower can sustainably handle monthly payments.

- **Collateral**: The value of the property being purchased plays a crucial role. The loan-to-value ratio (LTV) is calculated to ensure that the loan amount is appropriate relative to the property's appraised value. This is important because the property serves as security for the loan; it must be valuable enough to cover the loan amount in case of default.

Credit Scores and Loan Terms

Credit scores significantly influence the terms of the loan, including the interest rate. While conventional loans typically require a minimum credit score of 620, other loan types like FHA or VA loans might have different requirements. Higher credit scores may afford borrowers more favorable terms, and additional factors like cash reserves or extra income sources can compensate for higher debt-to-income ratios.

Underwriters assess several specific aspects of a borrower's credit history to determine their eligibility and the terms of the loan:

1. **Length of Credit History**: Longer credit histories provide more data for lenders to evaluate and can be indicative of good financial management if the history is positive.

2. **Credit Behavior and Management**: This includes how long borrowers have maintained good credit and their patterns in managing credit, which helps lenders predict future credit behavior.

3. **Late Payment History**: A history of late payments is a red flag for lenders as it suggests potential future delinquencies.

4. **Credit Utilization**: This refers to the amount of available credit that a borrower is using. High utilization can indicate that a borrower is overextended and may struggle to manage additional debt.

5. **Diversity of Credit**: Lenders also consider the types of credit a borrower has managed, such as credit cards, personal loans, and mortgage loans. A mix of credit types can show that a borrower has experience managing various forms of credit.

Loan-to-Value (LTV) Ratio

The Loan-to-Value (LTV) ratio is a crucial metric used by lenders to assess the risk of a mortgage loan. It represents the proportion of a property's value that is financed through a loan. This section explains how LTV ratios are calculated and utilized in determining the terms of a loan, including down payment requirements and interest rates.

Definition and Importance of LTV Ratio

The LTV ratio is calculated by dividing the mortgage amount by the lower of the property's appraised value or sales price. This ratio helps lenders determine the level of risk associated with a loan:

- **Lower LTV Ratios** indicate less risk for the lender as more equity is held by the homeowner, typically resulting in more favorable loan conditions such as lower interest rates or waived private mortgage insurance (PMI).
- **Higher LTV Ratios** suggest higher risk, as the borrower has less equity in the property, which could lead to stricter loan conditions.

LTV Ratio Calculation: Examples

Example 1:

- Property Sales Price: $600,000
- Appraised Value: $600,000
- Desired LTV Ratio: 75%

Calculation:

- $600,000 (Property Value) × 0.75 (LTV Ratio) = $450,000 (Loan Amount)
- Down Payment Required: $600,000 (Property Value) - $450,000 (Loan Amount) = $150,000

In this scenario, the buyer would need to make a 25% down payment, or $150,000, to meet the 75% LTV requirement.

Example 2:

- Property Sales Price: $575,000
- Appraised Value: $550,000 (Lower than Sales Price)
- Desired LTV Ratio: 80%

Calculation:

- $550,000 (Appraised Value) × 0.80 (LTV Ratio) = $440,000 (Loan Amount)
- Down Payment Required: $575,000 (Sales Price) - $440,000 (Loan Amount) = $135,000

In this example, due to the lower appraisal, the buyer would need to put down approximately 23.5%, or $135,000, to cover the difference between the sales price and the appraised value at an 80% LTV ratio.

Implications of LTV Ratios

- **Down Payment**: The LTV ratio directly affects the amount a buyer needs to put down. A higher appraised value relative to the sales price can reduce the down payment required, whereas a lower appraisal increases it.
- **Loan Terms**: Lenders might offer better interest rates and terms on loans with a lower LTV ratio.
- **PMI Requirements**: Loans with an LTV ratio above 80% typically require the borrower to purchase PMI, adding to the monthly cost of the mortgage until enough equity is built to lower the LTV ratio.

Understanding Private Mortgage Insurance (PMI)

Private Mortgage Insurance (PMI) is an essential component of the home financing process, particularly for borrowers who are unable to make a 20% down payment. This section explains the purpose of PMI, how it functions, and the conditions under which it can be terminated.

Purpose of PMI

PMI is designed to protect lenders from the risk of default by the borrower. When a borrower makes a down payment of less than 20% and has an LTV ratio higher than 80%, the loan presents a higher risk to the lender. In such cases, PMI is required to offset this risk, ensuring that the lender is protected against potential financial loss if the borrower fails to repay the loan.

PMI Requirements

PMI is generally required on conventional loans that do not meet the minimum equity requirements set by Fannie Mae and Freddie Mac. The criteria for requiring PMI include:

- **Down Payment Less Than 20%**: Typically, if a borrower's down payment is less than 20% of the home's value, the lender will require PMI.
- **LTV Ratio More Than 80%**: Loans with an LTV ratio over 80% are considered higher risk, necessitating PMI to secure the loan.

Calculation of Equity and LTV

Equity is calculated as the difference between the current market value of the property and the amount still owed on the mortgage. Here's how equity and LTV ratios interact:

- **Increasing Equity**: As the borrower pays down the mortgage or if the property value increases, equity in the property increases.
- **Decreasing LTV**: As equity increases, the LTV ratio decreases, reflecting a lower risk to the lender.

Termination of PMI

The termination of PMI can occur under certain conditions, offering potential savings for the borrower:

- **Automatic Termination**: Lenders are required by law to terminate PMI automatically when the mortgage balance reaches 78% of the original property value, provided the borrower is current on payments.
- **Borrower-Requested Termination**: Borrowers can request the removal of PMI when the principal balance falls to 80% of the original or current appraised property value. Approval may depend on current market conditions, additional payments made, or improvements to the property that increase its value.

Example Scenario

Consider a home with an appraised value of $400,000 and a mortgage loan amount of $360,000. This sets the LTV ratio at 90%.

- **PMI Requirement**: PMI is required due to the 90% LTV ratio.
- **PMI Termination Points:**
    - Automatic Termination: When the loan balance drops to $312,000 (78% of $400,000).
    - Borrower-Requested Termination: When the balance reaches $320,000 (80% of $400,000).

Debt-to-Income (DTI) Ratio

The Debt-to-Income (DTI) ratio is a crucial financial benchmark used by lenders to evaluate a potential borrower's ability to manage monthly payments and repay debts. This section explains what DTI ratio is, how it's calculated, and its implications for securing a mortgage.

What is the DTI Ratio?

DTI ratio measures the percentage of a borrower's gross monthly income that goes towards paying monthly debt obligations. This ratio is a key determinant in the lending process, influencing both the approval and conditions of mortgage loans.

- **Gross Income**: This is the total earnings before any deductions such as taxes, social security, and other benefits are applied.
- **Net Income**: Often referred to as "take-home pay," this is the income remaining after all deductions are made from the gross income.

Monthly Debt Obligations

Monthly debt includes obligations such as:

- **Credit Card Payments**: Only the minimum required payments are considered.
- **Loan Payments**: Includes auto loans, student loans, personal loans, and any other fixed debt payments.
- **Mortgage Payments**: For those already owning a home, existing mortgage payments are included.
- **Child Support and Alimony**: These are considered in the debt calculations.

Expenses like utilities, health insurance, and car insurance are not included in the debt calculations for DTI purposes.

Types of DTI Ratios

1. **Front-End DTI Ratio**: This ratio considers only housing-related expenses, which include the prospective mortgage payment, property taxes, homeowner's insurance, and any applicable homeowners association (HOA) dues.
2. **Back-End DTI Ratio**: This is more comprehensive and includes all minimum required monthly debt payments along with housing-related expenses. It provides a fuller picture of a borrower's financial obligations.

Calculation Examples

- Monthly Debt Payments: $4,000
- Gross Monthly Income: $12,000
- DTI Ratio Calculation: ($4,000 / $12,000) × 100 = 33.33%

This 33.33% DTI ratio suggests that the borrower uses 33.33% of their gross monthly income to cover monthly debt obligations.

Acceptable DTI Ratios

Lenders typically prefer different DTI ratios depending on their policies and the loan type:

- **Less than 36% (Back-End)**: Ideal scenario where a significant portion of income is not going towards debt repayment.
- **Front-End Ratio of 28%**: Preferably, no more than 28% of income should go towards the mortgage payment.

DTI Ratio Guidelines for Borrowers

- **DTI Ratio ≤ 35%**: Indicates manageable debt levels. Borrowers with this ratio are usually seen as low risk.
- **DTI Ratio 36% to 49%**: Acceptable but indicates room for improvement. Lenders may require additional eligibility criteria.

- **DTI Ratio ≥ 50%**: Considered high risk. Borrowers with such a ratio have limited financial flexibility, making it difficult to handle additional unforeseen expenses or economic downturns.

Principal, Interest, Taxes, and Insurance (PITI)

Principal, Interest, Taxes, and Insurance (PITI) encompass the core components of a typical mortgage payment and are crucial for determining the affordability of a home loan. This section breaks down each element of PITI and explains how these costs relate to a borrower's financial assessments.

Components of PITI

1. **Principal**: This is the portion of the payment that directly reduces the balance of the mortgage loan.
2. **Interest**: This is the cost paid to the lender for borrowing the principal amount.
3. **Taxes**: This refers to property taxes which are typically assessed by local governments and paid annually or semi-annually. For mortgage calculations, they are divided by twelve and added to the monthly mortgage payment.
4. **Insurance**: This includes homeowner's insurance, which covers damage and liability related to the home. Like taxes, the annual premium is typically broken down into a monthly cost.

These components are often bundled into a single monthly mortgage payment, making budgeting simpler for homeowners.

PITI and Mortgage Affordability

Mortgage lenders use PITI to determine the affordability of a mortgage for a prospective homeowner. It is a critical factor in calculating the front-end debt-to-income (DTI) ratio, which lenders use to evaluate a borrower's ability to manage monthly housing expenses.

- **Preferred PITI Proportion**: Lenders generally prefer that PITI does not exceed 28% of a borrower's gross monthly income. This threshold helps ensure that borrowers have enough income left each month to cover other living expenses and debts.

Example Calculation

Let's consider an example to illustrate how PITI influences mortgage affordability:

- Annual Gross Income: $108,000

- Monthly Gross Income: $108,000 / 12 = $9,000
- Monthly Mortgage Payment (PITI): $2,700

Front-End DTI Calculation:

- PITI Payment: $2,700
- Gross Monthly Income: $9,000
- Front-End DTI Ratio: ($2,700 / $9,000) x 100 = 30%

In this example, the front-end DTI ratio is exactly 30%, aligning with the typical lender's preference. This suggests that the mortgage is affordable under standard guidelines, assuming no other significant monthly debt obligations.

Additional Considerations

If the property requires homeowners association (HOA) fees, these should also be considered in the monthly housing costs, potentially affecting the affordability calculations. Lenders will add HOA fees to the PITI to form a more comprehensive view of the housing-related expenses.

Escrow Accounts in Real Estate Transactions

Escrow accounts play a pivotal role in real estate transactions, providing security and ensuring that funds are used appropriately according to the terms of the agreement. This section explains the two main types of escrow accounts used in real estate: real estate escrow accounts and mortgage escrow accounts.

Real Estate Escrow Accounts

1. **Purpose**: Real estate escrow accounts are essential during the closing process of a property sale. They are used to hold funds securely while the buyer and seller meet the conditions of the sale agreement.
2. **Function**: When a buyer makes an offer on a property, they often deposit earnest money into an escrow account to demonstrate their serious intent to purchase. This deposit is typically 1-10% of the property's sale price. The escrow agent (a neutral third party) holds these funds until all contractual obligations are met by both parties.
3. **Disposition of Funds**: At closing, the earnest money generally goes towards the purchase price of the property. However, if the buyer fails to fulfill their obligations under the contract, the earnest money may be forfeited to the seller as compensation.

Mortgage Escrow Accounts

1. **Purpose**: Mortgage escrow accounts are used by lenders to ensure that property taxes and homeowners' insurance premiums are paid on time. This safeguards the lender's interest in the property by preventing tax liens and lapses in insurance coverage.

2. **How It Works**: Each month, a portion of the mortgage payment is directed into the escrow account. This portion is typically calculated as one-twelfth of the total annual cost of property taxes and homeowners' insurance.

3. **Management and Adjustments**: Lenders often require a cushion, generally about two months' worth of escrow payments, to cover fluctuations in tax or insurance rates. If the actual expenses are lower than estimated, the surplus is usually refunded to the homeowner. Conversely, if there is a shortage due to increased tax rates or insurance premiums, the lender will notify the homeowner. The homeowner can then choose either to pay the difference in a lump sum or spread the extra cost over future monthly payments.

Example of Escrow in Action

Consider a buyer who is purchasing a home priced at $350,000:

- **Earnest Money Deposit**: The buyer might deposit $3,500 (1% of the purchase price) as earnest money.
- **Escrow Account at Closing**: This $3,500 is held in an escrow account until closing, where it will be applied to the purchase price, reducing the amount the buyer needs to finance.
- **Mortgage Escrow Account Post-Closing**: If the annual property taxes are $4,200 and the homeowner's insurance is $1,500, the lender will collect approximately $475 per month ($4,200 + $1,500 = $5,700 / 12 months = $475) into the escrow account to cover these bills.

How Mortgage Interest is Paid: Understanding Loan Structures

Mortgages are complex financial instruments, and understanding how interest on these loans works is crucial for both prospective homebuyers and those managing existing loans. This section breaks down the payment of mortgage interest, exploring different loan types and the concept of amortization.

Principal and Interest

1. **Principal**: This is the amount borrowed from the lender that still remains unpaid. It does not include the interest charged on the loan.

2. **Interest**: This represents the cost of borrowing the principal amount and is paid at a rate agreed upon by the lender and borrower.

Types of Mortgage Loans

- **Fixed-Rate Mortgage**: This loan type maintains the same interest rate throughout the duration of the loan, providing predictable monthly payments and stability against interest rate fluctuations.
- **Adjustable-Rate Mortgage (ARM)**: ARMs begin with a fixed interest rate for a preliminary period (typically 3, 5, 7, or 10 years), after which the rate adjusts annually. Initial rates are usually lower than fixed-rate mortgages, but the adjustment is tied to a specific financial index, which can increase or decrease based on broader economic changes.

Fixed/Adjustable-Rate Note

Some loan agreements allow borrowers to switch from a fixed-rate to an adjustable-rate loan, or vice versa, under specific conditions.

Annual Percentage Rate (APR)

APR is a broader measure of the cost to borrow money. It includes the interest rate plus any additional fees or costs associated with the mortgage, expressed as a percentage of the loan amount. It provides a more comprehensive view of the loan costs over time.

Interest Rate Lock

Borrowers can often lock in an interest rate for a period (commonly up to 90 days), securing the current rate even if rates rise before the loan is finalized. If the transaction does not close within this period, the locked rate may expire, potentially leading to a higher rate.

Amortization: The Structure of Loan Payments

Amortization is the process of spreading loan payments over time, which allows for a fixed end date to the loan. Payments are divided between the principal amount and interest:

- **Early Payments**: In the initial years, payments are primarily interest.
- **Later Payments**: Over time, the proportion of interest in each payment decreases while the principal portion increases.

Amortization Schedules

An amortization schedule provides a detailed breakdown of each payment throughout the life of the loan, showing how much of each payment is allocated toward principal versus interest.

The interest and principal

In an amortized loan, the relationship between principal and interest is inverse. Each month, the amount of interest charged depends on the remaining principal balance. As you gradually pay off the loan, the portion of your payment that goes towards interest decreases, while the portion that goes towards reducing the principal increases.

Special Amortization Cases

- **Partially Amortized Loan**: This type of loan includes regular amortization payments for a period, followed by a balloon payment (a large, lump-sum payment) at the end of the loan term.
- **Negative Amortization**: This occurs primarily with ARMs when the monthly payments are insufficient to cover the interest due. The unpaid interest is added to the principal, increasing the total debt owed.

Calculating Monthly Mortgage Payments

Calculating monthly mortgage payments involves determining the amount each month that will go towards both the principal and the interest based on the loan amount, the annual percentage rate (APR), and the term of the loan.

Example

Loan Details:

- Loan Amount: $450,000
- Annual Percentage Rate (APR): 4%
- Loan Term: 30 years (which equates to 360 total monthly payments)

Steps to Calculate the Monthly Payment:

1. **Find the Monthly Interest Rate**: The APR of 3% is divided by 12 (months) to find the monthly interest rate.
   - Monthly Interest Rate = 4% / 12 = 0.3333%

2. **Use an Amortization Chart**: The amortization chart provides a factor based on the APR and loan term used to calculate the monthly payment. For a $450,000 loan at 4% APR over 30 years, the factor from the chart is 4.77415.

   - Monthly Mortgage Payment Calculation = ($450,000 / $1,000) x 4.77415 = $2,148.37

This payment of $2,148.37 represents the total amount paid monthly towards both principal and interest.

Calculating Interest and Principal Payments:

- In the initial stages of repayment, a larger portion of the monthly payment is allocated towards interest. As the principal balance decreases over time, the interest component of the payment decreases, and more of the payment goes towards reducing the principal.

Origination Points and Fees

Origination Points: These are upfront fees charged by the lender to process the new loan, usually ranging from 1% to 3% of the loan amount. They are part of the closing costs and can sometimes be negotiated between the lender and the borrower.

Discount Points on Mortgage Payments

Discount points are an important financial tool in mortgage transactions that allow borrowers to reduce their interest rate and, consequently, their monthly payments. Understanding the cost and benefit of purchasing discount points is essential for making informed mortgage decisions.

What Are Discount Points?

Discount points, often simply called "points," are fees paid directly to the lender at closing in exchange for a reduced interest rate. Each point typically costs 1% of the total loan amount and usually lowers the interest rate by approximately 0.25%.

Example Breakdown

Consider a mortgage loan of $500,000 with an initial APR of 3.5% for a 30-year term. In this scenario:

- **Origination Point**: 1% of the loan amount, or $5,000, is charged by the lender to create the loan.
- **Discount Point**: An additional 1% of the loan amount, or another $5,000, is paid to lower the interest rate by 0.25%.

Total Points Cost: $10,000 (2% of the loan amount)

Financial Implications

- **Initial APR**: 3.5%
  - **Monthly Payment (No Points)**: $2,245.23 (principal and interest)
- **New APR after Buying 1 Point**: 3.25%
  - **Monthly Payment (With Discount Point)**: $2,176.03 (principal and interest)

Savings Calculation

- **Monthly savings**: $2,245.23 - $2,176.03 = $69.20
- **Over 30 years (360 payments)**: $69.20 × 360 = $24,912 total savings

Considerations Before Purchasing Points

1. **Break-even Point**: It will take just over 6 years for the buyers to recover the $5,000 spent on the discount point, calculated by dividing the cost of the point by the monthly savings.
   - **Break-even point in months**: $5,000 / $69.20 ≈ 72.25 months
2. **Long-Term Ownership**: Buying points is generally more beneficial for those who plan to stay in their home long enough to pass the break-even point. The longer you stay beyond the break-even, the more you save.
3. **Opportunity Cost**: Money spent on points could potentially yield a higher return if invested elsewhere. If the buyers do not intend to stay in the home through the full term of the loan, or if investment returns are projected to exceed the savings from lower interest payments, skipping the points might be advisable.

Decision-Making Strategy

Buyers should consider both their short-term financial ability and long-term housing plans when deciding whether to buy discount points. The decision should align with their overall financial strategy and the potential for changes in housing needs or financial circumstances over time.

Key Points to Remember

- **Amortization**: This process schedules periodic payments that pay off both interest and principal over the loan term.

- **Interest Calculation**: The interest for each month is calculated on the remaining principal balance, which means as the principal is paid down, less interest accrues.
- **Loan Term Impact**: The longer the term of the loan, typically, the lower the monthly payment but the higher the total amount of interest paid over the life of the loan.

Mortgage Loan Types

Understanding the different types of mortgage loans available can help borrowers choose the best option based on their financial situation and home buying goals. This section explores the various types of conventional loans, including conforming, nonconforming, and jumbo loans.

Conventional Loans

Conventional loans are mortgage loans offered by private lenders without government backing. They are considered secure for lenders, typically requiring a down payment of 20%, which results in an 80% loan-to-value (LTV) ratio, reducing the lender's risk. Here are the key characteristics:

- **Down Payment**: Usually 20%, though it can vary based on borrower creditworthiness and the specific lender's requirements.
- **Private Mortgage Insurance (PMI)**: Required if the down payment is less than 20% until the LTV ratio reaches 80%.

Conforming Loans

Conforming loans adhere to limits and other criteria set by Fannie Mae and Freddie Mac. They are called "conforming" because they conform to these standards:

- **Loan Limits**: Determined annually by the Federal Housing Finance Agency (FHFA) based on housing market trends. These limits can vary by region.
- **Secondary Market**: Conforming loans can be sold on the secondary mortgage market, which increases their availability and generally lowers interest rates.

Nonconforming Loans

Nonconforming loans do not meet the criteria set by Fannie Mae and Freddie Mac, usually because they exceed the established loan limits or differ in other qualifying aspects:

- **Higher Loan Amounts**: Often exceed the conforming loan limits set by the FHFA.
- **Cannot Be Sold on Secondary Market**: This restriction often results in higher interest rates compared to conforming loans.

Jumbo Loans

- **A Subset of Nonconforming Loans**: Specifically, jumbo loans exceed the loan limits set for conforming loans but may meet other conforming criteria.
- **Typically Higher Interest Rates:** Reflects the increased risk to lenders.

Importance of the House Price Index (HPI)

The HPI is crucial for several reasons:

- **Loan Limit Adjustments**: The FHFA uses the HPI to adjust the annual loan limits for conforming loans.
- **Market Analysis**: Provides insights into housing market trends, helping lenders, policymakers, and borrowers understand changes in home values across different regions.
- **Risk Assessment**: Aids in predicting trends in mortgage defaults, prepayments, and overall housing affordability.

Government-Backed Loans

Government-backed loans provide a crucial financing option, particularly beneficial for borrowers who might not qualify for conventional loans due to less stringent requirements concerning credit scores or down payments. These loans are guaranteed by the government, significantly reducing the risk to lenders and enabling more favorable lending conditions.

Federal Housing Administration (FHA) Loans

One of the most accessible types of government-backed loans is offered by the Federal Housing Administration. FHA loans are designed to make home buying more achievable for those with lower credit scores and smaller down payments.

Key Features of FHA Loans

- **Credit Score Requirements**: FHA loans are available to individuals with a minimum credit score of 500. The required down payment varies based on the credit score:

- **Credit Score 580 and above**: Minimum down payment of 3.5%.
  - **Credit Score 500 - 579**: Minimum down payment of 10%.
- **Loan Limits**: FHA sets maximum loan limits that it will guarantee, which generally align with the conforming loan limits set for conventional loans.
- **Debt-to-Income Ratios**:
  - **Front-end ratio (housing costs only)**: Capped at 31% of a borrower's income.
  - **Back-end ratio (total debts)**: Must not exceed 43% of a borrower's income.

These limits are designed to ensure borrowers are not overextending themselves financially.

Mortgage Insurance Premium (MIP)

- **Purpose**: The MIP compensates for the lower risk threshold and broader accessibility of FHA loans.
- **Payment Structure**: Includes an upfront payment at closing and an annual premium that is paid monthly.
- **Duration**: For most FHA loans, the MIP is required for the life of the loan or until it is refinanced into a non-FHA loan.

Benefits of FHA Loans

- **Lower Down Payments**: Making homeownership accessible to more people, especially first-time buyers or those without substantial savings.
- **Flexibility in Credit**: Accommodates borrowers with lower credit scores who are still capable of handling monthly mortgage payments.

VA Loans

The U.S. Department of Veterans Affairs (VA) provides loan guarantees for qualifying veterans, active-duty service members, and certain members of the National Guard and Reserves. This program is highly beneficial for military personnel looking to own a home.

Key Features of VA Loans

- **No Down Payment**: VA loans do not typically require a down payment, making home ownership more accessible for veterans.

- **No Private Mortgage Insurance (PMI)**: Unlike conventional loans, VA loans do not require PMI, which can significantly lower monthly payments.
- **Loan Guarantee**: The VA guarantees up to 25% of the conforming loan limit for the area, which mitigates lender risk and facilitates favorable lending terms.
- **Credit and Debt Ratios**: Many lenders require a minimum credit score of 620 and the maximum allowable debt-to-income ratio is 41%.

Eligibility

- **Service Requirements**: Eligibility for a VA loan is based on length and type of military service. For example, 181 days of active duty service or 90 continuous days under certain conditions are typical benchmarks for eligibility.

USDA Loans

The U.S. Department of Agriculture (USDA) supports homeownership in rural areas, aiming to boost rural economies. These loans are particularly targeted at low-income borrowers in designated rural areas.

Key Features of USDA Loans

- **No Down Payment Required**: Qualifying borrowers can obtain a USDA loan with little to no down payment.
- **Loan Terms**: USDA loans offer terms that can make monthly payments more affordable—33 years standard, and up to 38 years for very low-income borrowers.
- **Loan Guarantees**: The USDA can guarantee up to 95% of the loss of principal and interest, providing significant protection to lenders.

Eligibility

- **Geographical Requirements**: The property must be located in an eligible rural area as defined by the USDA.
- **Income Limits**: Borrowers must meet certain income thresholds which vary by region and family size.

Special Considerations for Government-Backed Loans

- VA and USDA loans provide opportunities for homeownership with benefits such as no down payment and reduced mortgage insurance costs, which can be especially helpful for first-time home buyers or those without significant savings.
- Borrowers should ensure they meet the specific service or geographical requirements to qualify for these loans.
- It's important for potential borrowers to understand not just the benefits but also any potential limitations or requirements, such as property location for USDA loans or military service for VA loans.

Other Loan Types

In addition to conventional and government-backed loans, there are several specialized types of loans that cater to specific financing needs during different stages of homeownership and property management. Here's a breakdown of some unique loan types:

Construction Loan

- **Purpose**: Construction loans are specifically designed to fund the building of a new home or a significant renovation project. They are unique because the loan amount is not disbursed in one lump sum but rather at various stages of the construction process.
- **Process**: The funds are released to the builder based on the completion of predetermined stages of the project. This type of loan is usually short-term and often has higher interest rates due to the perceived risk by the lender.
- **Conversion**: Once the construction is complete, these loans are generally converted into a conventional mortgage with typical loan repayment terms.

Home Equity Loan

- **Purpose**: A home equity loan allows homeowners to borrow against the equity they have built up in their home. Equity is the difference between the current market value of the property and the amount still owed on the mortgage.
- **Usage**: These loans are commonly used for major expenses such as home renovations, medical bills, or college tuition. The loan comes as a lump sum and is often at a fixed interest rate.

Bridge Loan

Purpose: Bridge loans, also known as swing loans, are temporary loans used to "bridge" the gap between the costs of new property acquisition and the sale of a previous property.

Features:

- **Short-term Nature**: Typically, bridge loans are short-term (up to one year), with relatively high interest rates and are secured by the borrower's existing property.
- **Payment Structure**: Borrowers may only need to make interest payments during the life of the loan, with the principal due in full once the old home is sold.

Owner Financing

- **Concept**: Also known as a land contract or contract for deed, in this arrangement, the seller acts as the lender. The buyer does not receive the actual deed until the final payment is made.
- **Advantages**: This can be beneficial for buyers who might not qualify for traditional financing due to credit issues or other financial constraints.

Sale Leaseback

- **Scenario**: In a sale leaseback arrangement, a property owner sells the property to a buyer but continues to live in or use the property as a tenant.
- **Benefits**: This arrangement can be useful for owners who need to unlock the equity in their home for cash but wish to continue living at the property. It's often used in commercial real estate as a way for businesses to free up capital while maintaining operations in the same location.

Purchase Money Mortgage

- **Definition**: A purchase money mortgage is provided by the seller of a property to the buyer as part of the purchase agreement.
- **Application**: This type of financing is particularly useful in scenarios where the buyer may not qualify for a traditional mortgage due to credit issues or other financial constraints.

Shared Equity Mortgage

- **Concept**: In a shared equity mortgage, a third party (often a relative or investor) provides funding assistance for purchasing a property in exchange for a share of the profits when the property is sold.

- **Common Use**: This is popular among real estate investors, especially those involved in house flipping, as it allows for shared investment risks and rewards without traditional lending.

Open-End Mortgage

- **Functionality**: An open-end mortgage allows borrowers to borrow against the equity in their home up to a certain limit, even after paying down the balance.
- **Example**: If a borrower has a loan limit of $200,000 and currently owes $150,000, they can potentially re-borrow up to $50,000.

Package Mortgage

- **Description**: A package mortgage includes financing for both real estate and personal property contained within the home, such as furniture.
- **Benefit**: This can be convenient for buyers who wish to purchase a fully furnished home, integrating all costs into one loan.

Blanket Mortgage

- **Purpose**: Blanket mortgages cover multiple properties under a single loan and are often utilized by developers to finance large projects like subdivisions.
- **Mechanism**: As individual lots are sold, the developer can pay off part of the blanket mortgage through partial release provisions.

Wrap-Around Mortgage

- **Structure:** A wrap-around mortgage involves a seller financing arrangement where the seller's existing mortgage is wrapped by a new mortgage extended to the buyer.
- **Payment Flow**: The buyer makes monthly payments to the seller, who then continues to make payments on the original mortgage.

Reverse Mortgage

- **Target Audience**: Available to homeowners over the age of 62, allowing them to convert part of the equity in their home into cash.
- **Payment Options**: Funds from a reverse mortgage can be received as a lump sum, fixed monthly payments, or a line of credit, providing financial flexibility during retirement.

Understanding the Primary Mortgage Market

The primary mortgage market is where loans originated, allowing borrowers to secure financing directly from lenders for various real estate purchases. This market is diverse, featuring several types of lenders who cater to different segments of the market—from residential to large commercial projects. Understanding the role of each lender can help borrowers choose the best lender for their needs.

Types of Lenders in the Primary Mortgage Market

1. **Commercial Banks**
   - **Function**: These are national banks that provide a broad range of consumer and business loans.
   - **Secondary Market Activities**: Many loans originated by commercial banks are designed for resale in the secondary mortgage market, which helps them manage risk and liquidity.

2. **Savings and Loan Associations (S&Ls)**
   - **Specialization**: Also known as thrifts or savings banks, S&Ls are community-based and focus primarily on residential mortgages.
   - **Regulatory Requirements**: By law, they must allocate the majority of their lending resources to residential financing.

3. **Credit Unions**
   - **Structure**: Member-owned cooperatives that offer savings accounts and provide loans primarily to their members, including auto and home loans.
   - **Benefits**: Typically offer favorable rates and terms due to their not-for-profit status.

4. **Insurance Companies and Investment Groups**
   - **Focus**: These entities generally invest in and finance large real estate projects like office buildings and shopping centers, not individual mortgages.
   - **Investment Strategy**: They look for large, long-term investments that match their need to pay out claims over time.

5. **Pension Funds**
   - **Investment Focus**: Similar to insurance companies, they invest in significant real estate projects and are more involved in commercial rather than residential loans.
   - **Goal**: To secure stable, long-term returns for retirees.

6. **Mortgage Bankers**

- **Operations:** Utilize in-house resources to process, underwrite, and fund loans.
- **Role**: Often service the loans they originate or sell them on the secondary market.

7. **Mortgage Brokers**

- **Function**: Act as intermediaries between borrowers and lenders.
- **Services**: They do not fund loans directly but match borrowers with lenders that best meet their needs based on their financial situation and borrowing criteria.

Interaction with the Secondary Mortgage Market

- **Loan Sales**: Lenders in the primary market frequently package and sell their conforming loans to entities in the secondary mortgage market, such as Fannie Mae and Freddie Mac.
- **Purpose**: This process helps to replenish their capital, enabling them to offer more loans to other consumers.
- **Liquidity and Funding**: Selling loans allows lenders to maintain liquidity and continue lending without having to wait for loans to mature over long periods.

Secondary Mortgage Market

The secondary mortgage market plays a crucial role in the housing finance ecosystem by enhancing liquidity and stability. This market involves entities known as Government-Sponsored Enterprises (GSEs), which purchase mortgages from lenders and package them into mortgage-backed securities (MBS). These securities are then sold to investors, which provides lenders with the capital to issue more loans, promoting broader accessibility to mortgage financing.

Key Players in the Secondary Mortgage Market

1. **Fannie Mae (Federal National Mortgage Association)**

- **Role**: Established in 1938, Fannie Mae's primary function is to stimulate homeownership by buying mortgages from larger commercial banks and other financial institutions.
- **Purpose**: By purchasing these loans, Fannie Mae provides the original lenders with liquidity to issue new mortgages, particularly focusing on assisting low- to moderate-income borrowers.

2. **Freddie Mac (Federal Home Loan Mortgage Corporation)**

   - **Establishment**: Created in 1970 to expand the secondary market for mortgages by buying loans from smaller banks that might otherwise struggle to provide financing on their own.
   - **Objective**: Similar to Fannie Mae, Freddie Mac supports homeownership for middle-income Americans through its purchasing and securitization activities.

3. **Ginnie Mae (Government National Mortgage Association)**

   - **Function**: Part of the U.S. Department of Housing and Urban Development since 1968, Ginnie Mae guarantees the timely payment of principal and interest on its mortgage-backed securities.
   - **Significance**: Ginnie Mae's guarantee enhances the safety of investments in its MBS, making them highly attractive to investors and thus supporting affordable homeownership.

4. **Farmer Mac (Federal Agricultural Mortgage Corporation)**

   - **Focus**: Specializes in the secondary market for agricultural loans, buying qualified loans from lenders to facilitate rural and agricultural financing.
   - **Impact**: By providing liquidity to rural lenders, Farmer Mac helps ensure that agricultural businesses and rural homeowners have access to affordable financing options.

Understanding Mortgage-Backed Securities (MBS)

- **Definition**: MBS are asset-backed securities secured by a collection of mortgages, originating from regulated financial institutions.
- **Process**: Once loans are purchased from primary lenders, they are pooled together and securitized into MBS, which are then sold to investors on the global markets.

The Distinction Between Mae and Mac

- **Fannie Mae and Ginnie Mae**: These GSEs primarily deal with government-backed loans, such as FHA and VA loans, which are designed to support specific populations in obtaining homeownership.
- **Freddie Mac and Farmer Mac**: These entities typically handle conventional loans, which are not insured or guaranteed by the federal government.

Conforming Loans

- **Criteria**: For a mortgage to be eligible for purchase by these GSEs, it must meet specific conforming loan limits and borrower qualifications.

- **Purpose**: These standards ensure that the loans acquired by GSEs are of high quality and match their risk tolerance and policy objectives.

Key Clauses in Security Instruments for Mortgages

Security instruments, such as mortgages and deeds of trust, include various clauses that outline the rights and responsibilities of both the borrower and the lender. These clauses are critical for protecting the interests of the lending institution and ensuring clear terms for the repayment and handling of the loan. Here, we'll explore some of the common clauses found in these legal documents.

Defeasance Clause

- **Purpose**: This clause ensures that once a mortgage loan is fully paid off, the borrower will receive clear title to the property. It legally binds the lender or trustee to release the lien from the property's title.
- **Effect**: Prevents the lender from claiming any further payments or interests from the borrower after the mortgage is completely settled.

Acceleration Clause

- **Trigger**: This clause comes into effect if the borrower defaults on the loan, typically after being delinquent for two to three months.
- **Outcome**: Allows the lender to demand immediate repayment of the entire outstanding balance of the loan. If the borrower cannot pay the full amount, this clause can lead to foreclosure.
- **Process**: The lender must first send an acceleration letter to the borrower, officially notifying them of the default and the lender's intent to accelerate the loan terms.

Due-on-Sale (Alienation) Clause

- **Activation**: This clause is activated when a property is sold or transferred to another party.
- **Requirement**: Mandates that the borrower must pay back the full remaining loan balance upon the sale or transfer of the property.
- **Purpose**: Protects the lender by preventing the new owner from taking over the existing loan without approval.

Power-of-Sale Clause

- **Function**: Grants the lender the authority to foreclose on the property and sell it without going through judicial proceedings, should the borrower default on the loan.
- **Jurisdiction**: The use and process of this clause can vary by state, as some states require judicial review for foreclosures.
- **Efficiency**: This clause facilitates a quicker foreclosure process, benefiting the lender by reducing legal costs and time.

Pre-payment Penalty Clause

- **Application**: This clause allows the lender to impose a penalty on the borrower if the loan is paid off early, compensating for the interest that would have been paid over the life of the loan.
- **Current Market**: While once common, pre-payment penalties are now rare in the mortgage market and are often regulated by state laws or financial regulations to protect consumers.

Understanding Foreclosure Processes

Foreclosure is a significant legal procedure that lenders use to recover the balance of a loan from a borrower who has stopped making payments. It results in the lender taking ownership of the property and usually selling it. The process and regulations surrounding foreclosures can vary significantly by state, but there are three main types that are commonly recognized:

1. Judicial Foreclosure

- **Process**: This type involves the court system. The lender must file a lawsuit against the defaulting borrower, and the court must issue a judgment for foreclosure. The property is then usually sold at a public auction.
- **Requirements**: The lender must prove that the borrower is delinquent.
- **Commonality**: This is the most common type of foreclosure, particularly in states that require a court review to initiate foreclosure proceedings.

2. Nonjudicial Foreclosure

- **Process**: In states that permit nonjudicial foreclosures, the process does not require court involvement. The lender can initiate foreclosure under the terms of a "power-of-sale" clause that must be included in the mortgage or deed of trust. This allows the lender to sell the property to recover the unpaid loan amount without court supervision.

- **Cost and Duration**: It is generally faster and less costly than judicial foreclosure.
- **Deficiency Judgment**: Most nonjudicial foreclosure states do not allow lenders to pursue deficiency judgments if the sale price of the property doesn't cover the full amount owed, although this can vary.

3. Strict Foreclosure

- **Process**: A less common form, strict foreclosure involves a court proceeding where the court orders the defaulting borrower to pay the mortgage within a certain period.
- **Outcome**: If the borrower fails to pay within the specified timeframe, the property's title is transferred directly to the lender without the need for sale.
- **Usage**: This type is only available in a few states and is typically used when the value of the property is less than the mortgage balance.

Legal and Financial Implications

- **Foreclosure Notice**: Typically, lenders will not start the foreclosure process until the borrower is at least 120 days delinquent, although this can vary based on the lender's policies and the state's laws.
- **Impact on Borrowers**: Foreclosure can severely impact a borrower's credit score and ability to obtain future loans.
- **Buying Foreclosed Properties**: Purchasing a foreclosed home can be an opportunity for buyers to find a property at a reduced price, but it comes with increased complexity and potential risks.

Tips for Dealing with Foreclosure

- **State Laws**: It's crucial for both borrowers and real estate professionals to understand the specific foreclosure processes and rights in their state.
- **Prevention**: Homeowners facing financial difficulties should seek advice early from financial advisors or legal counsel to explore options such as loan modification, refinancing, or selling the home before foreclosure becomes unavoidable.
- **Real Estate Professionals**: If you're involved in buying or selling a foreclosed property, thorough due diligence is essential. Understanding the state-specific foreclosure process and the property's legal status can help mitigate risks.

Financing and Credit Laws in Real Estate

Navigating the complexities of real estate financing requires a solid understanding of various laws designed to ensure fair lending practices and protect consumers. Key legislation includes the Truth in Lending Act (TILA), Regulation Z, and the Real Estate Settlement Procedures Act (RESPA). Each of these laws plays a vital role in regulating how financial information is disclosed and how real estate transactions are conducted.

Truth in Lending Act (TILA)

- **Purpose**: Enacted in 1968, TILA aims to promote the informed use of consumer credit by requiring clear disclosure of key terms of the lending arrangement and all costs.
- **Triggering Terms**: When specific terms such as down payment amount, number of payments, or specific interest rates are mentioned in advertising, full disclosure of all lending terms must be made to avoid misleading consumers.
- **Regulation**: TILA is implemented through Regulation Z, which also includes provisions related to credit advertising and effects how loan originators are compensated.

Regulation Z

- **Function**: Regulation Z provides specific guidelines for lenders in the application of TILA. It ensures that lenders provide consumers with clear and understandable information on the terms of credit.
- **Loan Originator Compensation**: This regulation prohibits compensation to loan originators that is based on the terms of the loan other than the amount of credit extended. Additionally, it forbids loan originators from steering clients towards less favorable loan terms simply to increase their own compensation.

Real Estate Settlement Procedures Act (RESPA)

- **Objective**: Established in 1974, RESPA aims to protect homebuyers from abusive practices during the real estate settlement process. It ensures that buyers are provided with detailed information about all costs involved in the real estate transaction.
- **Disclosure Requirements**: Lenders are required to give borrowers detailed disclosures at various stages of the settlement process. This includes the Loan Estimate and Closing Disclosure forms, which outline the charges likely to be incurred upon settlement.
- **Prohibitions on Kickbacks**: RESPA strictly prohibits the exchange of fees, kickbacks, or anything of value in exchange for referrals of settlement service business related to real estate transactions.

Practical Implications for Consumers and Professionals

- **For Consumers**: These laws ensure that borrowers receive timely and complete information about the costs and conditions of their mortgages, enabling them to make informed financial decisions.
- **For Real Estate Professionals**: Understanding and complying with these laws is crucial to avoid legal pitfalls and to foster trust and professionalism in real estate transactions. Real estate agents and brokers must be particularly cautious about their partnerships with lenders or other service providers to ensure compliance with RESPA's anti-kickback provisions.

The Equal Credit Opportunity Act (ECOA) and laws against predatory lending practices are essential for safeguarding consumers in the real estate financing market. These regulations are designed to ensure fair treatment, prevent discrimination, and protect consumers from unethical lending practices.

Equal Credit Opportunity Act (ECOA)

- **Purpose**: Enacted in 1974, the ECOA aims to prevent lenders from discriminating against loan applicants based on factors unrelated to their creditworthiness.
- **Protected Classes**: Under ECOA, it is unlawful for lenders to discriminate based on race, color, religion, national origin, sex, marital status, age (provided the applicant is old enough to enter into a contract), because all or part of the applicant's income derives from any public assistance program, or because the applicant has in good faith exercised any right under the Consumer Credit Protection Act.
- **Requirements**: Lenders must provide applicants with a notice of action taken within 30 days of receiving a completed application. This notice must include reasons for any denial or the right to learn the reasons if denied.

Predatory Lending Practices

Predatory lending refers to unethical practices by lenders that deceive, exploit, or discriminate against borrowers. These practices can lead to borrowers entering into loans that they may not fully understand or that are likely to be unaffordable, often resulting in detrimental financial consequences.

Common Forms of Mortgage Fraud

- **Illegal Property Flipping**: Involves purchasing properties and artificially inflating their value through false appraisals. These properties are then quickly sold, creating profit based on the inflated values.

- **Silent Second**: The buyer of a property takes out a second mortgage to cover the down payment and fails to disclose this loan to the primary lender. This can mislead the primary lender about the buyer's financial status and the property's equity.

- **Equity Skimming**: An investor uses a straw buyer to acquire a property, does not make mortgage payments, and rents out the property until it goes into foreclosure.

- **Straw Buyers**: Individuals who stand in for another person in a transaction without revealing the identity of the real buyer, often to manipulate the lending process.

- **Inflated Appraisals**: Occur when appraisers, in collusion with borrowers or other parties, provide misleadingly high property valuation reports to lenders.

- **Usury**: Charging interest at rates above those allowed by law.

The Equal Credit Opportunity Act (ECOA) and laws against predatory lending practices are essential for safeguarding consumers in the real estate financing market. These regulations are designed to ensure fair treatment, prevent discrimination, and protect consumers from unethical lending practices.

Legal and Practical Implications for Consumers

- **ECOA Protections**: Consumers should be aware that they are protected under ECOA from discriminatory lending practices and have the right to fair and equal credit access based on their financial capabilities.

- **Awareness of Predatory Practices**: By understanding what constitutes predatory lending, consumers can be more vigilant and avoid engaging with lenders who propose dubious loan terms or conditions that seem too good to be true.

- **Reporting and Redress**: Victims of discriminatory lending practices or predatory lending can seek legal redress. They can report such activities to the Consumer Financial Protection Bureau (CFPB) or state consumer protection agencies.

Understanding Qualified Mortgages

Qualified Mortgages (QMs) represent a category of loans that have certain stable features to make it more likely that borrowers will be able to afford their loans. QMs were developed as part of the Dodd-Frank Wall Street Reform and Consumer Protection Act of 2010. These mortgages comply with the "ability-to-repay" rule, a requirement that compels lenders to make a reasonable and good faith effort to determine that the borrowers can afford to pay back the loan.

Key Requirements of Qualified Mortgages

The Consumer Financial Protection Bureau (CFPB) sets standards for what constitutes a Qualified Mortgage. Adherence to these standards provides lenders with certain legal protections and helps ensure the financial stability of borrowers. Key aspects include:

1. **Debt-to-Income Ratio**: For a loan to be considered a Qualified Mortgage, the borrower's debt-to-income ratio (DTI) should not exceed 43%. This means monthly debt payments cannot be more than 43% of the borrower's pre-tax income.

2. **Points and Fees Limitation**: Points and fees charged on a QM cannot exceed 3% of the loan amount for loans above $100,000. This rule helps to prevent excessive charges that can make loans unaffordable.

3. **Loan Term**: QMs are limited to terms of 30 years or less. Longer loan durations can pose a greater risk of default.

4. **Prohibited Features**:

   - **Interest-Only Loans**: QMs cannot have terms that allow the borrower to pay only interest and no principal during any period of the loan.

   - **Balloon Payments**: Except under specific circumstances in rural or underserved areas, QMs cannot have balloon payments, where a large lump sum is due at the end of the loan term.

   - **Negative Amortization**: Payments that do not fully amortize the remaining balance are not allowed under QM standards. Each payment must bring down the principal owed.

Benefits of Qualified Mortgages

- **Consumer Protection**: By eliminating risky features like negative amortization and interest-only periods, QMs protect consumers from unexpected financial burdens that could lead to default.

- **Standardized Lending Practices**: QMs create a more stable and predictable lending market by standardizing the practices around mortgage loans.

- **Legal Protections for Lenders**: Lenders who issue Qualified Mortgages receive certain legal protections, such as a presumption of compliance with the ability-to-repay rule, reducing the risk of litigation.

Considerations for Borrowers

While Qualified Mortgages provide numerous protections, they may also restrict the availability of credit to certain borrowers, such as those with higher DTI ratios or those needing non-standard loan products. Borrowers should assess their financial situation to determine if a Qualified Mortgage fits their needs or if they might qualify under non-QM loan options available in the market.

TILA/RESPA Integrated Disclosures (TRID)

The TILA/RESPA Integrated Disclosure rules, commonly referred to as TRID, are critical regulations designed to ensure clarity and fairness in the mortgage process by requiring lenders to provide clear, timely, and standardized information to consumers about the costs and terms of their loans. Here's a closer look at the specifics of these disclosures and their impact on the mortgage process.

Key Components of TRID

1. **Loan Estimate (LE)**
   - **Purpose**: The Loan Estimate provides prospective borrowers with detailed information about the terms of the mortgage for which they are applying. This includes interest rates, monthly payments, and the total closing costs for the loan.
   - **Timing**: Lenders are required to provide this document within three business days after a borrower submits a loan application.
   - **Details Covered**: The LE includes costs such as the origination fees, services you cannot shop for, services you can shop for, taxes, government fees, prepaids, and initial escrow payments at closing.
2. **Closing Disclosure (CD)**
   - **Purpose**: This document offers final details about the mortgage. It is intended to confirm and clarify the terms and expenses the borrower will commit to.
   - **Timing**: The Closing Disclosure must be provided at least three business days before the loan closing, allowing borrowers ample time to review the terms and costs.
   - **Contents**: The CD finalizes the loan amount, interest rate, monthly payments, and a detailed list of closing costs.

Applicability of TRID

- **Relevant Transactions**: TRID rules apply to most residential mortgage transactions, including home purchases, refinancing, and home equity loans.

- **Comparative Review**: Borrowers can compare the initial Loan Estimate to the final Closing Disclosure to ensure there are no unexpected changes and that they fully understand their financial obligations.

Exemptions from TRID Rules

While TRID covers a broad range of mortgage transactions, certain loans are exempt:

- **Reverse Mortgages**: These are special types of home loans that allow older homeowners to convert part of the equity in their homes into cash without having to sell the home or pay additional monthly bills.
- **Home Equity Lines of Credit (HELOCs)**: These are revolving lines of credit secured by the equity in the borrower's home.
- **Manufactured Housing Loans (not secured by real estate)**: These loans might be secured by personal property rather than real estate.
- **Commercial and Business Loans**: Generally exempt, unless they are used to purchase or improve a rental property that includes one to four residential units.

Importance of TRID

TRID enhances consumer protection by ensuring transparency, which helps borrowers understand and manage their financial responsibilities more effectively. The standardized disclosure formats prevent surprises at closing, improve the borrower's ability to compare different loan offers, and facilitate better communication between the lender and borrower. Compliance with these rules is crucial for lenders to avoid regulatory penalties and for borrowers to ensure they engage in fair and understandable mortgage transactions.

Summary

In this chapter, we explored the comprehensive landscape of financing in real estate, detailing the mechanics behind various mortgage types and the regulatory framework ensuring fair lending practices. From understanding the roles of different mortgage lenders in the primary market to navigating the complexities of the secondary mortgage market, this chapter aimed to equip readers with the knowledge required to make informed financing decisions.

We delved into the specifics of government-backed loans, discussed the significance of Qualified Mortgages, and highlighted key legal protections under TILA, RESPA, and other consumer protection statutes. By providing a clear overview of these crucial elements, this chapter serves as a guide for both buyers and financial professionals to successfully manage the financing process in real estate transactions, ensuring compliance, transparency, and fiscal responsibility.

Chapter 5: General Principles of Agency

Agency principles are crucial, comprising approximately 13% of the exam, translating to about 10 questions.

Agency vs. Non-Agency Relationships

Agency Relationships

In an agency relationship, a real estate professional acts as an agent for a client, involving significant representation that necessitates exercising judgment or discretion. The specific responsibilities of an agent are elaborated later in this chapter.

Example: Consider a real estate agent, Jane, who is hired by the Smith family to sell their home. As their agent, Jane has a fiduciary duty to act in the Smiths' best interests, from advising on the listing price to negotiating with potential buyers.

Subagency

Subagency often develops when a second agent, not directly hired by the buyer, shows a property. While this agent assists the buyer in viewing the property, they owe their fiduciary duties to the listing broker and the seller, not to the buyer. Nevertheless, the buyer can anticipate honest treatment from the subagent. Modern real estate practices have shifted towards buyers generally having their own agents, reducing the prevalence of subagency.

Example: If agent Tom, who is showing a property, is not representing the buyer, his primary duty is to the seller and the listing broker. Although he should deal honestly with the buyer, his advice and actions are geared to favor the seller's position.

Non-Agency Relationships

Non-agency relationships occur when real estate professionals assist a consumer without representing them as agents. This assistance does not involve the exercise of professional judgment or discretion. The obligations of non-agents are regulated by state laws.

Example: Emily, a real estate professional, provides market data and listings to Paul, but she does not advise him on which home to buy or negotiate terms on his behalf. Her role is purely informational, and she does not have a fiduciary responsibility towards Paul.

Transactional Brokers

In jurisdictions that permit non-agency, transactional brokers or facilitators help in real estate transactions without representing either the buyer or the seller. They are compensated for facilitating the transaction but are not bound by agency duties. The specifics of this role can vary widely by state, so professionals are advised to be familiar with local regulations.

Example: In a state where non-agency relationships are recognized, Sarah acts as a transactional broker for a property sale. She organizes the necessary paperwork and coordinates communication between the buyer and seller, ensuring a smooth process, but she does not provide guidance or advocacy for either party.

Understanding the differences between agency and non-agency relationships, including subagency and transactional brokerage, is essential for real estate professionals and is a significant component of the licensing exam. This chapter will continue to explore these roles and their legal implications in the sections to follow.

Clients, Customers, and Consumers

In real estate transactions, understanding the distinctions between clients, customers, and consumers is fundamental. Each category has specific roles and responsibilities that real estate professionals must manage effectively.

Client (Principal)

A client, also known as the principal, is the individual or party whom the agent represents in a real estate transaction. This could be a buyer or a seller. The agent owes fiduciary duties to the client, which include loyalty, confidentiality, obedience, accounting, and diligence. These responsibilities ensure that the agent acts in the best interests of the client at all times.

Example: Let's consider a scenario where a real estate agent, Lisa, is hired by the Johnsons to help them sell their home. The Johnsons are Lisa's clients, and she is legally obligated to prioritize their interests, advise them effectively, and strive to secure the best possible terms in the sale of their property.

Customer

A customer in a real estate context is someone who interacts with an agent but does not have a formal agency relationship with that agent. Customers receive services and information but are not afforded the protective fiduciary duties owed to clients. Real estate professionals must treat customers with honesty and fairness, but they do not advocate on their behalf.

Example: In the previous scenario with Lisa and the Johnsons, suppose a potential buyer named Tom approaches Lisa to inquire about the property. Tom is a customer; he receives important information about the house from Lisa, but she does not negotiate on his behalf or offer him advice tailored to promote his best interests.

Consumer (Prospect)

Consumers, or prospects, encompass all potential clients and customers within the real estate market— essentially anyone who might consider buying or selling property in the future. Real estate professionals aim to convert consumers into clients by establishing relationships and demonstrating value.

Example: After the successful sale of the Johnsons' home, they recommend Lisa to a friend, Mr. Green, who is considering selling his house. Mr. Green is initially a consumer or prospect. If Lisa meets with him and they agree to terms, he will transition from being a consumer to a client, with Lisa assuming the full responsibilities of representation.

Real estate professionals interact with different categories of people—clients, customers, and consumers— each requiring a unique approach and level of service. Understanding these distinctions is vital for maintaining professional ethics and ensuring that all parties are treated appropriately throughout the buying or selling process. This knowledge is not only essential for daily operations but also critical for the real estate licensing exam.

Types of Agents and Their Responsibilities

Understanding the various types of agents and the scope of their responsibilities is essential for both real estate professionals and those studying for the real estate licensing exam.

Special Agents

A special agent in real estate has limited authority to act on a client's behalf. Typically, real estate agents and escrow officers fall into this category. They can perform specific tasks as directed by their client but do not have the authority to bind the client to a contract.

Example: A real estate agent like Alice can list a property for sale and work to find a buyer, but she cannot sign a sales contract on behalf of her client. Her role is limited to facilitating communication and negotiations between the buyer and seller.

General Agents

General agents have more comprehensive authority to handle a range of activities within a specific area for a client. A common example is a property manager, who may have the ability to bind the client to certain types of contracts related to the management of the property.

Example: As a property manager, Bob manages several rental properties for his client. He can make decisions on the client's behalf, such as signing lease agreements and handling tenant issues without needing to consult the property owner for each decision.

Universal Agents

Universal agents possess the broadest authority, typically granted through a power of attorney. These agents can make decisions that affect their principal's legal and financial status.

Example: If Carol has been given power of attorney by her elderly aunt, she can manage all of her aunt's affairs, including selling her home, managing her investments, and making health care decisions.

Agency Relationship Types in Real Estate Transactions

Single Agency

In a single agency arrangement, the agent represents only one party—either the buyer or the seller.

- Seller's Agents are contracted through a listing agreement to represent the seller's interests, aiming to secure the best price and terms for the sale of the property.
- Buyer's Agents represent the buyer's interests throughout the transaction. They may be paid directly by the buyer or through a commission shared with the seller's agent.

Dual Agency

Dual agency involves an agent or a brokerage representing both the buyer and the seller in the same transaction. This arrangement can lead to conflicts of interest, as the agent must remain neutral, which can dilute the level of advocacy provided to both parties.

- Single Licensee Dual Agency occurs when one agent represents both the buyer and seller, requiring explicit, written consent from both parties.
- Dual Licensee Dual Agency happens when two agents from the same brokerage represent each party independently. This setup helps mitigate the limitations of single licensee dual agency by allowing each client to receive full representation.

Real estate agents operate under different types of agency relationships that dictate their responsibilities and the extent of their authority. These relationships are crucial for ethical practice and are regulated by law to protect the interests of all parties involved in a real estate transaction. Understanding these distinctions is vital for anyone entering the real estate industry.

Agent Responsibilities to Clients: The OLD CAR Principle

Real estate agents, as fiduciaries, are trusted to act in their clients' best interests. Their duties can be effectively remembered using the acronym "OLD CAR," each letter representing a key aspect of their responsibilities.

Obedience

Agents are required to follow their clients' lawful and reasonable instructions. This obedience is limited to ethical and legal directives; agents must not follow instructions that are illegal or unethical. Additionally, agents must inform potential buyers of known material defects in a property, even if doing so could harm the seller's interests.

Example: If a client instructs their agent, Denise, not to disclose the existence of termites in the home, Denise must disregard this request and inform potential buyers of the infestation, as it is a material defect.

Loyalty

An agent must place the client's interests above all others, including their own. This includes seeking the best possible terms for the client, even if it results in a lower commission for the agent.

Example: Mark, a buyer's agent, discovers a home priced below market value that is perfect for his client. Even though securing this deal might reduce his commission, Mark prioritizes his client's interest and works to secure the property at the lower price.

Disclosure

Agents must disclose all relevant facts that could affect the client's decisions in a transaction. This includes not only the positives but also any negatives that could impact the client's position or decisions, such as potential conflicts of interest.

Example: An agent, Sarah, learns that a planned highway expansion might increase noise levels near a property she's selling. She must inform her client of this development as it could affect the property's value and the client's desire to proceed.

Confidentiality

Confidentiality involves safeguarding any information that could weaken the client's negotiating position if disclosed. This duty extends beyond the termination of the agency relationship.

Example: If a client confides in his agent, Tom, that he needs to sell quickly due to financial difficulties, Tom must keep this information confidential and not disclose it to potential buyers, as it could be used to negotiate a lower sale price.

Accounting

Agents are responsible for accurate handling of all client-related properties and funds. This includes ensuring that there is no improper mixing of client funds with the agent's personal funds and managing all paperwork and property related to the transaction carefully.

Example: Lisa, who is managing an earnest money deposit for a buyer, must keep these funds in a separate escrow account and not mix them with her own money or use them for personal expenses.

Reasonable Skill and Care

Agents must use their knowledge and skills to competently manage the real estate transaction. They should provide accurate and timely information, ensuring they act within their scope of expertise and referring clients to specialists when necessary.

Example: An agent, Jim, advises his clients to consult a lawyer for a complex legal issue arising during their transaction, ensuring they receive expert advice on a matter outside his expertise.

Understanding and adhering to the "OLD CAR" fiduciary duties is crucial for real estate agents. These principles guide ethical behavior and professional practice, ensuring that agents provide the highest standard of service to their clients, which is a foundational element of real estate practice and a critical area of knowledge for the licensing exam.

Agent Responsibilities to Customers

Honesty and Integrity

Agents must conduct themselves with honesty and integrity when dealing with customers. This includes being transparent about whom they represent (their clients) and what their responsibilities are to those clients. Agents should ensure that all interactions are conducted fairly, such as during property showings, and clearly communicate their agency relationships to avoid any confusion or misunderstandings.

Example: An agent should inform a potential buyer at the outset of a showing that they are working for the seller and are committed to achieving the best possible outcome for the seller.

Accounting

Similar to their duties to clients, agents must handle any property or funds belonging to customers with care. This includes securely managing keys, paperwork, or any deposits they might handle during the course of a showing or transaction. For example: If a customer leaves a security deposit for a rental application with the agent, the agent must ensure that these funds are handled appropriately, not commingled with other funds, and are fully accounted for.

Disclosure

Agents have a duty to disclose their agency relationship with their clients to customers before any confidential information is shared. They must also inform customers of any material facts that could affect their decisions related to the property. Understanding and adhering to state-specific disclosure requirements is crucial in this regard.

Example: An agent must inform a customer if they are representing the seller and should disclose any significant issues with the property, such as foundational problems or pest infestations, which could influence the customer's decision to proceed with a transaction.

These responsibilities are essential for maintaining professionalism in real estate transactions and ensuring that customers are treated fairly and ethically, even when they are not the agent's clients.

Establishing Agency Agreements

Agency agreements are essential for clarifying the relationships and responsibilities in real estate transactions. It's important for agents to understand and comply with state-specific laws that govern these relationships. Agency can be established in several ways:

Express Agency

Express agency occurs when an agency relationship is explicitly agreed upon, either in writing or verbally, between a real estate agent and a client. The form of agreement—written or oral—can depend on state laws, with written agreements generally being more enforceable and clear.

Example: A written contract where a buyer agrees to exclusively work with a real estate agent to find a property, outlining the agent's duties and compensation.

Implied Agency

An implied agency is formed through actions rather than formal agreements. This type of agency arises when the behavior of the agent and the client suggests that they have agreed to an agency relationship, even if there is no written or spoken agreement to that effect.

Example: If an agent repeatedly acts on behalf of a client and the client accepts this representation without a formal agreement, an implied agency may be established.

Agency by Ratification

This type of agency occurs after the fact when a client formally approves an agency relationship after an agent has already acted on their behalf. This can ratify what might initially have been an implied agency.

Example: A client signs a formal agreement approving past actions taken by an agent, thereby establishing a formal agency relationship that legitimizes previous informal activities.

Agency by Estoppel

Agency by estoppel can occur when a client allows an agent to act on their behalf in such a way that it appears an agency relationship exists. This prevents the client from later denying such a relationship, particularly in legal contexts where such denial could be unjust.

Example: If a client leads a third party to believe an agent is acting on their behalf and the third party relies on this assumption, the client may be estopped from denying the agency relationship.

Agency Coupled with Interest

In this arrangement, the agent has a personal interest in the property being sold, which goes beyond mere compensation for agency services. This type of agency does not end with the death or incapacitation of the principal.

Example: A real estate agent might agree to sell a piece of land at a reduced price in exchange for receiving an exclusive listing on future developed lots.

Key Recommendations:

- **Documentation**: To avoid ambiguity and legal issues, it is best to document all agency relationships in writing.
- **Communication**: Before entering into an agency agreement, general discussions about real estate are acceptable, but agents should avoid giving advice that could be construed as representing a client's interests.
- **Clarity in Role**: Understanding and clearly communicating the differences between responsibilities to clients versus customers helps prevent misunderstandings and ensures ethical practice.

Ensuring clear, written agreements and adhering to legal and ethical standards in all interactions will help real estate professionals maintain professionalism and protect the interests of all parties involved.

Agency Disclosure Laws in Real Estate

Agency disclosure laws are fundamental in real estate to ensure transparency and uphold the trust of all parties involved in a transaction. These laws require real estate agents to disclose who they represent to avoid conflicts of interest and ensure that all parties are aware of the agent's obligations and loyalties. Here are several key scenarios where disclosure is crucial:

Disclosure of Agency Relationships

Real estate agents must clearly disclose to potential buyers that they are representing the seller if they are the listing agents for the property. This clarity prevents buyers from mistakenly believing that the agent is working in their best interest, which is critical when buyers might inadvertently share sensitive information that could compromise their position in negotiations.

Example: If an agent is showing a house, they should inform the potential buyers at the outset that they are the seller's agent, especially before any discussions about the buyer's financial details or motivations.

Disclosure of Material Facts

Agents have a duty to disclose any facts that could influence the decisions of their clients. This includes any information that could affect the desirability or value of the property.

Example: If an agent knows that a property has a history of flooding, this must be disclosed to potential buyers, as it is a material fact that affects the property's value and livability.

Disclosure of Compensation Sources

Agents who receive compensation from parties other than their client must disclose these relationships. This is important for maintaining trust and ensuring that clients understand any potential biases or conflicts of interest that may affect the agent's advice.

Example: If an agent is offered a bonus by a seller or another broker for selling a property quickly, this incentive must be disclosed to the buyer if the agent represents them.

Personal Transactions

Real estate professionals must disclose their professional status and any personal interests when they are buying or selling properties themselves. This includes any familial, organizational, or financial interest they have in a property.

Example: If a real estate agent is buying a property and they also happen to be the real estate professional handling the listing, they must disclose their dual role to the seller and any potential buyers.

Additional Disclosures

- **Ownership Interests**: Agents must disclose if they have an ownership interest in a property being sold.
- **Family or Organizational Connections**: If there is a family or business relationship with the property owner, this must be disclosed to potential buyers or other parties involved in the transaction.

Listing Agreements in Real Estate

A listing agreement is a contract between a property seller and a real estate agent that establishes an agency relationship and outlines the duties and rights of each party. These agreements are typically written to ensure clarity and enforceability, though some jurisdictions do recognize oral agreements as binding. The listing agreement is crucial for detailing the agent's responsibilities, such as confidentiality, disclosing material facts, marketing the property effectively, and presenting all offers and counteroffers to the seller. There are four common types of listing agreements:

1. Exclusive Right-to-Sell Agreement

This type of agreement grants one brokerage the exclusive right to sell the property, and the listing agent receives a commission regardless of who actually procures the buyer. This is the most common type of listing agreement and includes definite start and end dates, which helps define the term of the agent's efforts.

Example: If a homeowner signs an exclusive right-to-sell agreement with an agent, and later a buyer who was introduced by a friend of the homeowner purchases the home, the agent is still entitled to the commission.

2. Exclusive Agency Agreement

Under an exclusive agency agreement, the property is marketed exclusively by one brokerage. However, this type differs from the exclusive right-to-sell in that if the seller finds the buyer themselves, they are not required to pay a commission to the brokerage.

Example: If a seller under an exclusive agency agreement manages to sell their home to a coworker without the aid of the agent, no commission is owed to the agent.

3. Open Listing Agreement

An open listing agreement allows the seller to enter into agreements with multiple agents. The agent who successfully brings a buyer who purchases the property receives the commission. If the seller finds their own buyer, no commission is due to any agent.

Example: A seller could work with several agents at the same time and only pay a commission to the agent who brings a buyer whose offer is accepted.

4. Net Listing Agreement

In a net listing, the agent agrees to sell the property for a set minimum price. Any amount obtained over this price is kept by the agent as their commission. However, net listings are illegal in many areas because they can create significant conflicts of interest, potentially leading to ethical dilemmas, such as the agent working against the seller's best interests by focusing on maximizing their own profits rather than selling the property at a fair market value.

Example: An agent agrees to sell a house for $300,000. If the property sells for $320,000, the agent keeps the $20,000 difference as their commission.

Buyer Agency Agreements in Real Estate

Buyer agency agreements are crucial in defining the relationship and responsibilities between a real estate agent and a homebuyer. These agreements typically outline the scope of the agent's duties, the type of property the buyer is interested in, and the terms of compensation. Here are the primary types of buyer agency agreements:

1. Exclusive Buyer Agency Agreement

This type of agreement binds the buyer to work exclusively with one brokerage or agent for the duration of the agreement. The broker earns a commission on any property the buyer purchases during the term, regardless of who actually finds the property. This agreement ensures that the agent is compensated for their time and efforts, even if the buyer ultimately purchases a property they found independently.

Example: If a buyer signs an exclusive buyer agency agreement and later purchases a home they discovered while driving through a neighborhood, the broker is still entitled to a commission because of the exclusivity clause.

2. Exclusive Agency Buyer Agency Agreement

In an exclusive agency buyer agency agreement, the broker is the exclusive agent for the buyer but only earns a commission if they are the one who locates the property that the buyer ultimately purchases. If the buyer finds a property on their own and arranges the purchase without the broker's assistance, no commission is owed.

Example: A buyer under an exclusive agency agreement finds a home through a personal connection and negotiates the purchase themselves without involving their agent. In this scenario, the agent would not receive a commission.

3. Open Buyer Agency Agreement

An open buyer agency agreement allows the buyer to work with multiple brokers simultaneously. The broker who successfully finds the property that the buyer purchases earns the commission. This type of agreement provides flexibility for the buyer but can result in less personalized service since multiple agents may be less motivated to invest extensive time in a non-exclusive relationship.

Example: A buyer works with several agents and also searches independently. The agent who shows the buyer the home they eventually decide to purchase is the one who receives the commission. If the buyer finds and purchases a home entirely on their own, no commission is paid to any agents.

Real Estate Commissions: Structure and Distribution

Real estate commissions are a vital aspect of the compensation structure within the real estate industry, typically representing 5% to 6% of a property's sale price. Understanding how these commissions are structured, who pays them, and under what conditions they are earned can clarify many of the financial interactions in real estate transactions.

Commission Split Between Agents

Commissions are usually split between the buyer's agent and the seller's agent, with each side typically receiving between 2.5% to 3%. However, the exact split can vary based on the agreement between the agents and their respective brokerages.

Who Pays the Commission?

In most cases, the listing broker (seller's agent broker) is responsible for paying both the seller's agent and the buyer's agent at closing. This payment structure is generally outlined in the listing agreement that the seller signs when they engage a broker to sell their property.

Example: If a home sells for $300,000 with a 6% commission, a total of $18,000 is paid in commissions. If split evenly, each agent could receive $9,000.

Exceptions to the Rule

There are exceptions where the buyer may pay their agent's commission directly. This is less common and usually occurs in specific market conditions or under particular agreements, such as when the buyer's agent is representing a buyer in a market where listings offer lower commissions or none at all.

Earning the Commission

Real estate agents earn their commissions when they produce a buyer who is ready, willing, and able to purchase the property under the terms agreed upon by the seller. The commission is typically paid at closing but is considered earned once an agreement is reached between the buyer and seller.

Procuring Cause

The concept of procuring cause is used to determine which broker rightfully earns the commission. It involves identifying the broker whose efforts directly led to the completion of the sale. This determination can become significant in disputes where multiple agents may have interacted with the buyer.

Example: If an agent showed a buyer a home and initiated negotiations that led to a sale agreement, but another agent later stepped in and the first agent's efforts were disregarded, the first agent might still be considered the procuring cause and thus entitled to the commission, depending on the specifics of the interaction.

Scenario: Seller Backs Out

In cases where a seller backs out of a deal after a ready, willing, and able buyer has been procured, the agents involved may still be entitled to their commissions because they fulfilled their contractual obligations.

Example: An agent secures a buyer willing to purchase a home at the asking price, but the seller decides not to proceed with the sale for personal reasons. The agent may still be entitled to a commission, as they successfully met their obligation of providing a qualified buyer, depending on the terms of their listing agreement.

Termination of Agency Relationships in Real Estate

Understanding how and when an agency relationship in real estate can be terminated is crucial for both agents and principals (clients). These terminations can happen under various circumstances, each with specific implications:

Expiration

Agency agreements typically include an expiration date, often set for six months from the start of the agreement. If no sale occurs within this period, the agreement simply expires, and the broker is not owed any compensation related to the sale of the property.

Example: If a listing agreement is set to expire on July 1st and no sale has occurred, the agency relationship ends on that date without further obligation from the seller.

Completion

The agency relationship terminates upon the successful completion of the transaction for which the agent was hired. Once the transaction closes, the agent is paid their commission, and their formal responsibilities end.

Example: When a home sale closes, the listing agent's role officially ends after the final closing documents are signed and the sale is recorded.

Force of Law

Certain uncontrollable events can also terminate an agency agreement, and no compensation is typically owed in these cases:

- **Bankruptcy**: If the principal or the agent declares bankruptcy.
- **Property Destruction**: Events such as fires, floods, or other disasters that destroy the property.
- **Incapacitation or Death**: If the principal or the agent dies or becomes legally incapacitated.
- **Condemnation**: If the property is seized under eminent domain.

Example: If a property listed for sale is completely destroyed by a natural disaster, the listing agreement is terminated as the subject of the contract no longer exists.

Mutual Agreement

Both parties can mutually agree to end the agency relationship at any time. This is often the simplest and least contentious method for termination.

Example: If both the agent and the seller find that their goals are not aligned, they may mutually decide to terminate the agreement before the expiration date.

Renunciation or Revocation

Either party may choose to end the agency relationship unilaterally:

- **Revocation by the Client**: The client may terminate the agency relationship at any time for any reason, such as a lack of trust or dissatisfaction with the agent's performance. Depending on the terms of the agreement, this may or may not involve a penalty.
- **Renunciation by the Agent**: The agent may also decide to withdraw from the relationship, possibly due to a conflict of interest or other professional reasons. This might also lead to legal or financial consequences depending on the circumstances.

Example: A seller may revoke an agency agreement due to dissatisfaction with the agent's lack of effort or poor communication, potentially facing a breach of contract penalty depending on the agreement's terms.

Post-Termination Duties

- **Accounting**: The agent's duty to account for all property and funds related to the transaction ends once these have been fully and properly managed.
- **Confidentiality**: The duty of confidentiality does not end with the termination of the agency; it persists indefinitely, protecting the client's private information forever.

Summary

This chapter has comprehensively explored the fundamental principles of agency in real estate, emphasizing the varied types of agency relationships and the distinct roles and responsibilities that accompany them. We examined the nuances of agency agreements, including express, implied, and those created by estoppel or ratification, and discussed the importance of clear, written contracts to avoid misunderstandings.

We also delved into the fiduciary duties encapsulated by the acronym OLD CAR—obedience, loyalty, disclosure, confidentiality, accounting, and reasonable skill and care—highlighting how these duties serve to protect client interests and maintain professional integrity. The termination of agency relationships and the conditions under which they may end were also clarified.

Chapter 6: Property Disclosures

Overview

This chapter is crucial for understanding the importance of property disclosures in the real estate process, covering approximately 6% of the exam, which translates into about 5 questions.

Importance of Property Condition in Transactions

Purchasing a home is a significant financial commitment, possibly one of the largest your clients will undertake. The state of the property not only affects its current market value but also influences future appreciation or depreciation. Thus, it is essential to advocate for thorough home inspections for all properties, including new constructions. Home inspections are vital as they provide a comprehensive report on the property's condition, identifying any defects, safety issues, or health hazards that may not be obvious or known to the seller.

Role of Home Inspections

Home inspections are pivotal for

- **Assessing true property condition**: Inspectors are trained to identify hidden problems that could cost buyers significantly in repairs and safety issues.
- **Safeguarding investments**: Including a home inspection contingency in the purchase agreement can protect a buyer's earnest money deposit, offering an exit strategy should significant issues arise.
- **Facilitating negotiations**: The results of a home inspection can be a powerful tool in negotiating the purchase price. Properties in excellent condition might fetch higher prices, while those requiring substantial work offer negotiation leverage for lower prices.

Market Dynamics and Property Condition

Properties requiring minor updates may appeal to buyers looking for slightly under-market-value homes they can personalize. Conversely, properties in need of extensive renovations often attract investors and house flippers. These buyers aim to purchase at low prices, renovate economically, and sell for a profit, capitalizing on the "fixer-upper" market. The dynamics of property condition and its impact on pricing strategies are critical for real estate professionals to master, enabling them to guide their clients effectively through buying and selling processes.

Additional Inspections and Property Surveys

In real estate transactions, the initial home inspection might reveal issues that necessitate further specialized inspections or detailed property surveys. This section will explore these additional evaluations, which are crucial for uncovering potential problems that could affect the transaction or future ownership.

Detailed Inspections

Following a general home inspection, certain areas may require more in-depth examination. These include:

- **Major Property Systems**: It is critical to ensure the functionality and safety of major systems such as HVAC, electrical, and plumbing. These systems are not only expensive to repair or replace but also pose significant risks if they malfunction.
- **Structural Integrity**: Inspectors assess the condition of the roof, foundations, and walls for signs of stress such as cracks or water damage. Other structural concerns include the integrity of windows, doors, and moisture issues in basements or crawl spaces.
- **Pest Infestation**: The presence of wood-eating pests like termites, carpenter ants, and certain beetles can severely compromise the structural integrity of a property. Identifying these pests early is essential for managing potential damage and remediation costs.
- **Environmental Hazards**: Residential properties may also harbor hazardous materials such as lead, radon, asbestos, or mold. These substances can pose serious health risks, and their removal often requires specialized remediation services.

Property Surveys

A property survey is an essential tool for defining a property's physical boundaries and legal constraints. Key elements of property surveys include:

- **Identifying Boundaries and Lot Size**: Surveys clarify the exact dimensions of a property, which is vital for future developments, renovations, or resolving disputes with neighbors.
- **Easements and Encroachments**:

- Easements grant a non-possessory right to use another's land for a specific purpose, like passing through or utility access. Understanding easements is crucial as they can affect how a property is used.

- Encroachments occur when a structure or object intrudes onto a neighboring property without permission. This can lead to legal disputes and may require resolution for a clear title.

Importance of Additional Inspections and Surveys

Conducting these specialized inspections and surveys is vital for several reasons:

- **Risk Management**: They help buyers avoid unforeseen liabilities and financial burdens associated with hidden property defects.

- **Negotiation Leverage**: Detailed knowledge about the property's condition and legal standing can serve as a powerful negotiating tool in the purchase process.

- **Long-term Satisfaction and Security**: Ensuring that all property aspects are thoroughly checked and legally sound provides peace of mind and security to the buyer, enhancing their ownership experience.

Material Facts, Defects, and Disclosure

In real estate, "material facts" refer to any information that could influence a buyer's decision to purchase a property or the price they are willing to pay. These facts can relate to both the physical condition of the property and its legal status.

Key Considerations for Material Facts

- **Variability in Impact**: Material facts affect buyers differently depending on their intentions and needs. For instance, an investor might be more willing to accept certain defects if they believe there is potential for profit after repairs, whereas a family looking for a home might prioritize the absence of major defects.

- **Examples of Material Facts:**
  - Structural integrity issues like a leaky roof or cracked foundation.
  - The age and condition of major systems such as heating or cooling.
  - Environmental hazards including mold or radon.
  - Legal impediments like easements or encroachments.
  - Future area developments that might affect the property's environment or value.

Latent Defects and Their Disclosure

Latent defects are hidden issues with a property that are not easily identifiable during a standard inspection. The requirements for disclosing these defects vary by state, highlighting the need for real estate professionals to be well-versed in local regulations.

- **Disclosure Requirements**: Depending on the state, the disclosure of latent defects may be mandatory, impacting the transparency and ethical considerations of a transaction.

Property Condition Disclosure Regulations

Property condition disclosures are typically governed by state laws, and most states require sellers to complete and provide specific disclosure forms to buyers.

Types of Disclosure Regulations

- **Disclosure States**: These require the disclosure of all known material facts and latent defects. Real estate agents and sellers must ensure all pertinent information is shared with potential buyers.
- **Disclaimer States**: Operating under a "buyer beware" approach, these states place the onus on the buyer to discover property defects. Sellers may not be required to disclose defects actively.
- **Option States**: In these states, sellers can choose to either disclose defects or disclaim any knowledge, leaving some room for buyer diligence.

Role of Real Estate Professionals in Disclosures

Real estate agents must navigate these disclosure requirements carefully:

- **Guidance on Disclosure Forms**: Agents should instruct sellers to be thorough and honest in their disclosures but must avoid filling out forms on behalf of sellers to prevent liabilities.
- **Ensuring Timely Disclosure**: Disclosures should be made before any contractual agreement is finalized, allowing buyers the opportunity to withdraw if undisclosed defects are discovered.

Agent Disclosure

Real estate agents play a crucial role in the process of property disclosures, adhering to specific legal requirements that vary by state. These obligations ensure that all parties are fairly informed about the property in question.

Understanding Agent Disclosure Requirements

- **State-Specific Laws**: Agents must be familiar with the disclosure laws relevant to their state. Some states require the disclosure of all known material facts, while others may only require disclosure of known adverse material facts.

- **Proactive Inquiries**: In many states, it's the duty of the listing agent to actively inquire about potential issues with the property—often referred to as "red flags"—to ensure they are aware of any material facts that must be disclosed.

- **The MAAP Standard**: Disclosures should adhere to the MAAP standard, ensuring that all disclosed information is:
  - **Material**: Significantly impacts a buyer's decision-making process.
  - **Adverse**: Relates to negative aspects that could affect the property's value.
  - **Actual**: Based on concrete knowledge of the property.
  - **Physical**: Pertains to the tangible conditions of the property that are observable.

Home Inspection Reports and Their Confidentiality

Home inspection reports are another critical element in the real estate transaction process, primarily serving the interests of the buyer.

Key Points on Home Inspection Reports

- **Ownership and Confidentiality**: The home inspection report is owned by the buyer, and its contents are typically confidential unless the buyer chooses to share them.

- **Disclosure of Inspection Findings**: In some states, there are specific exemptions that relieve parties from the obligation to disclose findings from home inspections. If a sale does not proceed due to issues identified in an inspection report, sellers and their agents often choose not to review the report to avoid the liability of having to disclose its contents to future buyers.

- **Handling Previous Inspection Reports**: Generally, there is no requirement for sellers to share previous inspection reports with new prospective buyers, underscoring the importance of each buyer conducting their own due diligence.

Role of Real Estate Professionals

Real estate professionals must navigate these complexities with a thorough understanding of legal requirements and ethical standards.

- **Educating Clients**: Agents should educate their clients, both buyers and sellers, about the importance of disclosures and the potential implications of withholding information.
- **Ethical Practices**: Maintaining ethical standards by ensuring all disclosures are complete and truthful enhances the professionalism of agents and protects all parties involved in the transaction.

Permits, Property Zoning, and Surrounding Areas

For buyers, verifying that all modifications and constructions on a property have been properly permitted is crucial. This ensures compliance with local building codes and can prevent legal and financial headaches in the future.

Key Points on Permits

- **Verifying Permit History**: Obtaining a complete permit record ensures that any additions or alterations to the property were done legally and inspected accordingly.
- **Consequences of Unpermitted Work**: Unpermitted additions or alterations might require dismantling for inspection, correction, or even restoration to their original condition, potentially incurring significant costs.

The Role of Zoning and Environmental Factors

Zoning laws and environmental factors play a significant role in property valuation and can affect the buyer's long-term satisfaction with their purchase.

Important Zoning and Environmental Considerations

- **Zoning Classification**: Buyers should confirm the property's zoning status and any planned changes to it or the surrounding area that could affect the property's value or usability.
- **Awareness of Surrounding Areas**: Potential buyers should be aware of:
  - Future developments like new roadways or shopping centers that might affect property values positively or negatively.
  - Proximity to sources of noise such as highways, train stations, or airports, which might necessitate disclosures depending on state law.
  - Nearby industrial facilities, especially those classified as Brownfields, which could pose environmental hazards.

Stigmatized Properties and Megan's Law

Certain aspects of a property's history, such as crimes, deaths, or even reputed hauntings, can affect its marketability, known as stigmatized properties.

Handling Sensitive Historical Information

- **Stigmatized Properties**: While most states do not require disclosure of stigmatization events like homicides or paranormal activities, real estate agents must be aware of any local laws that do require such disclosures.
- **HIV/AIDS and Fair Housing**: Disclosing that a previous occupant had HIV or AIDS is considered a violation of fair housing laws. Such medical conditions must never be disclosed.
- **Megan's Law**: This law facilitates public access to information about registered sex offenders. Real estate agents are not required to provide this information but should direct interested buyers to relevant resources where they can obtain it themselves.

Environmental Hazards and Their Impact on Real Estate

Environmental hazards can significantly influence the viability and safety of a property, affecting its insurability, value, and desirability. Real estate professionals must ensure that both buyers and sellers are well-informed about the potential environmental risks associated with a property.

Types of External Environmental Hazards

Understanding the various types of environmental hazards is crucial for conducting thorough due diligence and ensuring that a property is a sound investment.

Common Environmental Hazards Include

- **Mining Activities**: Properties near active or abandoned mining sites might be susceptible to subsidence or contamination.
- **Underground Storage Tanks**: Old or poorly maintained tanks could leak, leading to soil and groundwater contamination.
- **Groundwater Contamination**: This can result from various sources, such as industrial spills or agricultural runoff, and can affect the quality of drinking water.
- **Agricultural Pesticides**: Properties near agricultural areas may be exposed to pesticide runoff, which can affect soil quality and health.

- **Former Waste Disposal Sites**: Properties on or near old landfills or waste disposal sites may be exposed to various contaminants, posing health risks and affecting property value.

The Role of Insurance in Managing Environmental Risks

Insurance plays a critical role in managing the financial risks associated with environmental hazards. However, properties in high-risk areas may face challenges in obtaining affordable insurance.

Factors Affecting Property Insurability

- **Location in Regulated Areas**: Properties in flood zones, wetlands, or historical districts may have special insurance requirements and restrictions.
- **Weather Events**: Properties in areas prone to hurricanes, tornadoes, hailstorms, flooding, or fires typically require additional insurance coverage, which can be costly.
- **History of Claims**: Properties with a history of environmental claims, such as mold or water damage, might be more expensive to insure due to the higher perceived risk.

Due Diligence and Environmental Assessments

Buyers are encouraged to perform extensive environmental assessments to uncover any hidden risks associated with a property. This includes:

- **Professional Environmental Assessments**: Engaging environmental experts to evaluate the property can help identify potential hazards that are not immediately obvious.
- **Reviewing Historical and Government Records**: Checking for past environmental claims and consulting local environmental agencies for any known issues in the area.
- **Consulting the Comprehensive Loss Underwriting Exchange (CLUE) Database**: Insurance companies use this database to review the history of claims on a property, which can inform potential buyers about past issues and help assess future risks.

Addressing Interior Environmental Hazards

Interior environmental hazards such as mold, radon, asbestos, and lead pose significant health risks and can impact the livability and value of a property. Real estate professionals must be knowledgeable about these hazards to effectively guide their clients through the complexities of environmental safety in real estate transactions.

Common Interior Environmental Hazards

- **Mold**: Thrives in moist environments with poor air circulation. It is crucial to address water leaks or dampness promptly to prevent mold growth.
- **Radon**: A naturally occurring radioactive gas that can seep into buildings from the ground. It is colorless and odorless, making radon testing essential in areas where radon presence is known to be significant.
- **Asbestos**: Used in building materials before 1970 for its fire-resistant properties. Asbestos is hazardous when airborne, as inhaling asbestos fibers can lead to serious lung diseases. Only licensed professionals should handle or remove asbestos.
- **Lead**: Found in paint, plumbing, and other materials in many older homes. Lead exposure is particularly harmful to children, causing severe health problems including developmental issues and neurological damage.

Regulatory Requirements for Disclosure

The handling and disclosure of these hazards are regulated to protect public health.

Lead-Based Paint Disclosures

- **EPA Regulations**: For homes built before 1978, the United States Environmental Protection Agency (EPA) mandates that sellers provide buyers with a lead-based paint disclosure and a "Protect Your Family" lead safety pamphlet.
- **Seller Responsibilities**: Sellers must disclose any known presence of lead-based paint and provide any available reports from lead testing.
- **Agent Responsibilities for Sellers**: Agents must ensure that sellers comply with all lead disclosure requirements, including the provision of the EPA pamphlet and disclosure forms.
- **Agent Responsibilities for Buyers**: Agents representing buyers should verify that the lead safety pamphlet is provided and that the disclosure includes any known information or previous tests. Buyers should be advised of their right to a 10-day inspection period to conduct lead testing.

Importance of Environmental Testing

Testing for these hazards is a critical step in the home-buying process, particularly for older properties that are more likely to contain hazardous materials. Real estate professionals should encourage and facilitate environmental testing to ensure the safety of the property.

- **Professional Assessments**: Engaging certified inspectors to test for mold, radon, asbestos, and lead can identify hidden problems that could pose serious health risks or affect the property's value.
- **Informing Buyer Decisions**: Detailed environmental reports help buyers make informed decisions about proceeding with a purchase, negotiating repair terms, or potentially withdrawing an offer based on the findings.

Summary

This chapter has comprehensively addressed the critical role of property disclosures in real estate transactions, emphasizing the need for thoroughness, accuracy, and adherence to legal standards. Real estate professionals are tasked with ensuring that all parties are well-informed about the material facts and potential hazards associated with a property, from environmental risks to zoning and permit issues.

By mastering the intricacies of property condition disclosures, additional inspections, and the handling of stigmatized properties, agents can safeguard their clients' interests and facilitate transparent and ethical transactions. This chapter not only equips aspiring real estate professionals with the knowledge required to pass their licensing exam but also prepares them to navigate the complexities of real estate disclosures in their practical day-to-day operations, fostering professionalism and trust in their relationships with clients.

Chapter 7: Contracts

Overview

Contracts are foundational in real estate transactions, comprising a significant section of the exam, specifically 17% which translates to approximately 14 questions.

Defining a Valid Real Estate Contract

A real estate contract, to be considered valid and enforceable, must meet several key criteria set forth by law. It is a legally binding document between two or more parties who are engaged in the purchase, sale, exchange, or transfer of real estate property. Here are the fundamental requirements for a contract to be valid:

Legal Competency of Parties

For a contract to be enforceable, all parties involved must be legally and mentally capable of understanding the terms and implications of the agreement. Legal competency is defined by several factors:

- **Age**: All parties must be of legal age.
- **Mental Capacity**: Individuals must be able to comprehend the contract terms and their consequences.
- **Volition**: Parties must act out of their free will without coercion.

Contracts involving parties lacking these competencies are considered voidable at the discretion of the incompetent party but can still be enforceable against the competent party.

Voluntary Agreement

A contract must be entered into willingly by all parties. This means:

- There must be no evidence of mistakes, misrepresentation, fraud, duress, or undue influence.
- Any contract signed under such conditions is deemed invalid as it does not represent a true meeting of the minds.

Mutual Agreement

A key component of a contract is the clear offer and acceptance, often referred to as mutual agreement or meeting of the minds. This occurs when:

- All parties have a clear and full understanding of the contract terms.
- The contract outlines clearly who the parties are, the object of the contract, and the terms agreed upon.

Consideration

Consideration refers to something of legal value that is exchanged between the parties:

- This can include monetary terms, such as a buyer's commitment to pay a specified amount.
- It can also involve other forms of value, like a seller's promise to transfer ownership through a deed.
- The essence of consideration is that it represents something of value agreed upon by all parties involved.

Legal Purpose

Lastly, for any real estate contract to be valid, it must be for a legal purpose:

- The objective of the contract must be lawful within the jurisdiction where the transaction is taking place.
- Any agreement made for an illegal purpose will render the contract void and unenforceable.

The Importance of Written Agreements

Under the statute of frauds, real estate contracts must be in writing to be legally enforceable. Oral agreements, while they might hold moral weight, lack the legal standing in court necessary for enforcement. A written contract serves not only as a clear record of the agreement but also as a crucial tool in upholding the contract's terms in legal settings.

Understanding Void, Voidable, and Unenforceable Contracts

In real estate, the distinction between void, voidable, and unenforceable contracts is crucial. Each category has specific characteristics that determine the enforceability and validity of a contract. Understanding these differences is key for real estate professionals to navigate legal challenges effectively.

Void Contracts

Void contracts are fundamentally flawed due to the absence of one or more essential elements required for a valid contract. Characteristics include:

- **Lack of Essential Elements**: These contracts may lack a lawful object, mutual agreement, consideration, or involve parties who are not legally competent.
- **Legal Status**: Since essential elements are missing, void contracts are inherently invalid from the outset and cannot be enforced by any party.

Voidable Contracts

Voidable contracts initially appear valid but may be nullified or affirmed depending on the circumstances surrounding their execution. Key aspects include:

- **Potential for Nullification**: These contracts can be cancelled at the option of one of the parties, usually the one adversely affected by factors like lack of competence, misunderstanding, or misrepresentation.
- **Enforceability**: While voidable, these contracts are generally enforceable against the party not suffering from the defect unless and until the affected party chooses to void them.

Unenforceable Contracts

Unenforceable contracts may meet all the criteria of a valid contract but still fail to be enforceable in a court of law due to specific legal deficiencies. These include:

- **Presence of Legal Deficiencies**: Such deficiencies might include failure to meet the requirements of the statute of frauds (i.e., not being in written form when required), containing terms that are unfair, or violating public policy.
- **Legal Remedies**: Although these contracts might not be enforceable, the parties may seek other legal remedies or rectifications based on the principles of equity.

Severability in Contracts

The concept of severability is significant in dealing with contracts that contain unenforceable terms. It involves:

- **Preservation of Contractual Intent**: If one or more terms of a contract are found unenforceable, the remaining terms can still be upheld.
- **Judicial Review**: Courts often strive to salvage as much of the contractual agreement as possible, discarding only those portions that are explicitly illegal or contrary to policy.

Types of Real Estate Contracts

Real estate contracts are diverse, each serving specific purposes within the field of property transactions. Understanding the various types of contracts and their specific applications is crucial for real estate professionals. Here's an overview of the primary real estate contracts used in the industry.

Purchase Agreements

Purchase agreements, also known variably as real estate sales contracts, home purchase agreements, sales and purchase agreements (SPA), or real estate purchase contracts, are fundamental in real estate transactions. This type of contract is a binding legal document that sets forth the terms agreed upon by a buyer and seller. The signing of a purchase agreement effectively places the involved parties and the property under a legal obligation. There are three main types of purchase agreements:

- **State/Association Purchase Agreement**: This is the standard format used when real estate agents facilitate the transaction, adhering to local realtor guidelines.
- **General Purchase Agreement**: A simplified version often employed in transactions without a real estate agent.
- **Property-Specific Purchase Agreement**: Tailored for unique properties such as vacant land or mobile homes, addressing specific concerns and terms relevant to these types of transactions.

Real Estate Assignment Contracts

Used primarily within the realm of wholesale investment, assignment contracts are pivotal for transactions involving distressed properties. An investor secures a property under contract and assigns it to another buyer. The key term "assigns" indicates that the contract's rights and obligations are transferable to another party.

Lease Agreements

Lease agreements form the legal foundation between a property owner (landlord) and a tenant (lessee). This contract outlines the conditions under which the tenant occupies the residential property, including the rent amount, payment terms for utilities, and the security deposit. Clearly defining these terms is essential to prevent future legal disputes and ensure mutual understanding.

Power of Attorney (POA)

A Power of Attorney is a legal document granting one individual (the agent) the authority to act on behalf of another (the principal). This contract is particularly useful in situations where the principal cannot physically be present to sign necessary documents due to reasons such as absence from the country or incapacity. The POA can be:

- **Specific or General**: Depending on the breadth of powers granted.
- **Durable or Non-Durable**: Indicates whether the POA remains in effect if the principal becomes incapacitated.
- **Termination**: A POA generally terminates upon the principal's death or revocation by the principal, and in cases of spouses, often by divorce.

This contract type is invaluable for managing multiple investment properties or assisting family members who cannot manage their affairs. The selection of an agent is a critical decision, often a trusted individual like a spouse, family member, friend, or a neutral third party.

Essential Elements of a Real Estate Sales Contract

Real estate sales contracts are complex documents containing numerous mandatory and optional components that govern the terms of a property transaction. These components are crucial for defining the obligations and rights of each party involved, ensuring clarity and legal enforceability. Here's an in-depth look at the common elements found in a real estate sales contract:

Addendums (Riders)

Addendums, or riders, are attachments to the contract that modify or add further conditions to the agreement. These are often used to:

- Address specific circumstances that the standard contract does not cover.
- Include mandatory disclosures, such as homeowner association (HOA) rules or environmental hazards.

Buyer and Seller Information

This section contains the full legal names and contact information of all parties involved in the transaction. It establishes the identities of the buyer and seller, which is fundamental for any legal proceedings or communications.

Closing Costs

The contract outlines all fees associated with the transfer of the property beyond the purchase price. It specifies which party is responsible for various costs, including:

- Escrow fees
- Title search and title insurance fees
- Notary fees
- Recording fees
- Transfer taxes
- Additionally, taxes and insurance are typically prorated based on the closing date.

Closing Date

This is the specified date when the transfer of title occurs, marking the finalization of the transaction. It is crucial as it impacts financial calculations like prorations and other time-sensitive obligations.

Considerations

Anything of value that is exchanged between the parties, typically the property and the money, but can also include other valuable items or conditions agreed upon by the parties.

Contingencies

These are conditions that must be fulfilled before the transaction can be finalized. Common contingencies include:

- Approval of buyer financing
- Sale of the buyer's current home
- Satisfactory home inspections and repairs
- Property appraisal meeting required values for sales price and loan processing

Deed of Trust

A deed of trust is mentioned when property ownership is temporarily transferred to a neutral third party (a trustee) until the buyer's debt is fully paid. It specifies the type of deed to be transferred.

Earnest Money

Terms regarding the earnest money deposit are outlined, indicating the amount and conditions under which it is held. This acts as a security deposit to demonstrate the buyer's serious intent to complete the purchase.

Financing

Details about how the buyer intends to finance the purchase are specified, including whether the financing will be through a mortgage, cash, or by assuming the seller's mortgage. This section also contains any terms related to financing that the buyer must fulfill.

Inclusions and Exclusions

This part of the contract specifies which fixtures, appliances, or other personal property items are included or excluded from the property sale. Clarity here helps avoid future disputes over personal property.

Lead-Based Paint Disclosure

For homes built before 1978, a lead-based paint disclosure is mandatory, providing the buyer with information on potential risks and the option for lead-based paint inspection. This is crucial for health and safety compliance and legal transparency.

Mortgage Note

A mortgage note is a detailed document containing all the terms of the mortgage, including the loan amount, interest rate, payment schedule, and other conditions. This document is signed at closing and serves as a promise by the borrower to repay the borrowed amount according to the agreed terms.

Option to Terminate

This provision allows the buyer to legally withdraw from the contract under specific conditions, before a certain deadline. It offers a level of flexibility and security for the buyer, enabling them to back out if necessary conditions are not met or if unforeseen circumstances arise.

Property Details

The contract must include a comprehensive description of the property, encompassing:

- The legal address
- Detailed physical description
- Any relevant information that affects ownership or use

Property Taxes

Details concerning the property taxes that will apply to the property post-transaction are included. This section often explains how taxes are prorated based on the exact closing date.

Purchase Price

This is the total amount agreed upon by the buyer and seller for the property. It includes any initial deposits and additional costs that are part of the transaction, clearly outlining the financial commitment of the buyer.

Recording Fees

These are fees charged by governmental entities to record the change of ownership of the property. Recording fees ensure that the public record reflects the current ownership status and protects both buyer and seller legally.

Representations and Warranties

The seller provides statements about the property's condition, structural integrity, and other important factors. These assertions are crucial as they inform the buyer about what is being purchased and provide a basis for legal recourse if the information proves incorrect.

Seller Assist

In some cases, especially in a buyer's market, the seller may agree to cover some or all of the buyer's closing costs. This can be negotiated into the contract as an incentive for the buyer and can make the property more appealing.

Signatures

A real estate sales contract must be signed by all parties involved to be legally binding. Signatures confirm that all parties agree to the terms and understand their obligations and rights as set out in the contract.

Title Insurance

The contract specifies who (buyer or seller) will be responsible for purchasing title insurance. This insurance protects against losses that might result from disputes over property ownership or issues discovered during the title search.

Title Search

This is the process of examining public records to verify the seller's right to transfer ownership and to discover any claims, errors, liens, or other impediments on the property. A thorough title search helps prevent future legal issues regarding property ownership.

These elements collectively ensure that all aspects of the property transaction are transparent and agreed upon, mitigating future conflicts and ensuring that both parties are adequately protected.

How Contracts are Created in Real Estate

Real estate transactions rely heavily on various types of contracts, each playing a pivotal role in defining the rights and obligations of the involved parties. Understanding how contracts are formed and their operational mechanics is essential for anyone involved in real estate. Here's a breakdown of the primary types of contracts used in the industry:

Express Contracts

An express contract is one where the terms are clearly stated and agreed upon by the parties, either verbally or in writing. The intentions of each party are explicitly expressed, making the terms and obligations clear.

Example: A homeowner signs a written agreement with a real estate agent, authorizing the agent to list their home for sale. The contract explicitly outlines the terms, including duties, compensation, and the duration of the listing.

Implied Contracts

Implied contracts are formed based on the actions or conduct of the parties, rather than written or spoken words. These contracts rely on the assumption that a contract exists due to the behavior of those involved.

Example: A buyer makes an earnest money deposit on a home, and the seller begins making agreed-upon repairs before closing. These actions imply an understanding and agreement that the transaction will proceed.

Bilateral Contracts

A bilateral contract is a mutual exchange of promises whereby each party commits to fulfilling certain obligations. In real estate, most contracts are bilateral.

Example: A listing agreement between a seller and a real estate agent, where the seller agrees to pay a commission if the agent successfully finds a buyer.

Unilateral Contracts

In a unilateral contract, only one party makes a promise, which is not reciprocal until the other party decides to act on it. The non-promising party has no obligation until they choose to perform.

Example: An option contract gives a buyer the right to purchase a property at a specified price within a certain timeframe, but the buyer is not obligated to proceed. If the buyer exercises the option, the seller must complete the sale, turning it into a bilateral contract.

Ratified Contracts

A ratified contract occurs once all parties have agreed to the terms but have not yet completed the execution. It moves forward once actions such as the exchange of earnest money have taken place.

Example: After a buyer and seller agree on the sale price and terms, and the buyer deposits earnest money, the contract is considered ratified but not yet fully executed.

Executed Contract

An executed contract occurs when all parties involved have fulfilled their obligations as outlined in the agreement. For example, in real estate, this is achieved when the deed is officially transferred to the buyer and the seller receives the agreed-upon payment, completing the terms of the sale. Until these conditions are met, the contract remains executory, meaning it is still in the process of being completed.

Example: a real estate sale contract is executory from the time the agreement is signed until the deed exchange and payment completion.

How an Offer Becomes a Contract (Purchase Agreement)

Offer and Counteroffer

An offer in real estate is a written proposal from a potential buyer to purchase property under specific terms, facilitated by their agent and delivered to the seller's agent. The "OR" "EE" rule is key: the person making the offer (offeror) and the one receiving it (offeree). If the seller accepts the offer as is, a legally binding agreement is formed. However, if the seller proposes changes, this constitutes a counteroffer, effectively voiding the original offer and making the seller the offeror and the buyer the offeree.

Binding Acceptance

A binding acceptance occurs when an offer or counteroffer is signed by the offeree and returned to the offeror, either physically or electronically. This acceptance solidifies the agreement between the parties.

Purchase Agreement

Once all terms are agreed upon and signed by both buyer and seller, a binding written purchase agreement is established, detailing all conditions of the sale.

Notice, Delivery, and Acceptance of Contracts

Effective communication of contract terms is crucial to prevent breaches. The process includes:

Notice

Notice clauses in a contract specify how and when notifications related to the contract must be communicated between parties. These clauses define the methods of delivery (physical or electronic) and when a notice is deemed received.

Delivery

Delivery refers to the process of exchanging documents, such as when the buyer presents an initial offer or during ongoing negotiations with counteroffers.

Acceptance

Acceptance is only achieved when all parties involved have signed the contract, indicating full agreement on all terms.

Time is of the Essence

This legal concept obligates all parties to adhere strictly to the contract's deadlines. If no specific time frame is provided, actions must be performed within a "reasonable" period, as might later be interpreted by a court. For example: If a seller issues a counteroffer with a specific deadline for acceptance, and the buyer fails to respond by that deadline, the counteroffer becomes void, reverting the negotiation process.

Understanding the Uniform Electronic Transactions Act (UETA)

Electronic Signatures and UETA

The Uniform Electronic Transactions Act (UETA) grants legal recognition to electronic signatures and records, equating them with traditional paper documents and "wet" ink signatures. This law acknowledges an electronic signature as an electronic sound, symbol, or process that is attached to or logically associated with a record and is executed or adopted by a person with the intent to sign the document.

State Regulation

While UETA sets a federal standard, it allows individual states to opt-in and implement their own guidelines, which can vary. State laws regarding electronic signatures and documents take precedence over UETA if they are more specific or stringent. This means that electronic documents and signatures are legally binding if all parties involved agree to this method of signing, depending on the state's adaptation of UETA.

Practical Application

DocuSign is a popular platform that facilitates the collection of valid electronic signatures, streamlining contract processes across various industries, including real estate.

Managing Multiple Offers

In real estate transactions involving multiple offers, all proposals must be presented to the seller. When managing counter-offers, it is crucial that these are carefully reviewed and finalized before addressing other potential buyers to avoid legal complications, such as inadvertently agreeing to sell the property to multiple buyers simultaneously.

Counter-offers and Offers

- Counter-offers invalidate any previous offers and remain valid until accepted, rejected, or withdrawn.
- Offers transition into contracts only after both parties accept the terms and provide their signatures.

Back-up Contracts

Back-up contracts can be used to secure a secondary offer contingent upon the failure of the primary agreement. It is advisable for parties to consult with legal professionals before entering into such agreements to understand the implications fully.

Escalation Clauses

In competitive market conditions, buyers might use escalation clauses to automatically increase their offer above others up to a predetermined maximum limit. This strategy ensures they remain competitive without exceeding their budget. Escalation clauses are particularly useful in seller's markets where multiple bids might occur.

These clauses and strategies, facilitated by the flexibility offered by electronic transactions under UETA, play a vital role in modern real estate dealings, ensuring both compliance with legal standards and adaptability in dynamic market conditions.

Addendums, Amendments, and Contract Clauses in Real Estate Contracts

Real estate contracts are comprehensive documents that detail the terms of a transaction and the responsibilities of each party. When additional terms are agreed upon or changes need to be made to existing terms, this is done through addendums and amendments. Together with the main contract, these documents form the complete legal agreement between the parties.

Addendum

An addendum is an additional document that adds terms not originally addressed in the main contract. These can be used to include any agreed-upon conditions that were not contemplated at the time the original contract was signed. For example, if a seller wishes to continue living in the property post-closing for a certain period, a rent-back agreement can be arranged and added as an addendum to the original contract, where the seller agrees to pay rent to the new owner.

Amendment

An amendment modifies specific terms of an existing contract. Unlike an addendum, which adds to the existing content, an amendment changes the existing terms. For instance, if both parties agree to adjust the closing date of the transaction, an amendment would be executed to make this change official.

Key Differences:

- Addendums add to the contract.
- Amendments change elements of the contract.

Contract Clauses

Contract clauses are specific provisions or sections within a contract that detail particular aspects of the agreement. These clauses are crucial for defining the obligations and rights of each party. Commonly included clauses are:

- **Time is of the Essence**: This clause ensures that all parties involved are committed to adhering to the timelines specified in the contract.
- **Choice of Law**: Determines that any legal disputes arising from the contract will be resolved under the laws of a specific jurisdiction.
- **Indemnification**: Obligates one or both parties to compensate the other for any losses or damages arising from the contract.
- **Contingency Clauses**: Specify conditions that must be met for the contract to proceed, such as satisfactory home inspections, appraisals, or the sale of a previous home.
- **Arbitration Clause**: Requires that disputes be resolved through arbitration, rather than through court litigation.
- **Mediation Clause**: Encourages parties to attempt to resolve disputes through mediation before moving to arbitration or litigation.

- **Statute of Limitations Clause**: Defines the time frame within which any legal action related to the contract must be initiated.

Contingencies in Real Estate Contracts

Contingencies are critical conditions within real estate contracts that must be fulfilled before the transaction can be completed and legally binding. These provisions ensure that certain benchmarks are met, allowing for a smooth transition of property ownership under predefined conditions. Understanding the roles and responsibilities associated with contingencies is crucial for both buyers and sellers.

Key Components of Contingencies

Contingencies in a real estate contract typically involve three main elements:

1. **Responsible Party**: Identifies who is obligated to perform the actions necessary to meet the contingency.
2. **Required Actions**: Outlines the specific steps that must be taken to remove the contingency and move forward with the transaction.
3. **Deadline**: Sets a clear timeframe by which the contingency must be resolved.

Failure to satisfy a contingency by its deadline can lead to a breach of the agreement, rendering the offer void and potentially leading to the termination of the contract. Handling contingencies typically involves:

- If a buyer fails to meet a contingency (e.g., securing financing), they risk losing their earnest money deposit.
- If a seller fails to fulfill their part (e.g., ensuring repairs are done), the buyer may have the legal right to terminate the contract.

Common Types of Contingencies

Several commonly used contingencies protect the buyer and ensure the property meets their needs and investment criteria:

- **Appraisal Contingency**: Ensures the property is valued at or above the agreed sales price, safeguarding the buyer from overpaying.

- **Financing Contingency**: Allows the buyer to withdraw from the deal without penalty if they are unable to secure financing from a bank or other financial institution.
- **Home Inspection Contingency**: Gives the buyer the right to have the property inspected and to request repairs or withdraw from the purchase based on the findings.
- **Home Sale Contingency:** Dependent on the buyer selling their current home, providing security that they will have the funds necessary to proceed with the new purchase.

Market Impact on Contingencies

The prevalence and stringency of contingencies can vary with market conditions:

- In a buyer's market, buyers may have the leverage to include more contingencies, reflecting lower demand and greater choice.
- Conversely, in a seller's market, contingencies may be fewer or waived altogether by buyers eager to make their offers more attractive amid high competition.

Tips for Managing Contingencies

To effectively handle contingencies, parties should:

- Clearly understand and agree upon the specifics of each contingency, including the actions required and the timelines for completion.
- Keep thorough documentation of all communications and actions taken to satisfy the contingencies.
- Use written notices to formally communicate the fulfillment or issues related to each contingency, ensuring legal compliance and clarity.

Rights and Obligations of Parties to a Real Estate Contract

Real estate contracts, like all contracts, are governed by principles that ensure fair dealings and accountability among the parties involved. These principles are not always explicitly stated within the contract but are understood to apply through general contract law.

Implied Rights in a Contract

Parties entering into a contract inherently have certain rights that protect them from unfair practices. These rights include:

- **Freedom from Fraud or Misrepresentation**: All parties have the right to expect that the facts presented in the contract are truthful and not deceptive.
- **Freedom from Undue Influence**: The contract should not be the result of one party taking advantage of their power or influence over another.
- **Freedom from Duress**: Contracts should be entered into voluntarily, without coercion, threats, or pressure from the other party.

Obligations of Parties

In addition to rights, parties to a contract also have several obligations, which include:

- **Good Faith**: Parties are expected to act honestly and not engage in any behavior that could be considered deceptive or fraudulent.
- **Timely Compliance**: Parties must adhere to the timelines specified in the contract, especially when the contract states that "time is of the essence".

Breach of Contract and Remedies

A breach of contract occurs when one or more parties fail to fulfill their legal obligations as stipulated in the contract. Various remedies are available to the non-breaching party, depending on the nature of the breach and the terms of the contract.

Responses to Breach of Contract

- **Unilateral Rescission**: The non-breaching party may choose to terminate the contract altogether.
- **Accept Partial Performance**: Instead of rescission, the non-breaching party may accept incomplete fulfillment of the contract terms, usually in exchange for some form of compensation.
- **Sue for Damages**: The injured party may seek monetary compensation for any harm caused by the breach. This is often the most common remedy sought in breach of contract cases.
- **Specific Performance**: In some cases, the court may order the breaching party to perform their contractual obligations, rather than just compensating the other party with money.

Liquidated Damages

In real estate, contracts often include a liquidated damages clause, particularly to address potential breaches by the buyer. Such clauses typically limit the seller's damages to retaining the earnest money deposit, providing a predefined remedy and avoiding lengthy litigation.

Ending of Contracts in Real Estate: Execution and Termination

Contracts in real estate, as in other areas of law, can conclude in various ways depending on how the obligations of the parties are met or unmet. Understanding these mechanisms is crucial for navigating legal relationships and managing real estate transactions effectively.

Execution of Contracts

The most straightforward and desired conclusion of a contract is through execution:

- **Performance (Execution)**: This ideal scenario occurs when all parties fulfill their outlined duties, leading to the termination of their obligations. In real estate, this means the seller receives payment and transfers property ownership to the buyer at closing.
- **Partial Performance**: Sometimes, one party may fulfill only part of their contractual obligations. If the other party accepts this partial performance, the contract is considered executed to the extent agreed upon.
- **Substantial Performance**: In cases where a party completes all material aspects of their obligations but fails in minor, non-material respects, they may still claim execution. They can potentially recover damages for any loss incurred due to the minor unfulfilled aspects.

Termination of Contracts

Contracts can also end through various forms of termination, which do not involve complete performance by all parties:

- **Termination by Notice**: A party may terminate the contract according to terms laid out within the agreement itself, potentially owing compensation to the non-terminating party.
- **Release**: This occurs when one party formally agrees to relinquish the other from their obligations under the contract.

- **Rescission**: Either party may rescind the contract if certain conditions or contingencies are not met, effectively nullifying the agreement and reverting all parties to their pre-contractual state.

- **Mutual Agreement**: Contracts can be terminated by mutual consent, ideally documented through a written agreement to ensure clarity and legal proof.

- **Assignment and Delegation**: Assignment involves transferring one's rights and obligations to another party, often used in real estate for transferring purchase rights. Delegation occurs when duties under a contract are assigned to a third party, although the original party remains liable if the new party fails to perform.

- **Novation**: This is a complete replacement of an original contract with a new one, with new terms or parties, thereby voiding the previous agreement and releasing the original parties from their obligations.

Summary

In conclusion, this chapter provides a comprehensive overview of real estate contracts, exploring their formation, types, components, and the eventual conclusion through execution or termination. It underscores the importance of understanding various contract forms such as purchase agreements, lease agreements, and the roles of electronic transactions under laws like the UETA. This chapter also highlights the critical nature of contract clauses, addendums, and amendments, which allow for adaptability and specificity in legal agreements.

Moreover, it discusses the strategic use of contingencies and the legal implications of breaches, providing pathways to resolve potential disputes. For real estate professionals, mastery of this knowledge is essential, ensuring that they can navigate complex transactions with confidence and legal acumen, safeguarding the interests of all parties involved and facilitating smooth and successful property transfers.

Chapter 8: Leasing and Property Management

Overview

Leasing and property management encompass a vital component of real estate practice, accounting for 3% of the Salesperson Exam. This chapter explores the nuances of lease agreements, the rights and obligations of the parties involved, and the various types of leasehold estates.

Lease Agreements

A lease agreement is a binding contract that delineates the terms under which one party, the tenant or lessee, is granted the use of property owned by another party, the landlord or lessor. The tenant's right under the contract is termed a leasehold estate. Lease agreements ensure the tenant can use the property for a specified period in exchange for rental payments to the landlord.

Types of Leasehold Estates

Understanding different leasehold estates provides a framework for managing lease terms and conditions effectively:

1. **Estate for Years**: This lease specifies a fixed duration with defined start and end dates. The lease automatically terminates at the end of the period without requiring notice from either party. This type of lease remains valid through changes in property ownership or the death of the landlord.
2. **Periodic Estate**: Often structured as month-to-month arrangements, this lease continues indefinitely without a set end date. It renews automatically at the end of each period until legally terminated by either party, typically requiring a 30-60 day notice.
3. **Estate at Will**: This flexible arrangement allows either party to terminate the lease at any time with proper notice, and it also ends automatically upon the death of either party.
4. **Estate at Sufferance**: This occurs when a tenant remains in possession of the property without the landlord's consent after the lease term has expired, also known as a holdover tenancy.

Special Lease Agreements

Lease agreements can also include options to buy or obligations to buy, which add complexity and potential for future transactions:

- **Lease with Option to Buy**: This agreement gives the tenant the right, but not the obligation, to purchase the property either during the lease term or at its conclusion. It combines a bilateral lease agreement with a unilateral option contract.
- **Lease with Obligation to Buy**: Known as a lease/purchase agreement, this contract obligates the tenant to purchase the property at the end of the lease term, binding both parties not just to the lease but also to a subsequent sale.

Subleasing and Assignment

Tenants may transfer their lease rights to third parties through subleasing or assignment:

- **Sublease**: The original tenant becomes a sublessor, creating a new lease agreement with a sublessee for all or part of the leased premises.
- **Assignment**: The tenant transfers their entire interest in the lease to another party, provided the lease does not explicitly prohibit such a transfer.

The Four Most Common Commercial Lease Types

In the realm of commercial real estate, understanding different lease types is essential for both tenants and landlords to negotiate terms that align with their financial and operational objectives. This section outlines the four most common types of commercial leases, each characterized by different structures of rent and expense responsibilities.

Net Leases

Net leases involve tenants paying not only rent but also some or all of the property's operating costs, which include property taxes, maintenance, and insurance. This category includes several types of net leases:

- **Single Net Lease (N)**: The tenant is responsible for rent and one of the expense categories, typically property taxes.
- **Double Net Lease (NN)**: The tenant pays rent and two of the expense categories, often property taxes and maintenance.

- **Triple Net Lease (NNN)**: This lease requires the tenant to pay all three expense categories along with the rent. Triple net leases are commonly used for single-tenant commercial properties and have long-term lease agreements.
- **Absolute Net Lease**: An extension of the triple net lease, where the tenant covers all expenses, including major repairs like roofing and structural issues.

Gross Lease

In a gross lease, the tenant pays a fixed rental amount, and the landlord covers all property expenses, making financial planning simpler for the tenant. Gross leases are prevalent in office buildings and retail spaces. Variations include:

- **Modified Gross Lease**: A hybrid of net and gross leases, where the tenant pays base rent plus a negotiated portion of the operating expenses, allowing for shared financial responsibility on operating costs.

Percentage Lease

Common in the retail sector, especially malls, the percentage lease involves the tenant paying a base rent plus a percentage of their revenue. The additional payment kicks in after reaching a pre-agreed sales breakpoint, incentivizing landlords to support tenants' business success. The landlord typically handles all property expenses, similar to a gross lease.

Graduated Lease

A graduated lease allows for rent adjustments over the lease term, based on pre-determined factors such as market conditions, property value, or an economic index. This lease type is beneficial for businesses that expect their revenue to grow over time, starting with a lower rent that increases gradually. It also protects landlords by enabling them to adjust rent in line with property values and inflation.

Understanding Lease Differences

- **Net Leases**: Generally offer lower rent but include variable operating costs, transferring more responsibility to the tenant.
- **Gross Leases**: Typically have higher rent that is inclusive of all costs, providing clarity and simplicity for tenants.

- **Percentage Leases**: Offer lower base rent with additional costs tied to business performance, suitable for retail spaces.
- **Graduated Leases**: Feature rent that adjusts over time, suitable for businesses planning for growth.

Additional Commercial Lease Types

Beyond the primary commercial lease types, there are several specialized leases that cater to unique business needs or property types. Understanding these can help tenants and landlords find creative solutions for specific situations.

Ground Lease

A ground lease involves leasing the land while allowing the lessee to construct a building or other improvements on it. Typically, these leases last for a long time—50 to 99 years—and upon lease expiration, ownership of the improvements reverts to the landowner. This arrangement is beneficial for lessees who wish to develop a property without purchasing the land and for lessors who want to retain long-term ownership of the land.

Loft Lease

Loft leases involve renting large, open spaces that are often found in converted warehouses or industrial buildings. These spaces are popular among artists, startups, and businesses looking for flexible working environments. Tenants can personalize their space but are restricted from making structural changes, preserving the building's integrity.

Lease Purchase

Lease purchase agreements combine rental and purchase elements, where a portion of each rental payment is credited towards the eventual purchase price of the property. This option is ideal for tenants who plan to buy but currently lack the financial means to do so outright. It allows them to lock in a purchase price while building equity over time.

Sale and Leaseback

In a sale and leaseback arrangement, a property owner sells the building to an investor and then leases it back. This strategy is often used by companies needing to free up capital while continuing to use the property.

It benefits the seller by providing immediate access to equity and the buyer by offering a long-term tenant and a steady income stream.

Sub-Surface Leasing Rights

Sub-surface leases are agreements where a tenant, typically a mining or extraction company, leases the right to explore and extract natural resources like minerals, oil, or gas from a property. The landowner receives an initial payment and, if resources are discovered, a percentage of the profits from the extracted materials. If no resources are found, the lease simply expires.

Sale of a Leased Property (Transfer of Ownership)

When a landlord sells a property, the new owner must adhere to any existing leases, allowing tenants to remain until the lease expires. If the lease includes a renewal option, the new owner is also obligated to honor this provision. It is the responsibility of the selling owner to inform prospective buyers about any active leases. Upon acquiring the property, the new owner assumes the role of landlord, inheriting both the rights to receive rent and the duties of managing the property.

Landlord and Tenant Rights and Obligations under the Uniform Residential Landlord Tenant Act (URLTA)

The URLTA governs residential rental agreements to ensure fairness in lease contracts. It provides a model for states to adapt into their own landlord-tenant legislation, making it essential for parties involved in lease agreements to familiarize themselves with specific state guidelines.

Landlord Rights

Landlords are permitted to select tenants based on creditworthiness and can enforce lease terms if violations occur. They have several rights in the event of a lease breach:

- Sue for unpaid rent: Landlords can legally recover rent that has not been paid.
- Begin eviction proceedings: If tenants fail to comply with lease terms, landlords may initiate legal proceedings to remove them.
- Terminate the lease agreement: Landlords can end the lease if tenants fail to meet their obligations.

Landlord Obligations

Landlords must meet various responsibilities to ensure the property is safe, clean, and habitable:

- **Compliance with Building Codes**: Ensuring the property meets all local building standards.
- **Maintenance of Common Areas**: Keeping shared spaces in good condition.
- **Unit Preparation**: Making sure units are empty, clean, and undamaged for new tenants.
- Safety and Repairs: Maintaining all major systems and performing necessary repairs to keep the property habitable.
- **Financial Responsibilities**: Accurately managing rents and security deposits.
- **Legal Compliance**: Following fair housing, civil rights, and ADA regulations.
- **Management Duties**: Overseeing budgets and property management tasks.
- **Disclosure Requirements**: Providing tenants with contact information for management and addressing issues promptly.
- **Notice for Entry**: Informing tenants in advance about entry for repairs, except in emergencies.
- **Eviction Procedures**: Adhering to legal procedures when eviction is warranted.

Landlords are tasked with balancing their rights to manage their properties effectively while fulfilling their obligations to maintain safe and habitable environments. Likewise, tenants are expected to adhere to the lease terms and respect the property, ensuring a harmonious rental relationship.

Tenant Rights and Obligations Under the Uniform Residential Landlord Tenant Act (URLTA)

The URLTA aims to balance the rights and responsibilities of tenants and landlords, ensuring fair treatment and legal compliance in residential lease arrangements.

Tenant Rights

Tenants are entitled to quiet enjoyment and possession of the property, using it for its legally intended purposes without undue disturbance. If a landlord fails to fulfill their obligations, tenants have several rights under the URLTA, provided they give written notice to the landlord about the issues, indicating their intent to exercise their rights if the issues are not timely resolved:

- **Repair and Deduct**: Tenants may make necessary repairs themselves and deduct the costs from their rent, provided they keep receipts and include them with rent payments.
- **Alternative Housing**: If the rental lacks essential services, tenants may find temporary alternative housing. During this period, rent may be suspended until the landlord resolves the issue.
- **Sue for Damages**: In severe cases, tenants can sue the landlord to recover damages resulting from the landlord's failure to maintain the rental property as required.
- **Terminate the Lease**: If the landlord does not address the breach, tenants have the right to terminate the lease agreement.

Tenant Obligations

Alongside these rights, tenants have several obligations they must fulfill to maintain the terms of their lease and ensure a functional living environment:

- **Obey Laws and Regulations**: Tenants must adhere to all local laws and regulations affecting the property.
- **Pay Rent**: Timely payment of rent according to the lease terms is required.
- **Maintenance of Property**: Keeping the property safe, clean, and sanitary is a tenant responsibility.
- **Allow Access for Repairs**: Tenants must allow landlords or maintenance staff access to the property for repairs or maintenance as required by the lease.
- **Report Issues**: Any damages or maintenance issues must be reported promptly to avoid exacerbation of the problems.

Types of Eviction in Rental Agreements

Eviction is a legal procedure used by landlords to remove tenants from rental property under specific circumstances, such as non-payment of rent or violation of lease terms. The process and conditions for eviction are strictly regulated to protect both landlords and tenants.

Actual Eviction

Actual eviction is the formal process through which a landlord legally removes a tenant. This process requires the landlord to provide the tenant with a notice that outlines the reasons for eviction and the timeframe in which the eviction proceedings will begin. This notice must be given in accordance with state laws, which specify the number of days a tenant has to either remedy the issue or vacate the property.

Constructive Eviction

Constructive eviction occurs under more indirect circumstances. This type of eviction happens when a landlord does something, or fails to do something, that substantially interferes with the tenant's ability to use and enjoy the property. Examples include failing to provide essential services like water or electricity or not addressing significant maintenance issues. If these actions make the property uninhabitable, a tenant may have the right to leave the property, terminate the lease, and possibly sue for damages.

Constructive eviction is considered an illegal eviction method because it forces the tenant to leave without following the formal eviction process required by law. Tenants claiming constructive eviction must prove that the landlord's actions or inactions were severe enough to breach the implied covenant of quiet enjoyment that is fundamental to all rental agreements.

Essential Components of a Lease Agreement

A lease agreement is a comprehensive document that establishes the terms under which a rental relationship operates between a landlord and a tenant. Here are the common elements found in lease agreements:

Contact Information

This section includes essential details about the landlord and tenant, such as names, addresses, and contact numbers, ensuring both parties can communicate effectively throughout the term of the lease.

Property Details

This part describes the rental property in detail, including its address, square footage, available amenities, and other unique characteristics that identify the property.

Lease Terms

Specifies the duration of the lease with start and end dates, and details on the conditions under which the lease may terminate early or be renewed.

Rent Payments

Defines the amount of rent, due dates, and acceptable payment methods. It may also outline penalties for late payments and conditions for any rent adjustments.

Security Deposit

Details the required amount for the security deposit, conditions for its return, and circumstances under which the landlord can withhold part or all of this deposit.

Maintenance and Repairs

Outlines responsibilities for both landlord and tenant regarding maintenance and repairs, clarifying who is responsible for various types of maintenance tasks.

Rights and Obligations

Enumerates the legal and practical responsibilities of each party, ensuring that both understand their duties to maintain the property and abide by the law.

Restrictions

Lists any prohibitions such as alterations to the property, subletting without permission, or specific rules like no smoking or restrictions on installing additional appliances.

Occupancy Limits

Defines who and how many people can reside at the property, which helps maintain safety standards and compliance with local housing laws.

Utilities

Clarifies which utilities are included in the rent and which are the responsibility of the tenant. This section helps prevent disputes regarding utility payments.

Addendums

Includes additional clauses or conditions not covered in the main body of the lease, such as pet policies or parking rules.

Disclosures

Legal disclosures that might be required by local laws, such as information about lead-based paint, mold, or the property's rental history.

Notices

Details the requirements for advance notice given by the tenant or landlord for various situations, such as not renewing the lease or requesting entry to the property for repairs.

Property Management

Property managers play a crucial role in the real estate sector by acting as the intermediary between property owners and tenants. They operate as general agents with fiduciary responsibilities, similar to those of real estate agents. Understanding the core duties of a property manager, often remembered by the acronym OLD CAR, is essential for effective management and adherence to legal standards.

Fiduciary Duties of Property Managers

1. **Obedience:** Property managers must follow the lawful instructions of the property owner regarding the management of the property. This includes adhering to all directives that do not violate legal statutes.
2. **Loyalty:** The interests of the property owner must always be placed above those of the property manager or any third party. This means prioritizing the owner's needs and striving to achieve the best possible outcomes in all transactions and negotiations.
3. **Disclosure:** Property managers are required to inform the property owner of all material facts that could influence decisions or affect the property. This includes changes in market conditions, tenant issues, or anything else that could impact the owner's interests.
4. **Confidentiality:** Sensitive information about the property owner, such as personal and financial details, must be guarded closely. Property managers should ensure that no information that could harm the owner's negotiating position or privacy is disclosed.
5. **Accounting:** All funds and properties received on behalf of the property owner must be accurately recorded and reported. This includes maintaining clear, up-to-date records of all transactions, security deposits, and maintenance costs.
6. **Reasonable Skill and Care**: Property managers are expected to manage the property competently and with a level of professionalism that meets industry standards. This duty compels them to handle all aspects of property management, from tenant relations to maintenance and emergency responses, with diligence and appropriate expertise.

Property Manager Responsibilities

Property managers play a crucial role in the real estate industry, ensuring the smooth operation of rental properties while upholding the financial and legal standards required by owners. Their responsibilities are diverse and integral to maintaining property value and tenant satisfaction.

1. **Financial Management**: Property managers are responsible for creating and maintaining financial documents like operating budgets, cash flow reports, profit statements, and budget comparisons. These documents are essential for tracking the financial health of the property.

2. **Renting Properties**: This includes market research to set competitive rental rates and filling vacancies to ensure a steady income from the property.

3. **Marketing Properties**: Effective advertising and promotional activities are crucial to attract potential tenants.

4. **Tenant Screening**: Selecting the right tenants is vital. This process must comply with fair housing laws at the local, state, and federal levels to avoid discrimination.

5. **Rent Collection and Security Deposits**: Property managers handle rent collection and manage security deposits in accordance with legal requirements to prevent issues such as commingling or conversion of funds.

6. **Tenant Relations**: Maintaining a good relationship with tenants involves addressing their concerns and resolving disputes effectively.

7. **Property Maintenance**: This includes conducting preventive, corrective, and routine maintenance to keep the property in good condition and address any issues promptly.

8. **Risk Management**: Property managers must manage risks through strategies such as controlling, avoiding, retaining, and transferring risks. This includes regular property inspections and maintaining appropriate insurance policies.

9. **Regulatory Compliance**: Ensuring compliance with all local, state, and federal regulations is crucial to prevent legal issues and ensure the property meets all required standards.

Property Management Agreements

A property management agreement is vital for defining the relationship between the property owner and the manager. Key components of this agreement include:

- **Identification of Parties**: Clearly states the owner and the property manager involved.

- **Property Description**: Details the properties under management.
- **Terms of Agreement**: Includes start and end dates and conditions for termination.
- **Objectives**: Describes the owner's expectations from the manager.
- **Manager Duties**: Outlines the responsibilities and any limitations of the property manager.
- **Owner Responsibilities**: Specifies the obligations of the property owner.
- **Manager's Authority**: Defines the extent of the manager's general agency authority.
- **Reporting Requirements**: Specifies the frequency and type of reports required.
- **Compensation Structure**: Describes how the manager will be compensated, whether fixed, commission-based, percentage, or a combination.
- **Expense Allocation**: Details who is responsible for various expenses.
- **Antitrust Provision**: Ensures compensation and fees are negotiable.
- **Equal Opportunity Statement**: Affirms compliance with fair housing laws.

Managing Operating and Trust Funds in Property Management

Effective financial management is crucial for property managers, who often handle both operating funds and trust funds. Proper accounting practices and legal compliance are essential to maintain the integrity of these funds and ensure transparent and effective property management.

Operating Accounts

Operating accounts are essential for the daily financial operations related to property management. These accounts are used for:

- **Depositing Rental Income**: All rental payments received from tenants are deposited into these accounts.
- **Paying Expenses**: Expenses such as staff salaries, property maintenance, utilities, and repairs are paid out of operating accounts.

Trust Accounts

Trust accounts, or escrow accounts, are used to hold funds that belong to others, such as tenants or property owners. Key aspects of managing trust accounts include:

- **Security Deposits**: Held in trust accounts until they are needed for repairs after a tenant moves out.
- **Prepaid Rent**: Funds received in advance from tenants are kept in these accounts as required by law.

- **Commissions and Fees**: Property management commissions pre-collected from property owners are also held in trust accounts and are withdrawn according to the agreed schedule in the property management agreement.

Legal Requirements

It is legally mandatory to keep operating and trust funds separate to prevent misuse of funds:

- **No Commingling**: Trust funds must be kept separate from operating funds to avoid legal violations.
- **No Conversion**: Using trust funds for operating expenses or personal use is illegal and considered conversion.

Financial Reports

Property managers must also prepare various financial reports to measure and communicate the financial health of the properties they manage:

- **Annual Operating Budget**: Projects the expected annual income and expenses, helping in planning and resource allocation.
- **Cash Flow Report**: Provides a snapshot of the property's current financial status, showing incoming funds and outgoing expenses.
- **Profit and Loss Statement**: Outlines the property's financial performance over a specific period, detailing profits or losses.
- **Budget Comparison Statement**: Compares actual financial outcomes with those projected in the annual operating budget to assess performance against financial goals.

These financial reports are critical tools for property managers, providing insights into financial performance and aiding in strategic decision-making. They help ensure that all financial activities are accounted for and that the property is managed efficiently and profitably.

Fair Housing Laws and Property Management Compliance

Property managers and landlords are governed by a stringent set of federal, state, and local fair housing laws designed to prevent discrimination in housing-related activities. Understanding and adhering to these laws is crucial for maintaining legal compliance and promoting equitable treatment in housing.

Scope of Fair Housing Laws

Fair housing laws apply to a wide range of real estate activities, including:

- **Sale and Rental of Housing**: Ensuring that housing is made available without discrimination based on protected characteristics.
- **Real Estate Brokerage Services**: Requiring all brokerage activities to be conducted without discriminatory practices.
- **Appraisals and Financing**: Prohibiting discrimination in assessing the value of properties or providing financing.
- **Advertising**: Mandating that all housing advertisements should be free of any language indicating preference, limitation, or discrimination.

Prohibited Discriminatory Acts

Under fair housing laws, property managers and landlords must not:

- **Refuse to Sell or Rent**: Denying access to housing based on someone's inclusion in a protected class is illegal.
- **Vary Terms and Conditions**: Offering different leasing terms or conditions based on discriminatory factors is prohibited.
- **Discriminative Advertising**: Indicating any preference or limitation in housing ads based on protected characteristics is forbidden.
- **Coercion or Intimidation**: It's illegal to coerce, threaten, intimidate, or interfere with someone's enjoyment of housing rights.
- **Steering**: Guiding prospective tenants towards or away from certain housing based on protected characteristics restricts their free choice and is considered discriminatory.
- **Blockbusting**: Creating fear among property owners about neighborhood demographic changes to manipulate housing prices or availability is also illegal.

Americans with Disabilities Act (ADA)

The ADA requires landlords to make reasonable accommodations for tenants with disabilities. These accommodations ensure that individuals with disabilities can use and enjoy their living spaces just like anyone else. Examples of reasonable accommodations include:

- **Modifications**: Allowing tenants to make necessary modifications at their expense, such as installing grab bars or ramps.
- **Policy Deviations**: Permitting exceptions to policies like assigned parking spaces or allowing transfers to more accessible units.
- **Assistance Animals**: Recognizing that assistance animals are not pets and thus, not subject to pet policies or additional fees.

Compliance and Best Practices

To ensure compliance with these laws, property managers should:

- **Educate Themselves and Staff**: Regular training on fair housing laws is essential.
- **Review Advertising Materials**: Ensure all promotional content is neutral and inclusive.
- **Implement Standardized Procedures**: Use uniform application processes and criteria for all prospective tenants to avoid any form of discrimination.
- **Document Interactions and Decisions**: Keeping detailed records can help defend against accusations of discriminatory practices.

Summary

This chapter delves into the complexities of leasing and property management, highlighting the critical roles that lease agreements and property managers play in the real estate sector. It emphasizes the importance of understanding the different types of leasehold estates—ranging from fixed-term leases to more flexible arrangements like month-to-month tenancies—as well as specialized agreements such as ground leases and lease purchase options.

Furthermore, the chapter outlines the comprehensive responsibilities of property managers, from financial oversight to maintaining tenant relations and ensuring compliance with fair housing laws. Adhering to these standards and obligations ensures that properties are managed efficiently and ethically, providing stability and value for both property owners and tenants. Ultimately, mastering the content of this chapter equips real estate professionals with the knowledge and tools necessary to effectively navigate the intricacies of property leasing and management, fostering a professional and legally compliant real estate practice.

Chapter 9: Transfer of Title

Overview

The transfer of title involves the legal process by which ownership of property is transferred from one party to another. This chapter focuses on understanding the distinct roles of titles and deeds in property transactions, clarifying the concept of title status, and exploring the necessary steps to ensure a title is clear from encumbrances.

Understanding Title and Deed

Definition of Title

Title refers to the legal right to own, use, or sell property. Unlike physical objects, a title is a conceptual entity that signifies ownership rights. It is analogous to how a person's job title indicates their role or function, rather than being a tangible item.

Definition of Deed

A deed, in contrast, is a physical document that facilitates the transfer of the legal title of property from one individual (the grantor) to another (the grantee). This document is crucial as it ensures the continuity of property ownership through a recorded history, showing who has owned the land and property over time.

Title Status: Clear vs. Cloudy

Clear Title

A clear title, also known as a clean title, indicates that the property is free from liens, encumbrances, or legal questions concerning the ownership of the property. This status is essential in real estate transactions as it reassures the buyer of undisputed ownership.

Cloud on Title

Conversely, a cloud on title represents any issues or irregularities that might cast doubt on the legality of the ownership. These can include unresolved liens, disputes over property boundaries, errors in public records, and fraudulent activities, among others. Such clouds must be resolved before a property can be sold with a clear title.

Title Search and Abstract of Title

Title Search

To ensure a title is clear, a thorough search of public records is conducted. This search aims to uncover any claims or liens against the property. Following the search, a preliminary report, or title commitment, may be issued, promising insurance under specified conditions.

Abstract of Title

The abstract of title provides a summarized history of the title, detailing past ownerships from the current owner back to the original. This document is prepared after extensive research into public records and is essential for resolving any gaps in ownership.

Practical Example: Handling a Title Defect

Consider a scenario where during a title search, an unreleased mortgage lien from a previous owner is discovered. The current owner must ensure this lien is discharged to clear the title before proceeding with the sale. Typically, resolving such an issue might involve contacting the lender for a release document or seeking legal assistance to address the encumbrance.

Title Requirements – Marketable vs Insurable

Marketable Title

A marketable title is considered ideal in real estate transactions. It implies that the title is sufficiently clear of significant defects and encumbrances that would deter a reasonable buyer. While not necessarily perfect, a marketable title is largely free of liens except for a current mortgage, which is typically resolved with the proceeds from the sale. This type of title ensures that there is no substantial doubt regarding the ownership of the property, and all significant liens are expected to be cleared at closing.

Key Considerations

- **Mortgage Liens**: Common in marketable titles but cleared at the point of sale.

- **Liens and Encumbrances**: Should not persist past closing unless trivial or agreed upon in the sale terms.

Insurable Title

Insurable title, while containing known defects or clouds, can still be acceptable for property transactions because a title insurance company is willing to insure against these defects. This category is less stringent than marketable title but ensures that ownership and property value are not compromised by the known defects.

Key Features

- **Known Defects**: These are specifically outlined and insured against.
- **Insurance Coverage**: Provided despite the defects, offering buyer and lender reassurance against potential financial loss.

Title Insurance and Its Implications

Importance of Title Insurance

Title insurance plays a critical role in real estate transactions by safeguarding against financial losses from undiscovered or future claims against the title. It is beneficial for both buyers and lenders, with policies tailored to each party's exposure.

Policy Coverage and Exceptions

Title insurance policies detail what they do not cover through a schedule of exceptions, typically excluding:

- **Claims Not in Public Records**: Undocumented claims are not covered.
- **Post-Policy Liens**: Liens recorded after the policy's effective date.
- **Unrecorded Claims**: Including those by non-documented residents or tenants.

Handling Claims

In the event of a title claim, the insurance company may opt to settle the debt or legally challenge the claimant. If the title company resolves the claim, they might pursue reimbursement through a legal principle called subrogation, where they step into the shoes of the insured party to recover costs.

Example: Imagine a buyer discovers a previously unrecorded lien after closing. The title insurance covers the claim, paying out the required amount. The insurance company then uses subrogation to recover this amount from the person who originally caused the lien.

10 Essential Elements of a Valid Deed

In the realm of real estate, deeds are the documents through which property ownership is transferred. Governed by the statute of frauds, these documents must be in writing to be legally valid. A deed that does not include the necessary elements may fail to properly convey property rights. Here, we detail the ten essential components that constitute a valid deed.

Grantor

Grantor: The current owner transferring the property. This individual must be legally competent and of legal age—typically 18 years or older. Accuracy in the grantor's name throughout the deed is critical to avoid any discrepancies.

Grantee

The recipient of the property's title. The grantee must be clearly identified, with precise specifications if names are shared across generations (e.g., John Doe Jr. versus John Doe Sr.).

Granting Clause

This clause articulates the grantor's intention to transfer the property and outlines the rights being conveyed. It is crucial that the language in this section clearly supports the transfer of ownership.

Legal Description of the Property

A deed must include a detailed legal description of the property. This is not simply the street address but a formal description using one of the recognized methods: Metes and Bounds, Lot and Block, or the Rectangular Government Survey System (RGSS).

Consideration

The deed must state what the grantor receives in return for transferring the property, which could be monetary ("for ten dollars"), symbolic ("for love and affection"), or the actual sale price.

Exceptions and Reservations

This section details any rights the grantor retains and any encumbrances that remain with the property, such as easements or deed restrictions.

Habendum Clause

The Habendum Clause specifies the extent of the interest being granted to the grantee. It must be consistent with the granting clause and includes the phrase "to have and to hold."

Signature of the Grantor

The deed is not valid unless it is signed by the grantor, confirming their intent to transfer the property.

Acknowledgement

A notary public or other authorized official must verify the identity of the grantor and confirm that the signature was made willingly and knowingly.

Delivery and Acceptance

The final step in the validation of a deed involves its delivery to and acceptance by the grantee. The deed must be recorded in the local land records to finalize the transfer.

Example Scenario: Validating a Deed

Consider a situation where Jane Doe wishes to transfer a property to her nephew. The deed must accurately list her as the grantor and her nephew as the grantee, specify the legal description using an accepted method, state the consideration, and include all necessary clauses and acknowledgements. Upon signing, the deed must be delivered to her nephew and duly recorded.

Transfer of Ownership - Understanding the Three Main Types of Deeds

Deeds are essential instruments in the transfer of property ownership. They come in various forms, each serving different purposes and offering varying levels of protection to the parties involved. The "OR" "EE" mnemonic—where "OR" represents the giver (grantor) and "EE" the receiver (grantee)—helps remember the roles each party plays in these transactions.

General Warranty Deed

A general warranty deed offers the most comprehensive level of protection among deed types, making it highly favored in real estate transactions. It assures the grantee that the property title is clear and the grantor has the rightful ownership to convey it. This deed encompasses six covenants split between present and future assurances:

- **Present Warranties:**
  - **Covenant of Seisin**: Ensures the grantor has both title and possession.
  - **Covenant of Right to Convey**: Affirms the grantor's legal right to transfer the property.
  - **Covenant Against Encumbrances**: Guarantees the absence of undisclosed encumbrances.
- **Future Warranties:**
  - **Covenant of Warranty**: Obligates the grantor to defend the title against claims.
  - **Covenant of Quiet Enjoyment**: Promises undisturbed use and enjoyment of the property.
  - **Covenant of Further Assurances**: Pledges the grantor will rectify any future title defects.

Special Warranty Deed

The special warranty deed provides a more limited assurance than the general warranty deed, making it common in commercial real estate transactions. It covers only the period during which the grantor held the property, guaranteeing:

- No title defects arose under the current grantor's period of ownership.
- The property is free from undisclosed debts or encumbrances during that time.

Quitclaim Deed

The quitclaim deed offers the least protection of all deed types. It does not warrant or guarantee the quality of the grantor's title; it merely transfers whatever interest the grantor may have in the property. Common uses include:

- Resolving title disputes.
- Transferring property between family members.
- Clearing clouds on the title.

Example: Choosing the Right Deed

Imagine a scenario where siblings inherit a family home and decide to transfer ownership solely to one sibling. A quitclaim deed might be employed here to simplify the process, as it effectively transfers whatever interest the other siblings have without the need for extensive title guarantees.

Other Types of Deeds

Besides the primary deeds discussed earlier, there are other types of deeds used in specific circumstances in real estate transactions. Each serves a unique purpose and provides different levels of assurance and protection based on the situation.

Bargain and Sale Deed

A bargain and sale deed indicates that the grantor owns the property and has the legal right to transfer it, but it does not provide any warranty against liens or other claims. This type of deed is commonly used in scenarios such as tax sales or foreclosure sales where the property is sold without any guarantees regarding encumbrances.

Court-Ordered Deeds

Court-ordered deeds arise from legal proceedings and often do not require the consent of the property owner. These deeds are essential in handling properties under specific legal conditions:

- **Administrator's Deed**: Utilized to convey property when an owner dies intestate (without a will), handled by a court-appointed administrator.
- **Executor's Deed**: Employed to transfer property according to a deceased person's will.
- **Master Deed**: Common in the development of condominiums, used to delineate individual units within a larger property.
- **Sheriff's Deed**: Issued following an execution sale, such as for settling a judgment against the property owner or for unpaid taxes.

Deed of Trust

In transactions involving a loan, a deed of trust is used to place the legal title of the property in the hands of a third party, serving as a neutral holder until the borrower repays the loan. The third party, often a bank, escrow, or title company, ensures that the property title remains secure.

Grant Deed

A grant deed transfers ownership with limited assurances; specifically, it only covers the period that the seller owned the property. It offers more protection than a quitclaim deed but less than a general warranty deed. Buyers often supplement the protection a grant deed offers with title insurance, which covers potential title disputes from before and after the seller's ownership period.

Example: Handling a Foreclosure Sale

Consider a property being sold at a sheriff's auction due to unpaid taxes. The winning bidder would receive a sheriff's deed. This deed implies that the property was legally sold under court order but carries no warranties against any undisclosed liens or claims. The buyer would need to conduct thorough due diligence or secure title insurance to protect against potential undisclosed issues.

Actual vs Constructive Notice Importance of Recording Documentation

Recording deeds safeguards the buyer's ownership by providing constructive notice, which makes details of real estate transactions publicly accessible through record searches. This contrasts with actual notice, where an individual directly learns of property details that are not on public record.

Transferring distressed properties, such as through short sales, foreclosures, and REO (Real Estate Owned) sales, involves unique challenges due to the financial strain on the property owner. Extended title insurance is advised for these transactions due to potential issues like property condition and unresolved liens.

Transferring Distressed Properties - Short Sales, Foreclosures, & REO

Short Sales happen when a property is sold for less than what is owed on it. For instance, if a homeowner owes $300,000 but must sell the property for $275,000 due to financial hardship, the remaining $25,000 debt remains the homeowner's responsibility. Short sales are voluntary and require lender approval, often involving complex paperwork and extended closing timelines.

Foreclosures occur when a lender sells a property after the borrower fails to make mortgage payments. Typically, properties are sold at auction following notice and a period allowing the borrower to settle the default. If the sale doesn't cover the debt, lenders might pursue a deficiency judgment against the borrower. An alternative to foreclosure includes a deed in lieu of foreclosure, where the borrower voluntarily transfers the deed to the lender.

REO Properties are those that return to the lender's ownership after an unsuccessful foreclosure sale or if the borrower hands over the property to avoid foreclosure. The sale process for REO properties can be lengthy due to additional reviews like foreclosure audits. While title issues are common, lenders often resolve these before sale to facilitate the process.

Home Warranty Programs

These programs are particularly reassuring for buyers of existing homes, as they cover the costs of repairing or replacing systems and appliances that fail due to normal wear and tear. Sellers might also opt to offer these warranties to protect themselves from post-closing claims concerning the condition of the home. When disputes arise under home warranty claims, the first step is usually mediation, followed by arbitration if mediation does not resolve the issue.

Home Construction Warranties

Offered by builders, these warranties cover new constructions and provide safeguards against defects in workmanship, materials, and major structural elements like the foundation, which are typically covered for up to 10 years. Coverage for major systems such as heating, air conditioning, plumbing, and electrical is usually valid for 2 to 5 years. These warranties ensure that any defects found within these periods are addressed by the builder.

Warranty of Completion of Construction

This type of warranty is essential for homes financed with FHA or VA loans and is a prerequisite for builders. It guarantees that the home is built according to the specified plans and standards and covers the buyer against defects in equipment, materials, or workmanship. The warranty commits the builder to repair any covered defects and to restore any parts of the home damaged in fulfilling these obligations. It typically starts when the title is transferred to the buyer, the construction is completed, or the buyer occupies the home—whichever occurs first.

Closing Time - Completing the Transfer of Ownership

Role of the Escrow Agent

The escrow agent, or closing agent, plays a pivotal role as a neutral third-party in real estate transactions. Their main responsibilities include:

- **Management of Escrow Funds**: Overseeing the collection, holding, and distribution of all funds according to the agreement between the parties.
- **Handling of Transaction Documents**: Managing all paperwork and ensuring that all instructions from the parties involved are followed.
- **Title and Legal Coordination**: Conducting or overseeing the title search, coordinating with lenders, and ensuring all legal aspects of the transaction are complete.
- **Closing Activities**: Preparing and facilitating the closing meeting, providing the Closing Disclosure (CD), and recording necessary documents.
- **Financial Transactions**: Verifying the funding of the buyer's loan, arranging for the payoff of the seller's loan, distributing funds, and filing necessary tax forms.

Understanding Closing Costs

Closing costs are additional expenses incurred during the transfer of property ownership that are not included in the property's sale price. These costs can include:

- **Loan-Related Fees**: Origination fees and points charged by the lender.
- **Title and Insurance**: Costs for title searches, title insurance, and other related fees.
- **Appraisal and Legal Fees**: Payments for property appraisals, surveys, and legal counsel.
- **Taxes and Prepayments**: Transfer taxes, and upfront payments for property taxes and insurance.

Loan Estimate and Closing Disclosure

- **Loan Estimate (LE)**: Provided within three business days of applying for a loan, this document gives an estimate of closing costs.
- **Closing Disclosure (CD)**: Delivered at least three business days before closing, detailing actual closing costs.

Debits and Credits in Closing

- **Buyer Debits**: Include the purchase price, loan fees, insurance premiums, and taxes.
- **Buyer Credits**: May consist of earnest money deposits, mortgage financing, and seller concessions.
- **Seller Debits**: Include items such as real estate commissions, loan payoff costs, and fees for clearing the title.
- **Seller Credits**: Typically the sale price of the property and any taxes or utilities prepaid by the seller.

Example Scenario: Closing Process

Imagine a scenario where the buyers and sellers meet at the closing table. The escrow agent reviews the final Closing Disclosure with both parties, ensuring all financial transactions are clearly understood. The buyers and sellers verify all debits and credits, ensuring that funds from the mortgage lender are correctly allocated and all fees are accounted for. Once all documents are signed and recorded, the escrow agent distributes funds accordingly, marking the successful transfer of property ownership.

Allocating Expenses - Proration

Proration in real estate involves the division of ongoing property-related expenses between the buyer and seller at the time of closing. This ensures that each party pays only for the period during which they hold property ownership. Prorated items can include property taxes, rents, homeowners association (HOA) dues, and utility charges.

Types of Prorated Expenses

- **Accrued Expenses**: These are costs that have been incurred but not yet paid at the time of closing. Examples include property taxes accrued up until the closing date. The seller is responsible for these expenses up to the day of closing and are typically debited to the seller and credited to the buyer.
- **Prepaid Expenses**: These expenses have been paid in advance by the seller before the closing. An example could be a seller who has prepaid the property taxes for the full year. The buyer would reimburse the seller for the portion of the tax period that falls after the closing. These are debited to the buyer and credited to the seller.

Proration of Rent and HOA Dues

For properties that generate income through rentals or have associated HOA dues, proration is calculated similarly:

- **Rental Income**: If a property is leased, rent is prorated based on the amount of time the tenant will occupy the property under the new ownership. The calculation involves determining the daily rent and multiplying it by the number of days the tenant occupies the property during the transition period.
  - **Daily Rent Calculation**: Monthly rent divided by the number of days in the month.
  - **Prorated Rent Calculation**: Daily rent multiplied by the number of days of occupancy under each owner.

- **HOA Dues**: Similar to rent, if HOA dues are paid in advance, the buyer compensates the seller for the portion of the dues that cover the period after closing.

Special Considerations

- **Utility Costs**: Utilities such as fuel for heating (propane or oil) are also prorated based on the amount remaining in the tank at closing. The buyer reimburses the seller for the value of the unused fuel, ensuring the seller only pays for what they consumed.
- **Mortgage Interest and Insurance**: These are only prorated if the buyer is assuming the seller's loan. Otherwise, the new owner arranges their own mortgage and insurance payments starting from the date of closing.

Scenario: Closing on a Rental Property

Imagine a scenario where a buyer is closing on a rental property on the 15th of the month, with monthly rent set at $1500:

- Daily Rent: $1500 ÷ 30 = $50
- Prorated Rent for Buyer: $50 × 11 (days from closing to end of month) = $550

In this case, the buyer would be credited the amount the tenant owes for the period they own the property, and the seller would be debited for the rent accrued up until the day of closing.

Property Taxes

Property taxes are determined based on the assessed value of a property and serve as a significant revenue source for local governments. Property owners encounter tax implications at various stages of ownership:

- **Acquisition**: At the time of purchase, homeowners may be able to deduct points paid and prepaid interest.
- **Ownership**: During ownership, deductions for property taxes, mortgage interest, and potentially depreciation are available.
- **Sale**: The sale of a property can trigger a reassessment, possibly raising taxes. Additionally, capital gains tax may be levied on the profit from the sale, though federal laws allow exclusions for primary residences ($250,000 for individuals and $500,000 for married couples filing jointly).

- **Title and Liens**: It's crucial to review the title commitment to ensure no existing tax liens are against the property.

Calculating Property Taxes at Closing

The responsibility for property taxes is prorated at closing, ensuring each party pays only for the time they own the property. This calculation involves determining the daily rate of property taxes and adjusting based on the exact closing date.

Transfer Taxes

Transfer taxes are levied when property ownership is transferred and the deed is recorded. The responsibility for paying these taxes can fall on either the buyer or seller, depending on their agreement. Rates vary significantly by location and can be calculated as a percentage of the sale price or as a flat rate per thousand dollars of the sale price.

- **Percentage Example**: For a property sold for $500,000 with a transfer tax rate of 0.04%, the tax would be calculated as $500,000 × 0.0004 = $200.
- **Dollar Amount Example**: For a property selling at $600,000 with a rate of $2.00 per $1,000, the calculation would be 600 × $2.00 = $1,200.

FIRPTA - Foreign Investment in Real Property Tax Act

When real property in the U.S. is sold by a non-resident foreign person, FIRPTA requires the buyer to withhold 15% of the gross sales price. This withholding is intended to cover potential capital gains tax liabilities and is handled by the closing agent, although the buyer must ensure it's carried out correctly. After filing a U.S. tax return, the seller may recover any overpayment through a refund, depending on their tax liabilities.

Practical Considerations

Understanding these tax implications is essential for real estate professionals to provide accurate advice and ensure compliance with tax regulations during property transactions. This knowledge helps protect all parties involved and ensures a smooth transfer process.

Summary

In conclusion, Chapter 9 has comprehensively explored the essential mechanisms and legal frameworks that govern the transfer of property ownership. We have dissected the critical roles of deeds and the variance in their protections, from general warranty deeds to quitclaim deeds, and detailed the significance of accurately managing closing procedures through escrow agents. Moreover, the chapter has highlighted the importance of understanding prorations, property taxes, and transfer taxes to ensure transparent and fair financial dealings during property transactions.

The in-depth discussion of these topics prepares real estate professionals to adeptly navigate complex transactions, ensuring they can offer expert guidance and foster trust with clients. As the real estate landscape continues to evolve, the knowledge encapsulated in this chapter will remain vital for professionals seeking to uphold integrity and efficacy in facilitating the seamless transfer of property titles.

Chapter 10: Practice of Real Estate

Overview

This chapter, constituting approximately 13% of the Salesperson Exam, equips candidates with the necessary knowledge to navigate complex legal responsibilities and ethical practices in real estate transactions. Understanding and managing trust/escrow accounts, adhering to fair housing laws, and avoiding prohibited conduct are crucial competencies assessed through about 10 questions in the exam.

Trust and Escrow Account Management

Agent Responsibilities

Real estate professionals are entrusted with managing escrow accounts that safeguard funds such as earnest money deposits and rental security deposits. These accounts, distinctly separated from an agent's operating funds, are critical for maintaining financial integrity and trust in real estate transactions.

- **Escrow Accounts**: These are special accounts where funds are held until the transaction requirements are fulfilled. The funds, including earnest money, must be deposited timely into the correct account following the acceptance of a purchase offer as per state guidelines.
- **Earnest Money**: This is a security deposit made by a buyer to demonstrate commitment to the purchase. It is crucial that agents deposit these funds into the designated escrow account for each specific transaction.
- **Regulatory Compliance**: Agents must adhere strictly to state laws regarding escrow funds, ensuring there is no commingling (mixing escrow funds with personal or firm's funds) or conversion (using funds for purposes other than intended).

Role of Escrow Agents

An escrow agent acts as a neutral third-party, ensuring that all financial transactions and contractual terms are completed before funds and property titles are exchanged. These agents can be individuals or entities such as title companies, brokers, or attorneys. They play a pivotal role in:

- Disbursing funds post satisfaction of all transaction conditions by the involved parties, including lenders.
- Managing disputes or transaction failures by requiring explicit instructions from both parties involved, or adhering to state laws in the absence of mutual agreement.

Prohibited Conduct in Real Estate Practices

Ethical Standards and Fair Housing

Agents must engage in practices that uphold integrity and fairness, strictly avoiding behaviors that discriminate or manipulate market dynamics.

- **Blockbusting**: This unethical practice involves persuading homeowners to sell their property cheaply by instilling fear of demographic changes affecting property values. Such actions not only undermine market stability but also violate fair housing laws.
- **Steering**: Directing clients towards or away from certain neighborhoods based on the demographics of the area is known as steering. Agents must present all suitable options to clients, letting them choose freely without influence, to maintain compliance with fair housing regulations.
- **Redlining**: This illegal practice involves denying financial services like loans or insurance to individuals based on their geographic location, irrespective of their eligibility. Such discriminatory practices are prohibited as they unjustly restrict access to financing based on demographics rather than individual creditworthiness.

Understanding Fair Housing Laws

Fair housing laws form the backbone of equitable real estate practices, ensuring that all individuals have the opportunity to acquire housing without facing discrimination. This section delves into the legal frameworks that protect various classes, the evolution of these laws, and the activities covered under these protections.

Protected Classes Under Federal Law

Federal fair housing legislation identifies seven protected classes to shield individuals from discrimination in housing-related activities. These classes are:

- Race

- Color
- Religion
- National origin
- Sex
- Disability
- Familial status

Covered Transactions

The scope of fair housing laws encompasses a variety of housing-related transactions, ensuring non-discriminatory practices in:

- **Financing**: Ensuring equitable access to housing loans and mortgages.
- **Appraisals**: Objective valuation of properties without bias.
- **Advertising**: Marketing of properties should be inclusive, without preference to any particular group.
- **Brokerage Services**: Providing unbiased assistance in buying or renting properties.
- **Sales and Rentals**: Offering housing without discrimination in terms or conditions.

Prohibited Acts

To enforce these protections, certain actions are explicitly prohibited under fair housing laws, including:

- **Refusing to Sell or Rent**: Denying a person housing based on their inclusion in a protected class.
- **Interference with Housing Rights**: Engaging in coercion, threats, or intimidation that impedes another's housing rights.
- **Discriminatory Advertising**: Signaling any preference or limitation in housing ads related to protected classes.
- **Unequal Terms**: Offering different leasing or purchasing terms based on discriminatory factors.

Historical Milestones in Fair Housing Legislation

- **1866**: The Civil Rights Act makes it illegal to discriminate based on race or color in property transactions.
- **1968**: Title VIII of the Civil Rights Act, also known as the Fair Housing Act, extends protections to include national origin and religion.

- **1974**: The Housing and Community Development Act includes sex as a protected class.
- **1988**: The Fair Housing Amendments Act adds familial status and disability, mandating reasonable accommodations for individuals with disabilities and protecting families with minors.
- **1974**: The Equal Credit Opportunity Act (ECOA) prohibits credit discrimination, ensuring that loan decisions are based solely on financial merit.

State-Specific Protections

It is crucial for real estate professionals to understand that states may extend these protections further. For instance, some states include marital status, sexual orientation, and mental disability as additional protected classes. Practitioners must be familiar with both state and federal regulations to ensure full compliance.

Acts and Exemptions in Fair Housing Laws

Fair housing laws, while comprehensive, include specific exemptions and acts designed to address particular scenarios in real estate practices. This section explores these exemptions and related regulations, such as the Americans with Disabilities Act (ADA), which play pivotal roles in shaping equitable housing opportunities.

Specific Exemptions in Fair Housing

- **Private Clubs**: These entities may offer housing exclusively to their members without extending offers to the general public, maintaining their private status.
- **Religious Organizations**: Sponsored housing can be restricted to members of the organization, provided that the organization does not discriminate against any protected class in its membership criteria.

Mrs. Murphy Exemption

This exemption applies to properties with four or fewer rental units where the owner resides in one of the units. Such properties are exempt from the federal Fair Housing Act, assuming:

- No discriminatory advertising is used.
- Real estate agents are not involved in the housing transaction.

Housing for Older Persons Act of 1995

This act allows certain facilities to legally discriminate based on familial status. To qualify, housing must be designed for seniors, and specific conditions must be met to ensure compliance. These communities are permitted to exclude families with minor children, supporting environments tailored for older adults.

The Americans with Disabilities Act (ADA)

The ADA is crucial in ensuring accessibility and non-discrimination for individuals with disabilities across various areas, including housing:

- **Scope**: The ADA covers all commercial and public facilities, requiring them to be accessible to individuals with disabilities.
- **Standards for Accessible Design (SAD)**: These standards are mandatory for new constructions and modifications of existing buildings, ensuring they are accessible.
- **Community and Public Spaces**: Buildings and public spaces must meet ADA compliance, with stringent requirements for newer constructions post-1990.

Enforcement and Compliance

U.S. Department of Housing and Urban Development (HUD)

HUD is responsible for enforcing ADA requirements relating to public housing, assistance, and referrals. It plays a central role in ensuring compliance across housing practices.

Office of Fair Housing and Equal Opportunity (OFHEO)

OFHEO, under HUD, actively enforces fair housing laws. It handles complaints related to discrimination, which can be filed up to one year after the alleged incident. Key processes include:

- **Complaint Review**: Initial examination to determine if there is a basis for the complaint.
- **Investigation**: Gathering evidence and notifying alleged violators to determine if a fair housing violation has occurred.
- **Resolution**: If a violation is found, the responsible parties may face lawsuits, fines, or other penalties, including suspension or revocation of real estate licenses.

Truth in Advertising in Real Estate

Real estate advertising must adhere strictly to ethical standards and legal requirements to maintain trust and integrity in the industry. This section outlines the principles of non-discriminatory advertising, the risks of misrepresentation, and the importance of data security in marketing properties.

Non-Discriminatory Advertising

Legal and Ethical Standards

The U.S. Department of Housing and Urban Development (HUD) stipulates clear guidelines on acceptable practices in real estate advertising to prevent discrimination:

- **Prohibited Practices**: Using words, phrases, visuals, or mediums that inherently discriminate or limit access based on any protected class is illegal.
- **Inclusive Advertising**: Marketing efforts should aim for inclusivity, avoiding any language or imagery that could be perceived as exclusive or discriminatory.

Federal Trade Commission (FTC) Regulations

The FTC enforces broad consumer protection laws against deceptive and unfair advertising practices:

- **Deceptive Advertising**: Ads must not mislead a reasonable consumer and should represent the truth about the services or properties offered.
- **Penalties for Non-compliance**: Violations can result in cease-and-desist orders, corrective advertising, civil penalties, and other consumer remedies.

Misrepresentation in Advertising

- **Negligent Misrepresentation**: Occurs when false information about a property is provided inadvertently by someone who should have known better. This can lead to voidable contracts if the buyer relies on this misinformation to their detriment.
- **Intentional Misrepresentation**: Involves deliberate omission or distortion of material facts, qualifying as fraud.

Puffery vs. Misrepresentation

- **Puffing**: Refers to the exaggeration of a property's attributes as a selling point. While not illegal, it is generally viewed as less credible by consumers.
- **Ethical Advertising**: It is preferable to present properties honestly, highlighting positives while transparently discussing any limitations.

Confidentiality and Data Security

Protecting Client Information

- **Security Measures**: Implementing and enforcing robust security policies is crucial to safeguard client data against identity theft and unauthorized access.
- **Secure Disposal**: Confidential information must be disposed of securely to prevent potential litigation risks.
- **Online Safety Practices**: Real estate professionals should exercise caution by avoiding unknown links and ensuring all client communications are secure.

Advertising Requirements Checklist

To ensure compliance and maintain ethical standards, real estate professionals should adhere to the following checklist:

1. **Broker Affiliation**: Clearly indicate broker affiliation in all advertisements to provide transparency.
2. **Avoid Discriminatory Content**: Refrain from using any language or visuals that might imply discrimination.
3. **Client Data Protection**: Take proactive steps to secure client information, including caution against phishing and ensuring secure communication channels.
4. **Financial Safety**: Advise clients against wiring funds to unverified parties to prevent fraud.

Real Estate Agent Employment

Real estate agents have the option to work under the supervision of brokers either as employees or independent contractors. Each arrangement has distinct implications for work practices, compensation, and legal responsibilities. This section delineates the fundamental differences between these employment types and outlines the benefits and responsibilities associated with each.

Employment Models for Real Estate Agents

Employee Agents

1. **Work Structure:**

   - Employees must adhere to specific work hours and processes as defined by the brokerage firm.

   - Training and professional development are typically structured and mandated by the employer.

2. **Compensation and Benefits:**

   - Employee agents are compensated based on time worked, not solely on sales output.

   - Paychecks from brokerage firms are subject to federal and state tax deductions.

   - Benefits such as health insurance, retirement plans, and worker's compensation are often provided.

3. **Supervision and Compliance:**

   - Brokerage firms are responsible for the strict supervision of their employee agents.

   - They must ensure that unlicensed personnel do not engage in activities requiring a real estate license.

Independent Contractors

1. **Autonomy and Flexibility:**

   - Independent contractors set their own hours and choose their methods of working to align with personal career goals.

   - They are responsible for their own business expenses and operational decisions.

2. **Financial Considerations:**

   - No withholding of taxes by the brokerage; contractors must manage their own tax obligations.

   - Eligibility to deduct business expenses from their income taxes, which can provide significant financial advantages.

3. **Brokerage Relationship:**

   - While independent, contractors must still adhere to some brokerage rules, such as maintaining membership in relevant real estate associations.

   - The supervision provided by brokers is generally limited to ensuring compliance with licensing laws.

Tax Regulations and Compliance

IRS Guidelines

The Internal Revenue Service (IRS) sets forth specific criteria that define the broker-independent contractor relationship:

- **Contractual Agreement**: There must be a written agreement stating that the agent is not treated as an employee for federal tax purposes.
- **Independent Contractor Status**: To maintain this status, brokerage firms should avoid:
    - Providing tools and materials necessary for the agent's work.
    - Offering traditional employment benefits like health insurance or retirement plans.
    - Compensating based on hours worked rather than sales or commission.
    - Imposing requirements regarding work location, hours, or mandatory participation in meetings.

Due Diligence in Real Estate Practice

Due diligence in real estate involves a comprehensive understanding and adherence to local, state, and federal regulations that govern the industry. Real estate agents must maintain a high standard of professional conduct, ensuring they operate within their legal scope of practice to provide accurate and reliable service to clients. This section highlights the critical elements of due diligence and outlines the responsibilities of agents in maintaining legal and ethical standards.

The Importance of Legal Knowledge and Compliance

Research and Understanding

Real estate agents are expected to thoroughly research and comprehend the laws relevant to their areas of operation. This includes, but is not limited to:

- Zoning laws
- Property rights
- Fair housing regulations
- Contract laws

Maintaining this knowledge is part of the duty of reasonable skill and care, ensuring that agents can advise their clients effectively and refer them to specialists when necessary.

Clear and Accurate Communication

- **Fact vs. Opinion**: Agents must clearly distinguish between facts and personal opinions when discussing properties and transactions. Misrepresentation, even unintentional, can lead to serious legal consequences.
- **Avoid Absolutes**: Using terms like "guarantee" or making unfounded claims can mislead clients and should be avoided to maintain trust and professional integrity.

Scope of Practice for Real Estate Agents

Contractual Documentation

- **Use of Pre-approved Forms**: Agents should always use attorney-prepared forms and documents provided by their brokerage, local REALTOR® association, or state authorities.
- **Limitations on Legal Advice**: Real estate agents must not draft contract language or advise clients on legal aspects of contract signing as it can constitute unauthorized practice of law.

Guidelines for Contract Preparation

1. **Standardized Forms**: Utilize forms that are standardized and vetted by legal professionals to avoid errors and legal oversights.
2. **Referral to Specialists**: When complex legal issues arise, refer clients to qualified attorneys to ensure that their interests are adequately protected.

Licensed Activities vs. Clerical Tasks and Compliance with DNC Regulations

Understanding the distinction between activities that require a real estate license and those that are considered clerical is critical for maintaining compliance with real estate regulations. Additionally, adherence to the Do-Not-Call (DNC) Registry rules is essential for ethical practice and legal compliance in real estate communications.

Licensed Activities vs. Clerical Tasks

- **Licensed Activities**: These include tasks that require professional judgment and knowledge such as negotiating, drafting contracts, and hosting open houses. Only licensed real estate agents can perform these duties.
- **Clerical Tasks**: These are supportive in nature and do not require a real estate license. Tasks such as scheduling appointments, making copies of listing information, and following up on transaction-related items like appraisals and inspections fall into this category.

Common Violations

Delegating tasks that require a license to an unlicensed assistant is a frequent regulatory violation. It's imperative that real estate professionals clearly understand and respect the boundaries of licensed and unlicensed work to avoid legal repercussions.

Compliance with the Do-Not-Call Registry

The Federal Telephone Consumer Protection Act established the DNC Registry to protect consumers from unsolicited telephone marketing. Real estate agents must adhere to several critical rules:

- **Prohibited Actions:** Calling before 8 a.m. or after 9 p.m., making anonymous or automated calls, and calling cell phones without consent are strictly forbidden.
- **Restrictions on Calling**: Real estate agents cannot contact individuals on the DNC list to promote buying or selling property unless specific conditions are met.

Relationship with Past Clients

- **Exclusion Period**: Agents have an 18-month window following the last transaction with a client during which they can contact them even if their number is on the DNC list. Beyond this period, explicit written permission is needed to continue communications.
- **Penalties for Violations**: Violations can result in fines up to $40,000 per incident. Brokerage firms may also face extended periods of court-ordered supervision for repeated infractions.

Best Practices for Compliance

- **Brokerage Policies**: Implement and follow strict brokerage policies regarding DNC compliance to avoid potential violations.

- **Use of Technology**: Leverage technology wisely to ensure all communication complies with DNC regulations and maintain records of client consents and interactions to safeguard against potential legal challenges.

Different Roles of Real Estate Agents

Real estate agents play diverse roles in the property market, each tailored to specific aspects of buying and selling real estate. Understanding these roles is crucial for clients and agents alike to ensure that everyone involved in a transaction receives the best possible representation.

Listing Agents (Seller's Agents)

Listing agents specialize in representing sellers and have a variety of responsibilities aimed at maximizing the sale price of a property:

- **Market Analysis**: They prepare a Comparative Market Analysis (CMA) to set a competitive asking price.
- **Marketing**: This includes creating listings, using the MLS, and organizing professional photography and marketing materials.
- **Showings and Open Houses**: They schedule and sometimes supervise these events to showcase the property.
- **Negotiations and Paperwork**: Listing agents negotiate contract terms and ensure all paperwork is timely and accurately completed.
- **Client Representation**: They act as intermediaries between the seller and potential buyers or buyer's agents.

Buyer's Agents

Buyer's agents focus on representing the buyer's interests in real estate transactions:

- **Understanding Client Needs**: They listen to the client's specific desires for a property including budget, size, and location preferences.
- **Property Search**: Buyer's agents find properties that match the client's criteria and organize viewings.
- **Negotiations**: They handle negotiations regarding price and terms, and coordinate property inspections and repairs.

- **Guidance Through Closing**: Buyer's agents guide their clients through the paperwork and closing processes.

Dual Agents

Dual agency occurs when one agent represents both the buyer and the seller, or when both agents involved work for the same brokerage. This role requires careful balancing of both parties' interests:

- **Conflict of Interest**: Dual agents must manage a potential conflict of interest with transparency and fairness.
- **State Regulations**: Some states have regulations that restrict or forbid dual agency due to the inherent conflict of interest.

Transaction Agents

Transaction agents facilitate real estate transactions without representing either party:

- **Neutral Party**: They ensure that all aspects of the contract preparation and signing are conducted fairly and legally.
- **Facilitation**: Their role is to help both parties complete the transaction smoothly without providing advocacy for either side.

Realtors

Realtors are real estate agents who are members of the National Association of Realtors (NAR) and adhere to its Code of Ethics:

- **Ethical Standards**: Realtors commit to higher ethical standards which can enhance trust and professionalism.
- **Benefits**: Membership provides access to additional resources such as training, networking opportunities, and discounts.

Understanding Antitrust Laws in Real Estate

Antitrust laws are crucial in maintaining fair competition within the real estate industry. These laws prevent practices that could limit competition or lead to monopolistic control, ensuring that consumers have access to diverse choices and fair prices. This section explains the primary antitrust statutes affecting real estate and outlines common violations and their penalties.

Federal Antitrust Laws

1. **The Sherman Act (1890)**: This foundational law aims to prevent the formation of monopolies and other activities that restrain trade.
2. **The Clayton Act (1914)**: It bolsters the Sherman Act by prohibiting mergers and acquisitions that would lead to monopolistic structures.
3. **The Federal Trade Commission Act (1914)**: Establishes the FTC, which investigates and penalizes antitrust violations.

Common Antitrust Violations in Real Estate

Price Fixing

Price fixing occurs when real estate agents or brokers collude to set prices for their services rather than allowing market forces to determine them independently. This practice is illegal under antitrust laws because it prevents natural market competition.

Market Allocation

This involves an agreement among brokers to divide the market geographically or by client type to avoid competing with each other. Such arrangements restrict consumer choice and distort market pricing.

Tie-In Arrangements

In these scenarios, a real estate service is provided only on the condition that another service is purchased from a specific provider. Tie-ins limit the consumer's options and violate antitrust regulations.

Group Boycotting

Group boycotting occurs when several parties agree not to do business with a specific individual or company. While an individual broker can choose their business associates freely, conspiring with others to exclude a party is illegal.

Per Se Violations

Certain actions, such as bid-rigging and horizontal customer allocation, are considered per se violations of antitrust laws. These are inherently illegal, with no need for further investigation to establish their unlawfulness.

Penalties for Antitrust Violations

- **Individuals**: May face up to 10 years in prison and fines up to $1 million.
- **Corporations**: Could incur fines of up to $100 million, or more if penalties are tied to the gains from or losses caused by the violation.
- **Brokerage Firms**: Those found guilty of antitrust violations might be placed under court-ordered supervision for up to a decade.

Summary

This chapter has comprehensively explored the varied and critical aspects of practicing real estate, from understanding the responsibilities associated with trust and escrow accounts to navigating the complexities of fair housing laws and antitrust regulations. It has emphasized the importance of ethical practices, the necessity for adherence to legal standards, and the role of real estate professionals in facilitating transparent and fair transactions.

As we have seen, maintaining professionalism, ethical integrity, and a deep understanding of legal obligations not only enhances the reputation of real estate professionals but also safeguards the interests of consumers, ensuring a trustworthy and efficient real estate market.

Chapter 11: Real Estate Calculations

Overview

Understanding basic mathematical operations is crucial for real estate professionals. Approximately 10% of the questions on the Salesperson Exam (about 8 questions) focus on calculations relevant to real estate transactions. Mastery of addition, subtraction, multiplication, and division is foundational for tackling these questions effectively.

Key Concepts in Real Estate Mathematics

Calculations

A calculation in real estate is the mathematical process of determining quantities or values, such as calculating the total cost, the size of an area, or the commission earned on a transaction.

Equations

An equation is a statement of equality between two expressions and often includes an equals sign ("="). In real estate, equations are used to determine values like closing costs, interest rates, or property values.

Formulas

A formula is a concise way to express information symbolically, as in a mathematical or chemical formula. In real estate, formulas are used to compute values such as area, volume, or financial sums. A commonly used formula might be for calculating interest: Interest = Principal x Rate x Time.

Practical Tips for Real Estate Calculations

- **Practice Recalculation**: When learning a new formula or calculation method, it is beneficial to manipulate the equation to solve for different variables. This enhances understanding and accuracy.
- **Rounding Off**: It's important to round off figures appropriately to avoid discrepancies in financial calculations, ensuring clarity and preciseness in your documentation.

Triangle Method for PART, TOTAL, and RATE

In real estate mathematics, the triangle symbol is a helpful mnemonic that shows the relationship between three key elements: PART, TOTAL, and RATE.

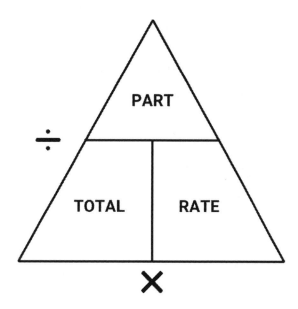

- **PART = TOTAL x RATE**: Used to determine a portion of a whole, like a commission amount.
- **TOTAL = PART / RATE**: Helps find the total when a part and its rate are known.
- **RATE = PART / TOTAL**: Useful for finding the rate when the part and the total are known.

Examples of Real Estate Calculations

1. Calculating Commission on a Property Sale
   - **Scenario**: You sell a property for $600,000, earning a commission rate of 3%.
   - **Calculation**: $600,000 x 0.03 = $18,000 commission.
2. Determining Property Sale Price from Commission
   - **Scenario**: You earn a commission of $20,000 at a 3% rate.
   - **Calculation**: $20,000 / 0.03 = $666,667 sale price.
3. Calculating Commission Rate from a Sale
   - **Scenario**: From a property sale at $900,000, you earn a commission of $27,000.
   - **Calculation**: $27,000 / $900,000 = 0.03 (or 3%).

Conversions in Real Estate Calculations

Real estate finance heavily relies on the use of percentages and decimals to express rates, proportions, and other financial metrics. Being proficient in converting these figures is key to ensuring accuracy in your calculations.

Converting Percentages to Decimals

To transform a percentage into a decimal:

- Divide the percentage by 100. For example, 50% becomes
- $50 \div 100 = 0.50$
- Alternatively, move the decimal point two places to the left. For instance, 2.5% becomes 0.025.

Converting Decimals to Percentages

To change a decimal to a percentage:

- Multiply the decimal by 100. For example, 0.50 becomes
- $0.50 \times 100 = 50$
- Move the decimal point two places to the right. For example, 0.0025 becomes 0.25%.

Real Estate Financial Examples Using Conversions

1. **Down Payments**
   - Typical Scenario: 20% of the sales price is required as a down payment.
   - **Example**: For a home priced at $400,000, the down payment would be $400,000 x 0.20 = $80,000.
2. **Loan-to-Value Ratio**
   - Typically, loans cover 80% of the home's appraised value.
   - **Calculation**: $400,000 x 0.80 = $320,000 for the loan amount.
3. **Real Estate Commissions**
   - Commissions usually range from 5% to 6%, with agents on each side getting 2.5% to 3%.
   - **Example**: A $400,000 home sale at a 6% commission yields $400,000 x 0.06 = $24,000 total commission.

4. **Discount Points**

- Each point costs 1% of the loan amount and lowers the annual percentage rate by about 0.25%.
- Example: $300,000 x 0.01 = $3,000 per discount point.

5. **Debt-to-Income Ratios**

- Front-end (housing costs only): 28% of gross monthly income.
- Back-end (all debts): 36% of gross monthly income.
- **Example**: For an $8,000 monthly income, the maximum front-end is $8,000 x 0.28 = $2,240, and the back-end is $8,000 x 0.36 = $2,880.

6. **Capitalization Rate (Cap Rate)**

- A good cap rate ranges from 5% to 10%.
- Calculation: $30,000 ÷ $300,000 = 10%.

Handling Fractions in Real Estate

A fraction represents a portion of a whole. In a fraction like 1/4, the bottom number, or denominator, indicates that the whole is divided into four equal parts, while the top number, or numerator, shows that we are considering one of those parts. While fractions are not commonly used in real estate, understanding how to convert them is still useful. To convert a fraction into a decimal, you divide the numerator by the denominator.

- 1/4 = 0.25 (25%)
- 1/2 = 0.50 (50%)
- 3/4 = 0.75 (75%)

Formulas for Calculating Mortgage Interest

Understanding mortgage interest calculation is essential for real estate professionals. It ensures accurate financial planning and helps clients make informed mortgage decisions.

Mortgage Interest Calculation Basics

When calculating mortgage interest, it's essential to consider the timing of the payments. Mortgage payments are usually made monthly, but interest rates are often expressed as an annual percentage rate (APR). The loan term typically spans several years. Interest calculations thus need to bridge these different time frames, using the principal amount and the interest rate.

Formula for Monthly Mortgage Interest

The interest for each mortgage payment is calculated using the monthly interest rate multiplied by the remaining loan balance (principal). The steps to derive this are:

1. Convert the APR to a Monthly Rate: Divide the annual rate by 12 (months).
   - **Example**: For an APR of 4.25%, the monthly interest rate would be:
   - $0.0425 \div 12 = 0.00354167$ or 0.354167%.
2. **Calculate Monthly Interest**: Multiply the monthly rate by the current loan balance.
   - Initial Calculation: $500,000 x 0.00354167 = $1,770.84 (interest for the first month).
3. **Determine Principal Paid**: Subtract the interest from the total monthly payment.
   - $3,000 - $1,770.84 = $1,229.16 (principal reduction in the first month).

Example Calculations for Subsequent Payments

To understand how the balance changes with each payment, consider the calculations for the second month:

1. **Update Remaining Principal**: Subtract the principal paid from the initial loan balance.
   - $500,000 - $1,229.16 = $498,770.84 (remaining principal after the first month).
2. **Calculate Second Month's Interest**: Apply the monthly interest rate to the updated principal.
   - $498,770.84 x 0.00354167 = $1,765.58 (second month's interest).
3. **Principal Paid in the Second Payment**: Subtract the second month's interest from the monthly payment amount.
   - $3,000 - $1,765.58 = $1,234.42 (principal reduction in the second month).

Total Interest Paid Over the Loan Term

To estimate the total interest paid over the life of the loan, you would:

1. **Calculate Total Payments Over the Term**: Multiply the monthly payment by the total number of payments.
   - $3,000 x 360 = $1,080,000 (total amount paid over 30 years).
2. **Subtract the Original Loan Amount**: To find the total interest paid.
   - $1,080,000 - $500,000 = $580,000 (total interest paid).

Simple Interest Formula

For simpler interest calculations that don't account for compounding, use the simple interest formula:

$A = P \times (1 + r \times t)$

- A: Total accrued amount (principal + interest)
- P: Principal amount
- r: Annual interest rate (as a decimal)
- t: Time period in years

This formula is generally used for shorter loans or interim calculations where compounding is not considered.

Property, Transfer, and Recording Tax Calculations

Understanding how to accurately calculate various property-related taxes is essential for real estate professionals. This knowledge ensures compliance with local regulations and assists clients in understanding potential costs associated with property transactions.

Property Tax Calculations

Property taxes are typically based on the appraised value of the property, a tax assessment ratio that varies by state, and a specific tax rate which might be expressed per dollar amount of value or as mills (millage rates).

Example of Property Tax Calculation

- **Property Value**: $700,000
- **Assessment Ratio**: 35%
- **Tax Rate**: $18 per $1,000 of assessed value, equivalent to 18 mills or a 0.018 tax rate.

Steps:

1. **Calculate the Assessed Value**: $700,000 x 35% = $245,000
2. **Calculate Annual Property Tax**: $245,000 x 0.018 = $4,410

Transfer Tax Calculations

Transfer taxes are levied when property ownership is transferred from one party to another. The tax rate may be a percentage of the sale price or a fixed dollar amount per unit value of the property price.

Percentage Rate Example

- Sale Price: $500,000
- Transfer Tax Rate: 0.06%

Steps:

1. **Convert the tax rate to a decimal:** 0.06% = 0.0006
2. **Calculate the Transfer Tax:** $500,000 x 0.0006 = $300

Dollar Amount Rate Example

- Sale Price: $600,000
- Transfer Tax Rate: $2.00 per $1,000

Steps:

1. **Convert the property price into units of $1,000**: $600,000 ÷ 1,000 = 600
2. **Calculate the Transfer Tax**: 600 x $2.00 = $1,200

Recording Tax Calculations

Recording taxes apply to the recording of legal documents such as deeds or mortgages and are often quoted per $100, $500, or $1,000 of the property or loan value.

Deed Recording Tax Example

- Sale Price: $800,000
- Recording Tax Rate: $2.50 per $1,000

Steps:

1. **Convert the sale price into units of $1,000**: $800,000 ÷ 1,000 = 800
2. **Calculate the Deed Recording Tax**: 800 x $2.50 = $2,000

Mortgage Recording Tax Example

- Loan Amount: $650,000
- Recording Tax Rate: $2.00 per $500

Steps:

1. **Convert the loan amount into units of $500**: $650,000 ÷ 500 = 1,300
2. **Calculate the Mortgage Recording Tax**: 1,300 x $2.00 = $2,600

Allocating Expenses Between Buyers and Sellers

Proration involves dividing property-related expenses between the buyer and seller at the time of closing. Understanding how to calculate prorated amounts is crucial for real estate professionals to ensure fair and accurate expense allocation.

Key Concepts for Proration Calculations

Prorated expenses can be either prepaid (already paid by one party) or accrued (not yet paid). In real estate exams and practical applications, it's essential to know whether to use a statutory year (360 days) or an actual calendar year (365 or 366 days in a leap year). Furthermore, it is important to determine who—buyer or seller—is responsible for the day of closing. Unless specified otherwise, calculations typically assume the seller owns the closing day.

Calculation Requirements

1. **Per Diem Rate (Daily Rate)**: The daily cost of the prorated item.
2. **Responsibility Duration**: Number of days each party is responsible for the expense.
3. **Nature of the Expense:** Whether the item is accrued or prepaid.
4. **Coverage Period**: Typically, this is annual, but may vary depending on the expense.

Example Calculations

Property Tax Proration

Scenario: The closing date is August 15, 2024, and the annual property tax bill is $4,000 due on December 31, 2024. The property tax is paid in arrears, and 2024 is a leap year.

Steps:

1. **Calculate the Per Diem Rate**: $4,000 ÷ 366 days = $10.93 per day
2. **Days Responsible (Seller)**: From January 1 to August 15, 2024, inclusive (since the seller is responsible for the closing day): 228 days
3. **Days Responsible (Buyer)**: From August 16 to December 31, 2024: 138 days
4. **Calculate Prorated Amounts**:
   - Seller: 228 days x $10.93 = $2,492.04
   - Buyer: 138 days x $10.93 = $1,508.34

Rent Proration

Scenario: A tenant's lease begins on April 4, 2024, with monthly rent of $2,400 due on the first of each month. The landlord is responsible for the closing day.

Steps:

1. Calculate Daily Rent: $3,000 ÷ 30 days = $100 per day
2. Days Responsible (Tenant): From May 10 to May 31, 2024: 22 days
3. Calculate Prorated Rent for May: 22 days x $100 = $2,200

Buyer Funds and Closing Costs

At closing, buyers need to ensure that they have all necessary funds ready to complete the property purchase according to the terms of the contract. These funds typically consist of personal contributions, mortgage funds, and any deposits made earlier in the process.

Understanding 'Cash to Close'

The term 'cash to close' encompasses all the financial contributions a buyer must make at the closing of a real estate transaction. This includes:

1. **Down Payment**: The portion of the purchase price the buyer pays out of pocket.
2. **Closing Costs**: Various fees associated with the purchasing of the property, such as lender fees and recording fees.
3. **Earnest Money**: A deposit made by the buyer to show their good faith when the contract is signed. This amount is credited toward the total 'cash to close'.

4. **Credits**: Any credits agreed upon during negotiations or as specified in the contract.

Key Buyer Closing Expenses

- **Lender Fees**: Costs charged by the lender for processing the mortgage.
- **Recording Fees**: Fees paid to the local government to record the new deed and mortgage.
- **Initial Escrow Payment**: Funds to start the escrow account, which typically covers property taxes and homeowner's insurance for the first year.

Interest Owed at Closing

Depending on the date of closing, buyers may also owe interest for the period between the closing date and the end of the month, as mortgage payments are typically due on the first of the month and cover the previous month. This is known as "per diem" interest.

Example: The closing date for a property is set for September 15th, with the buyer's initial mortgage payment scheduled for November 1st. It's important to note that mortgage payments are made in arrears, meaning the payment on November 1st covers the mortgage for October. The buyer has a loan amount of $600,000 with an annual percentage rate (APR) of 4.5%. Since the closing day is considered the buyer's responsibility, the interest due at closing needs to be calculated using a statutory/banker's year.

Calculation: First, determine the annual interest: $600,000 × 0.045 = $27,000 (annual interest). Next, calculate the daily interest rate: $27,000 / 360 = $75 (daily interest). Finally, calculate the interest for the closing month: $75 (daily rate) × 16 (days in September from closing to month-end) = $1,200 (interest owed at closing).

Seller Proceeds

Calculating the proceeds a seller receives from a real estate transaction involves several steps to deduct applicable commissions, fees, and any remaining mortgage balance from the sales price. This process ensures that all financial obligations are met at the time of sale.

Calculation of Seller Proceeds

Step 1: Deduct Real Estate Commission

- Sales Price: $500,000
- Commission Rate: 6%

- Calculation: $500,000 x (1 - 0.06) = $470,000
- Result: Net proceeds after commission are $470,000.

Step 2: Adjust for Contributions Toward Buyer's Closing Costs

- Seller Contribution: $7,000
- Adjusted Proceeds: $470,000 - $7,000 = $463,000

Step 3: Deduct Existing Mortgage Balance

- Remaining Mortgage: $150,000
- Net Proceeds After Mortgage: $463,000 - $150,000 = $313,000

Calculation of Mortgage Interest Owed

Interest Calculation Details

- Annual Percentage Rate (APR): 4.25%
- Loan Balance: $150,000
- Closing Date: December 15th

Monthly Interest Rate Calculation

- Annual to Monthly Conversion:
- 4.25% / 12 = 0.3542% or 0.003542
- Monthly Interest Amount: $150,000 x 0.003542 = $531.30

Daily Interest Calculation

- Daily Interest: $531.30 / 30 = $17.71 per day

Interest for the Month of Closing (from the last payment date to closing date)

- Days from December 1st to December 15th: 15 days (since the last payment covered November and was paid on December 1st)
- Interest for 15 Days: $17.71 x 15 = $265.65

Total Net Seller Proceeds Calculation

- Final Deduction of Mortgage Interest: $313,000 - $265.65 = $312,734.35

Calculating Equity

Equity is a fundamental concept in real estate that represents the value a homeowner has built up in their property. It is calculated as the difference between the current market value of the property and the total debt secured by it, such as a mortgage. Understanding how to calculate and interpret equity is essential for real estate professionals, as it impacts decisions related to selling, refinancing, or accessing equity.

Definition of Equity

Equity is the financial stake that an owner has in their property. It can increase through appreciation of the property value or by paying down the mortgage balance. Conversely, it can decrease through a fall in market value (depreciation) or by taking on more debt, such as a home equity loan.

Inverse Relationship with Loan-to-Value (LTV)

Equity and LTV ratio have an inverse relationship:

- As equity increases, the LTV ratio decreases.
- As equity decreases, the LTV ratio increases.

This relationship is important because a lower LTV ratio often qualifies homeowners for better borrowing terms.

Example Calculation of Equity

A couple bought their primary home 8 years ago for $600,000. They currently owe $350,000 on their mortgage. The home's market value has appreciated, and they have agreed to sell the home for $900,000.

Steps to Calculate Equity

1. **Determine the Current Market Value**:
   - Current market value of the property: $900,000
2. **Subtract the Outstanding Loan Balance**:
   - Loan balance: $350,000
3. **Calculate Equity:**
   - Equity = Current Property Value - Loan Balance
   - $900,000 - $350,000 = $550,000

The couple has accumulated $550,000 in equity from their original purchase. This amount reflects the increased market value minus the remaining loan balance. Understanding this calculation is crucial for making informed financial decisions regarding property investment, sale, and leveraging property for additional finance.

Investment and Rental Property Calculations

Investment properties require specific approaches for valuation, particularly when they generate rental income. For smaller residential properties (four units or fewer), the Gross Rent Multiplier (GRM) method is commonly used. For larger residential or commercial properties (five units or more), the Gross Income Multiplier (GIM) method is applicable. Understanding these methods is crucial for real estate professionals who assess the value of rental properties.

Gross Rent Multiplier (GRM)

The GRM is a valuation tool that relates the sales price of a property to its gross rental income. It is used primarily for quick appraisals of smaller residential properties.

Example: Calculating GRM and Estimated Property Value

Scenario: A four-unit property generates $12,000 in total monthly rental income ($3,000 per unit). Three comparable properties provide a basis for determining the GRM.

1. **Comparable Property Calculations:**
   - Comp 1: $800,000 sale price / $10,000 monthly rent = 80 GRM
   - Comp 2: $960,000 sale price / $12,000 monthly rent = 80 GRM
   - Comp 3: $1,200,000 sale price / $15,000 monthly rent = 80 GRM
   - **Average GRM**: (80 + 80 + 80) / 3 = 80 GRM
2. **Estimated Value of Subject Property:**
   - 80 GRM x $12,000 monthly rent = $960,000

Gross Income Multiplier (GIM)

The GIM method is similar to GRM but is used for properties with five or more units and is based on annual income, making it suitable for larger residential or commercial valuations.

Example: Using GIM to Estimate Property Value

Scenario: A 10-unit property generates $300,000 in annual gross income ($2,500 per unit per month). An appraiser estimates the value of a similar property with a higher income.

1. **Determine GIM from a Comparable Sale:**
   - Sale price / Gross annual income = GIM
   - $1,500,000 / $300,000 = 5 GIM
2. **Calculate Estimated Value for Subject Property:**
   - 5 GIM x $300,000 annual income = $1,500,000

Key Points for Exam Preparation

- **GRM:**
  - Used for properties with four or fewer units.
  - Based on monthly rental income.
  - **Formula**: Sales price / Gross monthly rent.
- **GIM:**
  - Used for properties with five or more units.
  - Based on annual rental income.
  - **Formula**: Sale price / Gross annual income.

Determining Rental Property Depreciation

Depreciation is a crucial accounting tool used to allocate the cost of a rental property over its useful life. For real estate, it pertains only to the building portion of a property, as land does not wear out and thus does not depreciate. The Internal Revenue Service (IRS) outlines specific criteria and methods for property depreciation, which are vital for property owners to understand for tax purposes.

Criteria for Claiming Depreciation

To claim depreciation on a property, the following IRS criteria must be met:

1. **Ownership**: The individual claiming depreciation must own the property.
2. **Income Production**: The property must be used to generate income.

3. **Useful Life**: The property must have a determinable useful life exceeding one year.

4. **Depreciable Asset**: The property must be something that wears out, decays, or becomes obsolete.

Standard Depreciation Method for Residential Rental Property

The IRS mandates that residential rental properties be depreciated at a rate of 3.636% per year over a period of 27.5 years.

Steps to Calculate Depreciation

Step 1: Determine the Cost Basis

This includes the purchase price plus permissible closing costs such as legal fees, recording fees, surveys, transfer taxes, and title insurance.

Step 2: Separate Land and Building Costs

The value must be split between land (non-depreciable) and buildings (depreciable). This can often be based on the fair market value at the time of purchase or on property tax assessments.

Step 3: Calculate Annual Depreciation

Divide the depreciable cost by the useful life of the property.

Example Calculation

Scenario: A rental property is purchased for $800,000 with an additional $12,000 in closing expenses. The land is valued at $160,000.

Calculations:

1. Total Cost Basis:
   - $800,000 + $12,000 = $812,000
2. Building Value (Depreciable):
   - $812,000 - $160,000 = $652,000
3. Annual Depreciation:
   - $652,000 ÷ 27.5 = $23,709.09

Assessing the Financial Impact

Determining Taxable Income from Rental Property

- Gross Rental Income: $60,000 annually
- Other Expenses: $15,000 (not including depreciation)
- Net Income Before Depreciation:
    - $60,000 - $15,000 = $45,000
- Net Taxable Income:
    - $45,000 - $23,709.09 = $21,290.91

Tax Savings from Depreciation

- Tax Rate: 22%
- Annual Tax Savings:
    - $23,709.09 x 22% = $5,216 (rounded)

Land Measurement and Conversion

Understanding land measurement is crucial for real estate professionals. Measurements in real estate are typically stated in terms of square feet, square miles, perimeter, frontage, linear miles, acres, and hectares. Each of these measures has specific applications and importance in various aspects of real estate from valuation to zoning.

Key Units and Conversions

It is essential to be familiar with the basic units and conversions used in land measurement:

- 1 Township = 36 Square Miles
- 1 Square Mile = 640 Acres (1 Section of a Township)
- 1 Acre = 43,560 Square Feet (essential for exam memorization)
- 1 Hectare = 107,639 Square Feet, or approximately 2.47 Acres
- 1 Linear Mile = 5,280 Feet (essential for exam memorization)

Formulas for Calculating Land Measurements

- **Acres**: Square Feet÷43,560

- **Square Feet**: Acres×43,560
- **Linear Mile**: Linear Feet÷5,280
- **Linear Feet**: Linear Miles×5,280

Practical Examples

Example 1: Calculating the Size of a Land Parcel

Scenario: A property is being subdivided into a parcel that is a half-mile square.

Steps:

1. **Calculate the Side Length in Feet:**
   - Half a mile in feet:
   - 5,280 feet×0.50=2,640 feet
2. **Calculate the Total Square Footage:**
   - 2,640 feet×2,640 feet=6,969,600 square feet
3. **Convert Square Feet to Acres:**
   - 6,969,600 square feet÷43,560 square feet per acre=160 acres

Example 2: Estimating Land Value

Scenario: A parcel of land measures three-quarters of a mile by 3,190 feet, priced at $2,500 per acre.

Steps:

1. **Calculate the Dimensions in Feet:**
   - 5,280 feet × 0.75 = 3,960 feet
2. **Calculate the Total Square Footage:**
   - 3,960 feet × 3,190 feet =12,632,400 square feet
3. **Convert to Acres and Calculate Value:**
   - 12,632,400 square feet ÷ 43,560 square feet per acre = 290 acres
   - $2,500 (price per acre) × 290 (acres) = $725,000 (property value)

Example 3: Determining Frontage

Scenario: A parcel is 10,000 square feet and 80 feet deep.

Steps:

1. Calculate Frontage:

   - 10,000 square feet÷80 feet deep=125 feet of frontage

These examples demonstrate the practical application of land measurement concepts in real estate. Mastery of these concepts enables real estate professionals to accurately assess property dimensions, calculate potential uses, and determine value, thereby providing better service to clients and enhancing their professional competence.

Measuring Structures (Homes and Buildings)

When it comes to real estate, the accurate measurement of homes and buildings is essential for valuation, marketing, and ensuring compliance with building standards. The American National Standards Institute (ANSI) Z765 provides guidelines for measuring residential properties, which real estate professionals must understand and apply.

ANSI Z765 Standards for Measuring Structures

Key Standards

1. **Contiguity**: Both finished and unfinished spaces must be attached to the main property via hallways or stairways to be included in the total measurement.
2. **Exterior Measurements for Detached Structures**: Measurements should be taken at floor level to the exterior finished surface of the outside walls.
3. **Inclusion of Stairwells and Closets**: These areas are counted in the total square footage.
4. **Flooring Considerations**: Treads and landings should be included in the square footage of the floor above.
5. **Ceiling Height Requirements:**
   - Standard height: At least 7 feet.
   - Beamed ceilings: At least 6 feet 4 inches under the beam.
   - Slanted ceilings: At least 7 feet high over 50% of the finished floor area.

Measuring Tips:

- For irregular shapes, divide the area into basic geometric shapes (squares, rectangles, triangles), calculate each area, and sum them for the total area.

Key Conversions and Formulas

- **Conversions:**
  - 1 linear foot = 12 inches
  - 1 square foot = 144 square inches
  - 1 linear yard = 3 feet
  - 1 square yard = 9 square feet
- **Area Calculations:**
  - Square or Rectangle: Area = Length x Width
  - Triangle: Area = (Base x Height) ÷ 2
  - Circle: Area = π (3.14) x Radius²

Definitions of Property Areas

Livable Area (Gross Living Area, GLA)

GLA is considered the conditioned area of a home that is heated or cooled. It generally includes:

- Finished attics and basements if they meet the ceiling height requirement.
- Excludes unfinished spaces like basements, attics, and garages unless they meet specific criteria.
- Enclosed exterior areas only if they use the same HVAC system as the house.
- Additional finished structures only if connected by a hallway or stairway.

Usable and Rentable Area

- **Usable Area**: The specific space within a building that a tenant occupies exclusively.
- **Rentable Area**: Comprises the usable area plus a pro-rata share of building common areas like lobbies, restrooms, and corridors, which tenants pay rent on.

Practical Application

When applying these standards and principles, real estate professionals should adhere to the specific guidelines set forth by ANSI and other regulatory bodies to ensure accuracy and consistency in property measurements. This precision is crucial not only for sales and leasing but also for property management and appraisal processes.

Rules of Real Estate - Patterns and Percentages

Understanding various real estate rules of thumb can offer valuable insights into the decision-making processes for buying, selling, and investing in properties. These rules provide quick, often percentage-based guidelines that help assess the viability and potential profitability of real estate investments. While these rules are not exhaustive and should not replace detailed analysis, they serve as helpful starting points.

Common Real Estate Rules of Thumb

1% Rule

- **Application**: Evaluates rental properties.
- **Guideline**: The monthly rent should be at least 1% of the purchase price.
- **Example**: A property priced at $400,000 should generate at least $4,000 per month in rent.

2% Rule

- **Application**: A stricter version of the 1% rule for assessing rental properties.
- **Guideline**: The monthly rent should be at least 2% of the purchase price.
- **Example**: A property priced at $800,000 should generate at least $16,000 per month in rent.

4-3-2-1 Rule

- **Application**: Used for appraising land or sites.
- **Guideline**: Value distribution from front to back of the property (40%, 30%, 20%, 10%).

5% Rule

- **Application**: Helps decide between renting and buying.
- **Guideline**: Multiply home value by 5%, divide by 12 to find the breakeven rent.

- **Example**: If the rent is lower than the calculated figure, renting is advised; if higher, buying is preferable.

10% Rule

- **Application**: Relates interest rates to borrowing power.
- **Guideline**: A 1% increase in interest rates reduces borrowing capacity by 10%.

30% / 30% / 3% Rule

- **Application**: Guides home affordability.
- **Guideline**:
    - Spend no more than 30% of gross income on mortgage payments.
    - Have at least 30% of the home's value in cash/semi-liquid assets.
    - Buy a home not exceeding three times the annual household income.

50% Rule

- **Application**: Estimating operating expenses for rental properties.
- **Guideline**: Half of the gross rental income should be assumed as operating expenses.

70% Rule

- **Application**: Used by home flippers.
- **Guideline**: Spend no more than 70% of the after-repair value of the home, minus the cost of renovations.

Practical Use of These Rules

While these rules of thumb provide quick assessments, they should be used with caution. Real estate markets are influenced by numerous factors, including location-specific dynamics, economic conditions, and individual property characteristics, which might not always align with these general guidelines.

Practice Questions Introduction

You've worked through the essential theories and gained a comprehensive understanding of the real estate concepts covered in this guide. Now, it's time to put that knowledge to the test. This section contains a variety of practice questions designed to mirror the format and complexity of the actual real estate licensing exam.

Mock Exams

We have included five full-length mock exams in this guide. Each mock exam is designed to simulate the real test conditions, giving you a comprehensive practice experience. These exams will help you gauge your readiness, manage your time effectively, and reduce exam-day anxiety. After completing each mock exam, review the detailed explanations for each answer to reinforce your understanding and identify areas for improvement.

Approach to Practice

Remember, practice is crucial to mastering the material and achieving success. Use these questions to:

- **Identify Weak Areas**: Understand where you need more review.
- **Reinforce Knowledge**: Solidify your grasp on key concepts.
- **Build Confidence**: Gain the assurance needed to tackle any question.

Let's get started on this final phase of your preparation. You've come this far—now, let's ensure you pass your exam with flying colors.

Mock Test 1

Question 1 - Mock Test 1

A type of advertisement where the broker's identity is not disclosed is called a:

A. Concealed Ad

B. Personal Ad

C. Phantom Ad

D. Blind Ad

Question 2 - Mock Test 1

A lien on property imposed without the owner's agreement, often due to unpaid debts like taxes or judgments, is known as a:

A. Involuntary lien

B. Supplementary lien

C. Voluntary lien

D. Attachment lien

Question 3 - Mock Test 1

_____ sets the fundamental requirements for safe building practices.

A. Building codes

B. Condemnation

C. Eminent domain

D. Escheat

Question 4 - Mock Test 1

_____ prevents a party from contradicting their earlier stance or actions:

A. Routing

B. Estoppels

C. An order of restriction

D. Commingling

Question 5 - Mock Test 1

A statutory lien ensuring priority payment for construction or repair work on land is termed a:

A. Mechanic's lien

B. Judgement lien

C. Assessment lien

D. Tax lien

Question 6 - Mock Test 1

Encouraging homeowners to sell due to the entry of minority groups into the neighborhood is known as:

A. Navigating

B. Panic peddling

C. Commingling

D. Puffing

Question 7 - Mock Test 1

The borrower's monthly expenses as a fraction of their gross monthly income is called the:

A. LOAN-TO-INCOME RATIO

B. DEBT-TO-INCOME RATIO

C. LOAN-TO-VALUE RATIO

D. DEBT-TO-VALUE RATIO

Question 8 - Mock Test 1

An issue that might hinder the transfer of property ownership is known as:

A. A writ of execution

B. Cloud on title

C. Lis pendens

D. Injunction

Question 9 - Mock Test 1

The process by which land increases due to water deposition is called:

A. Accretion

B. Appropriation

C. Accession

D. Land augmentation

Question 10 - Mock Test 1

The lawful entitlement to own and use a parcel of land is referred to as:

A. Title

B. Deed

C. Estoppel

D. Eminent domain

Question 11 - Mock Test 1

When financing a home, the type of interest typically applied is:

A. Simple interest

B. Additional interest

C. Compound interest

D. Direct interest

Question 12 - Mock Test 1

According to RESPA and TRID, the lender must submit a thorough Loan Estimate disclosure at the time of loan application or within three business days (but no later than seven days before closing) to:

A. The property seller

B. Neither buyer nor seller

C. The property buyer

D. Both the buyer and seller

Question 13 - Mock Test 1

In assessing a home loan application, a lender's primary concern is:

A. The availability of lending funds

B. Standard lending practices

C. Economic forecasts

D. The degree of risk

Question 14 - Mock Test 1

The Truth in Lending Act's right of rescission applies to:

A. Business funding

B. Construction loans

C. Consumer credit

D. Farming credits

Question 15 - Mock Test 1

The Federal National Mortgage Association (FNMA) was established to:

A. Buying Title-II loans to keep the market liquid
B. Fund large-scale builders in metropolitan areas
C. Provide financing for FHA Title-II loans where banks abstain
D. Oversee lending association activities

Question 16 - Mock Test 1

The distinction between MIP and PMI is:

A. No difference, they are identical
B. PMI is the traditional form of mortgage insurance
C. MIP is exclusive to VA mortgages
D. PMI covers conventional loans, while MIP is for FHA loans

Question 17 - Mock Test 1

Using property as collateral for a loan while maintaining possession is known as:

A. A subordination agreement
B. An impound account
C. Hypothecation
D. Purchase Money Mortgage

Question 18 - Mock Test 1

When a person gives his/her property as security for a debt, but does not give up possession, he/she has _____.

A. conveyed the property
B. devised the property
C. hypothecated the property
D. converted his fee simple title to equitable title

Question 19 - Mock Test 1

Comparing a straight note to an installment note, the straight note:

A. Features equal reductions in principal each year
B. Results in a higher overall interest rate than an installment loan
C. Excludes principal repayments until the final payment
D. Includes principal repayments throughout, including the final payment

Question 20 - Mock Test 1

With an FHA graduated payment mortgage, the element that changes over the loan term is:

A. The yearly rate
B. The interest rate
C. The finance charge
D. The monthly payments

Question 21 - Mock Test 1

What action effectively cancels an original offer?

A. Revocation through any listed means

B. Enacting a loss provision

C. Completing the terms

D. A counter offer

Question 22 - Mock Test 1

If a seller wishes to withdraw from an exclusive right to sell contract with a broker, they can:

A. Not cancel, as it's a binding agreement

B. Terminate the agreement without any consequences

C. Revoke the agency created by the listing contract, but may be liable for damages

D. Be compelled to proceed with the sale

Question 23 - Mock Test 1

A commercial property lease requires a tenant to pay $4,000 a month plus 3% of gross monthly sales. This kind of lease is known as a:

A. Percentage lease

B. Fixed-rate lease

C. Land lease

D. Comprehensive lease

Question 24 - Mock Test 1

Altering part of a contract or substituting it with a new agreement is known as:

A. Confirmation

B. Novation

C. Consent

D. Delegation

Question 25 - Mock Test 1

Until when must an agent present new offers to a seller?

A. Until the agent feels further offers are unnecessary

B. Until the close of escrow

C. Once the sale process initiates

D. Until the broker believes enough offers have been received

Question 26 - Mock Test 1

When does a purchase contract become effective after acceptance by the seller?

A. Following official document notarization

B. Once the broker receives their commission

C. Upon informing the buyer of the acceptance

D. Immediately after acceptance

Question 27 - Mock Test 1

A buyer working with multiple buyer's agents under a setup where compensation is due only upon transaction completion is engaged in:

A. An exclusive representation contract

B. A sole purchasing agent agreement

C. A collective listing arrangement

D. An open buyer agency agreement

Question 28 - Mock Test 1

A buyer discovering their home utilizes a septic system only after sale closure has the right to:

A. Keep quiet

B. Challenge the title company for oversight

C. Rescind the contract

D. Pursue the agent's professional license

Question 29 - Mock Test 1

The complete transfer of a tenant's lease interest to another party is termed:

A. Conveying a primary residence

B. Assumption

C. Handing over

D. Assignment

Question 30 - Mock Test 1

A contribution by the landlord towards customizing rental space for a tenant is called:

A. Advanced payment

B. Tenant improvement allowance

C. Prepaid rent

D. Pre-occupancy modification agreement

Question 31 - Mock Test 1

When Douglas grants a property "to Stephen for life," Douglas retains which type of interest?

A. An interest in remainder

B. A re-entry right interest

C. A reversionary interest

D. An interest for the duration of life

Question 32 - Mock Test 1

An easement represents:

A. A combination of a lien and an encumbrance

B. Land ownership rights

C. A debt claim

D. An encumbrance, but not a lien

Question 33 - Mock Test 1

A judgment lien filed in a county generally affects:

A. All debtor's property statewide

B. Real property only within that county

C. Personal property only within that county

D. Both the debtor's real and personal property located in that county

Question 34 - Mock Test 1

If a company provides building supplies and is not compensated for such materials, it may file a(n):

A. Claim for payment deficiency

B. Certificate of stopping work

C. Pre-litigation claim notice

D. Mechanic's lien

Question 35 - Mock Test 1

A woman hiking on her friend's property in autumn has been granted:

A. A zoning permit

B. An essential access easement

C. Waterfront usage rights

D. A license

Question 36 - Mock Test 1

The four unities required for joint tenancy include:

A. Timing, Ownership, Tolerance, and Equity

B. Timing, Equity, Ownership, and Obligation

C. Time, Title, Interest, and Possession

D. Timing, Possession, Equity, and Tolerance

Question 37 - Mock Test 1

After purchasing a store building, Leslie and Vivian became joint tenants. Vivian died testate. The shop is presently owned by Leslie:

A. In severalty

B. With survivorship rights intact

C. Alongside Vivian's inheritors

D. In a trust arrangement

Question 38 - Mock Test 1

A man gives his sister a life estate. When his sister passes away, the property will go to his niece in accordance with the conditions of the man's transfer. Which of these BEST sums up

the niece's involvement with the property while her sister was alive?

A. A buyback option

B. A life tenure by another's life

C. Remainder

D. A return interest

Question 39 - Mock Test 1

A piece of property was jointly owned by three friends. Following his death, one of the friends' interests became a part of his inheritance as per his will. The deceased friend was a:

A. Tenant in common

B. Joint tenant

C. Sole proprietor

D. Married couple's joint owner

Question 40 - Mock Test 1

Ownership in severalty means the property:

A. Excludes corporate entities

B. Can be owned by more than one person

C. Owner may sell, will, or lease the property to another person

D. Excludes spousal co-ownership

Question 41 - Mock Test 1

In the Government Rectangular Survey System, a section of standard size includes:

A. 6 square miles

B. 36 square miles

C. 1 square mile

D. 100 acres

Question 42 - Mock Test 1

Which of the following methods is used to handle discrepancies between the subject property and the comparables in the market data approach to appraisal?

A. A market average is used to alter the comparables

B. The subject property has been modified to meet the comparables' criteria

C. A price range is created by averaging the values of the subject properties

D. The comparables are adjusted to the characteristics of the subject property

Question 43 - Mock Test 1

Which of the following is the meaning of the phrase reconciliation?

A. Analyzing and weighing the findings obtained by the different approaches to value to arrive at a final estimate of value

B. The method by which an appraiser ascertains a piece of land's highest and best usage

C. Calculating depreciation by dividing the land's worth from the property's overall value

D. Value loss resulting from any source

Question 44 - Mock Test 1

What does Economic, environmental, and external obsolescence refer to?

A. Obsolescence that is reasonable and economically feasible to correct

B. Outdated items and changes in technology

C. Lack of maintenance and ordinary wear and tear

D. Factors outside of the property lines that affect the property's value

Question 45 - Mock Test 1

A home's bearing wall:

A. May be built with a doorway at any angle

B. Is often not altered while renovating

C. All of the above options are correct

D. None of the above

Question 46 - Mock Test 1

Which of the following methods of estimating value leads to establish the value's upper bounds?

A. Market comparison

B. Comparable sales

C. Income

D. Replacement

Question 47 - Mock Test 1

The practice of expressing expected future advantages of ownership in dollars and discounting them to their present value at a rate that attracts purchase capital to comparable assets is known as which of the following?

A. Comparable

B. Deduction

C. Capitalization

D. Cost

Question 48 - Mock Test 1

When evaluating retail centers, the social fiber of the community and distances from schools are referred to as:

A. The Market Data Approach

B. Site Analysis

C. Neighborhood analysis

D. Social analysis

Question 49 - Mock Test 1

What is the best example of functional obsolescence?

A. Residential building constructed adjacent to a factory

B. Steep, narrow stairway in a 1 3/4 story home

C. Residential home with Central air conditioning

D. Peeling paint

Question 50 - Mock Test 1

A retail shopping center's space is rented by a pizza business. To cook the pizzas, the proprietor fastens a huge iron pizza oven to the ground. The oven has a(n):

A. Real Property

B. Trade Fixture

C. Rental Fixture

D. Fixture

Question 51 - Mock Test 1

When a buyer receives a quitclaim deed from the seller, the buyer can be assured that:

A. The property is free from all encumbrances

B. The buyer has acquired the property, albeit with the seller retaining certain rights

C. The seller was in possession of the property

D. All of the seller's interests in the property belong to the buyer

Question 52 - Mock Test 1

A grant deed would not be considered valid from the start if:

A. The recipient of the property lacks legal competence

B. The person transferring the property lacks legal competence

C. The deed was executed on a public holiday

D. The deed was not officially recognized by a notary or other official

Question 53 - Mock Test 1

The right to alienation refers to:

A. Laws governing inheritance and estate distribution

B. The capability to execute and deliver a deed

C. The ability to devise property through a will

D. The right to transfer an interest in real property

Question 54 - Mock Test 1

The deed covenant assuring the grantor owns the property and has the right to sell it is known as:

A. The covenant against encumbrances

B. The covenant of seisin

C. The perpetual warranty covenant

D. The covenant of further assurance

Question 55 - Mock Test 1

A lien resulting from legal judgments, estate or inheritance taxes, decedent's debts, or federal income taxes is categorized as:

A. Consensual

B. Equitable

C. Designated

D. General

Question 56 - Mock Test 1

In a foreclosure sale, which lien is given precedence?

A. Delinquent property taxes

B. The original lender or mortgage holder

C. Construction or material suppliers who filed a notice after starting work

D. The earliest lien recorded

Question 57 - Mock Test 1

A borrower fell behind on his home mortgage loan payments, and the lender secured a court judgment to foreclose on the property. The home sold for $164,000 during the foreclosure sale, with an unpaid loan total of $178,000. What must the lender do to recover the remaining $14,000 owed by the borrower?

A. Seek a deficiency judgment

B. Request a default judgment

C. File a lawsuit for damages

D. Pursue specific performance action

Question 58 - Mock Test 1

When is the Title to real property is conveyed by deed?

A. When signed by the person selling the property

B. When filed in public records by the person receiving the property

C. When signed by the recipient and returned to the seller

D. When delivered to and accepted by the grantee

Question 59 - Mock Test 1

A title insurance policy covers the risk of loss for a variety of causes, but which of the following dangers is not covered?

A. Failure of a spouse to sign the deed

B. A zoning ordinance, regulation or plan

C. Forgery in the property's document chain

D. An unpaid municipal charge not listed in the policy

Question 60 - Mock Test 1

An individual cannot obtain the Title to real property through:

A. Prescription

B. Succession

C. Escheat

D. Land patent

Question 61 - Mock Test 1

A unique characteristic of real estate as an economic product is:

A. Its rapid conversion into cash

B. Its swift adaptation to supply and demand changes

C. its susceptibility to swings in the local economy

D. The simple exchange of one property for another

Question 62 - Mock Test 1

Which type of real estate users prioritizes neighborhood quality, service access, amenities, and lifestyle most in their property demands?

A. Commercial retailers

B. Corporate offices

C. Manufacturing and logistics sectors

D. Residential homeowners and renters

Question 63 - Mock Test 1

In Florence, where new construction is booming, the most immediate effect on the real estate market would likely be:

A. A surge in demand and price increases

B. An increase in vacancies leading to price drops

C. A simultaneous reduction in absorption rates and vacancies

D. A drop in available supply compared to demand

Question 64 - Mock Test 1

Which factor is considered a direct local influence on a real estate market?

A. Nationwide changes in money availability
B. Federal interest rate adjustments
C. The migration of significant employers into or out of the area
D. International trade deficits or surpluses

Question 65 - Mock Test 1

A construction moratorium represents:

A. Local government's real estate market intervention independent of demand forces
B. A natural outcome when demand surpasses supply
C. A municipal endorsement of laissez-faire market principles
D. An effort to curb escalating prices through regulatory measures

Question 66 - Mock Test 1

In the context of market economics, "vacancy" refers to:

A. Ownerless properties
B. A comprehensive listing of available properties
C. A lack of certain user groups in the market
D. Unoccupied spaces of a specific type at a given moment

Question 67 - Mock Test 1

"Base employment" in real estate demand analysis signifies:

A. The lowest employment tier by wage or status
B. The number of persons employed in base industries in an area
C. Employment figures on military installations
D. The total workforce potential across sectors

Question 68 - Mock Test 1

The traditional view of real estate's illiquidity stems from:

A. Its immovable physical nature
B. The definition of real estate as land
C. Challenges in quickly converting properties into cash
D. Its immobility

Question 69 - Mock Test 1

A construction boom signals that market prices:

A. Have been on the rise
B. Are in decline
C. Are balanced
D. Have surpassed the existing supply

NATIONAL REAL ESTATE LICENSE EXAM PREP

Question 70 - Mock Test 1

Declining rental prices in a commercial real estate market suggest that:

A. Demand has surpassed the available space
B. Market conditions are balanced
C. The market is over-supplied
D. Employment numbers are growing

Question 71 - Mock Test 1

Miller, a principal real estate broker, facing a lawsuit for conversion, is accused of:

A. Mixing client funds with personal funds
B. Not keeping the client trust accounts sufficiently funded
C. Not reconciling client trust accounts promptly
D. Misappropriately using client funds for personal use

Question 72 - Mock Test 1

A real estate conservation area implies:

A. Restrictions on certain real estate actions to preserve area stability
B. A ban on removing large trees without permission
C. Limited development to protect green spaces
D. The creation of buffer zones for conservation

Question 73 - Mock Test 1

The Civil Rights Act of 1866 outlaws housing discrimination based on:

A. Religious beliefs
B. Gender
C. Race
D. Marital status

Question 74 - Mock Test 1

A broker found guilty of steering would have:

A. Advised buyers on offering prices
B. Insisted on transporting buyers to property viewings
C. Showed properties based on buyers' preferred locations
D. Directed buyers towards properties in a predominately minority community because the buyers were of the same race

Question 75 - Mock Test 1

To calculate net operating income for a property, a property manager must deduct which of the following from the effective gross income?

A. Reserve funds for replacements
B. Mortgage or loan payments
C. Payments made to property owners
D. Operational expenses

Question 76 - Mock Test 1

Usury is best described as:

A. Issuing loans without co-signers

B. Charging illegal interest rates

C. Property capable of serving multiple purposes

D. Offering loans with variable interest rates

Question 77 - Mock Test 1

Stephen Douglas, who has been instructed by a court to cease burning leaves due to a lawsuit from his neighbors, received a court order known as:

A. A notice of pending legal action

B. A request for an exception

C. An injunction

D. A directive for release

Question 78 - Mock Test 1

Engaging in which of the following actions violates fair housing laws concerning periodic tenancy?

A. Mandating references from previous landlords for all tenants

B. Requiring a good credit score and reliable income from all tenants

C. Asking for advance rent payments from all tenants

D. Demanding a co-signer solely from single tenants

Question 79 - Mock Test 1

Under anti-discrimination laws, which of the following statements are prohibited?

A. Comments about nationality

B. Inquiries about future family planning

C. Remarks regarding gender

D. All the provided options

Question 80 - Mock Test 1

Which scenario necessitates having a real estate license?

A. Providing a matching service for property buyers and sellers for a fee

B. An executor handling the sale of an estate's property

C. A homeowner selling their property

D. A resident manager collecting rent for a property owner

Question 81 - Mock Test 1

The principal's key duty towards a broker in an agency relationship primarily involves:

A. Following orders

B. Maintaining secrecy

C. Keeping accurate records

D. Compensation

Question 82 - Mock Test 1

The authority to set the listing price ultimately rests with the:

A. Real estate agent

B. Sales associate

C. Property evaluator

D. Owner

Question 83 - Mock Test 1

The nature of the relationship between a property manager and the property owner is best described as a:

A. Representation of both parties

B. Joint venture

C. Specific task representation

D. General agency

Question 84 - Mock Test 1

Johnson, a real estate broker, has listed a property. Suzie, a salesperson at broker Sims, received an offer. Donna, a salesperson for broker Johnson, had the offer accepted. Who will receive the commission?

A. Johnson

B. Donna

C. Suzie

D. Sims

Question 85 - Mock Test 1

The responsibility to safeguard any funds received on behalf of others is an aspect of the fiduciary duty known as:

A. Informing

B. Following instructions

C. Accounting

D. Skill and care

Question 86 - Mock Test 1

The amount a broker can charge as commission for selling a house is:

A. Specified by law

B. Agreed upon in the broker's contract with his principal

C. A fixed percentage of the sale price

D. Based on prevailing local practices

Question 87 - Mock Test 1

Real estate agents typically act as representatives of:

A. The party covering the commission

B. The party with whom a written contract has been signed

C. The property owner

D. The purchaser

Question 88 - Mock Test 1

In representing seller Jones, real estate broker Smith is required to:

A. Adjust contract terms unilaterally

B. Dismiss insufficient offers autonomously

C. Provide loyal service

D. Offer legal counsel

Question 89 - Mock Test 1

Agency relationships cannot be terminated by:

A. The seller ending the listing to deal directly with a prospective buyer

B. Doubting the broker's effectiveness

C. Questioning the seller's performance

D. The property's destruction

Question 90 - Mock Test 1

Ethical practices for a real estate licensee essentially signify:

A. Legal awareness and compliance

B. Business proficiency

C. The licensee's honesty and fairness in dealing with the public, clients and associates and customers

D. High regard among peers and the public

Question 91 - Mock Test 1

An agent named Taylor sells 2/3 of an acre for $24,000 and earns a 7% commission. If Taylor splits the commission with the broker 55-45, how much does Taylor receive per square foot?

A. $0.026 / SF

B. $0.021 / SF

C. $0.018 / SF

D. $0.032 / SF

Question 92 - Mock Test 1

Lots in the Westfield subdivision are selling for approximately $0.50 per square foot. The Robinsons want to build a 2,600 square foot home on a 1 1/2-acre corner lot. The custom builder can build the home for $125 per square foot. What will the completed property cost the Robinsons?

A. $357,670

B. $370,000

C. $325,000

D. $32,670

Question 93 - Mock Test 1

Maria owned a 1/3 acre lot. She wanted to construct a 150' × 60' tennis court on the lot. What approximate percentage of the lot will be left over, if any, when she has completed the construction?

A. 62%

B. 38%

C. 45%

D. 25%

Question 94 - Mock Test 1

A developer plans to develop an 18-acre subdivision. He estimates that the streets and common areas will take up about 1/3 of the overall area. If the minimum lot size is 10,000 square feet, how many lots can the developer include on this property?

A. 50

B. 54

C. 52

D. 60

Question 95 - Mock Test 1

A homeowner wants to insulate the new family room in his basement. He has been told that 4 inches of insulation would do the job. The walls are all 8 feet high and measure 15 feet, 15 feet, 20 feet, and 20 feet in length, respectively. How many rolls will he need if each roll measures 4" × 2' × 40'?

A. 7

B. 8

C. 6

D. 10

Question 96 - Mock Test 1

John plans to mulch the flower area around his house. The house measures 50' × 35', and he plans to mulch an area 10 feet in width to form a big rectangle all around the perimeter. What is the square footage of the resulting mulched area?

A. 1,500 SF

B. 2,100 SF

C. 2,750 SF

D. 3,000 SF

Question 97 - Mock Test 1

Calculate how many acres are in the Southwestern 1/4 of the Southeastern 1/4 of the Eastern 1/2 of Section 12.

A. 20 acres

B. 40 acres

C. 80 acres

D. 10 acres

Question 98 - Mock Test 1

Homeowner Alex owns the Northeastern 1/4 of the Southeastern 1/4 of the Southwestern 1/4 of the Section 12. How many acres is that property?

A. 5 acres

B. 10 acres

C. 40 acres

D. 20 acres

Question 99 - Mock Test 1

Bakery Bliss has a percentage lease on its 1,800 SF space in Midtown Plaza. The terms are $1.40 per SF per month rent plus 1.75% of the store's gross income. If monthly sales averaged $41,500 last year, how much annual rent did Bakery Bliss pay last year?

  A. $43,420
  B. $30,240
  C. $21,525
  D. $38,955

Question 100 - Mock Test 1

A home appreciated 4 1/4% one year, then 5 1/3% the next year, and then 6 1/2% in the third year. What was the average appreciation over the 3-year period expressed as a decimal?

  A. 5.36%
  B. 16.08%
  C. 7.00%
  D. 5.50%

Mock Test 2

Question 1 - Mock Test 2

The reduction in value from everyday wear and use is known as:

A. FUNCTIONAL OBSOLESCENCE

B. EXTERIOR DETERIORATION

C. PHYSICAL DETERIORATION

D. ECONOMIC OBSOLESCENCE

Question 2 - Mock Test 2

The illegal practice by a real estate agent of blending personal finances with client funds is called:

A. QUIET TITLE ACTION

B. COMMINGLING

C. CONVERSION

D. ESCHEAT

Question 3 - Mock Test 2

A document detailing a company's financial performance, including earnings and expenditures over a specific period, is:

A. REVENUE REPORT

B. BALANCE SHEET

C. PROFIT AND LOSS STATEMENT

D. NET DIFFERENTIAL STATEMENT

Question 4 - Mock Test 2

Rights concerning the use of flowing water from rivers or streams are:

A. LITTORAL RIGHTS

B. RIPARIAN RIGHTS

C. DUE PROCESS

D. BUNDLE OF RIGHTS

Question 5 - Mock Test 2

Fixtures within a business premise, considered personal property, are:

A. Business lien

B. Trade fixture

C. Trade source

D. Business item

Question 6 - Mock Test 2

A wall that carries not only its own weight but also the load from other parts of the building is:

A. Support wall

B. Hip wall

C. Load-bearing wall

D. Foundation wall

Question 7 - Mock Test 2

Property rights for land adjacent to oceans and lakes are termed:

A. Avulsion

B. Riparian

C. Littoral

D. Accretion

Question 8 - Mock Test 2

A type of lease where the tenant covers the rent plus property expenses like taxes, insurance, and maintenance is:

A. SANDWICH LEASE

B. NET LEASE

C. GROSS LEASE

D. PERCENTAGE LEASE

Question 9 - Mock Test 2

Value growth in property due to external community or area developments rather than direct improvements to the property itself is called:

A. WAIVER

B. VALUE

C. YIELD

D. UNEARNED INCREMENT

Question 10 - Mock Test 2

A provision that allows a later mortgage to become more important than an existing one is:

A. Open-end clause

B. Acceleration clause

C. Release clause

D. Subordination clause

Question 11 - Mock Test 2

Under the Federal Truth-in-Lending Law, credit costs on certain loans are expressed as:

A. A monthly rate

B. An annual percentage rate

C. The highest possible rate

D. The lowest possible rate

Question 12 - Mock Test 2

A mortgage requiring $875.70 monthly for 20 years, with a large final payment ($24,095), is identified as:

A. Accelerated

B. Variable

C. Balloon

D. Wraparound

Question 13 - Mock Test 2

The primary purpose of the FHA is to:

A. Guarantee qualified borrowers against default

B. Create a secondary market for mortgages

C. Provide insurance for home loans made by approved lenders

D. Insure all home equity loans for qualified borrowers

Question 14 - Mock Test 2

Denying a Savings & Loan application from Mr. and Mrs. Sparks would breach the Federal Fair Housing Act if based on:

A. Insufficient income

B. Age

C. Minority background

D. Excessive borrowing history

Question 15 - Mock Test 2

Jones has a mortgage payment plan that allows him to pay less than the real amount required to pay off the debt and interest. He is at risk for:

A. Shared equity

B. Scaled payments

C. Negative amortization

D. Mortgage modification

Question 16 - Mock Test 2

The mortgage clause allowing the lender to demand full repayment upon default is termed:

A. An acceleration clause

B. Legal action clause

C. Loss clause

D. Step-up clause

Question 17 - Mock Test 2

A mortgage with steady payments not covering the full balance, resulting in a remaining sum, refers to:

A. Final settlement payment

B. Quick repayment

C. Escalation payment

D. Balloon payment

Question 18 - Mock Test 2

What is a Purchase Money Mortgage?

A. A release of the primary mortgage

B. Financing on bought personal property

C. A mortgage given from buyer to seller to secure the purchase price

D. Part of a payment plan sale

Question 19 - Mock Test 2

The Federal Reserve Board raises cash reserve requirements to:

A. Market securities

B. Stimulate borrowing

C. Increase taxes

D. Decrease loan activity

Question 20 - Mock Test 2

Which of the following types of loans were most likely obtained by buyers who bought a home for $142,500 and received a loan for 100% of the purchase price?

A. VA-guaranteed

B. FHA-insured

C. Wraparound

D. Conventional

Question 21 - Mock Test 2

All the following are required in an exclusive listing contract, except:

A. The final contract price

B. All relevant parties' signatures

C. Detailed property description

D. A defined termination date

Question 22 - Mock Test 2

A verbal agreement to buy a house, accompanied by a $500 earnest money check, is considered:

A. Finalized

B. Unenforceable

C. Invalid

D. Legally binding

Question 23 - Mock Test 2

The legal action that forces a seller to complete a sale is known as:

A. Specific performance

B. Property repossession

C. Execution order

D. Eviction order

Question 24 - Mock Test 2

Essentially, a listing agreement is a/an:

A. Employment contract

B. Purchase agreement

C. One-sided contract

D. Selling option

Question 25 - Mock Test 2

All listing types except one require the broker to directly facilitate the sale to earn a commission. The exception is:

A. A non-exclusive listing

B. An exclusive-right-to-sell listing

C. There are no exceptions; all require direct facilitation

D. An exclusive agency listing

Question 26 - Mock Test 2

Which of the following is not essential for creating a contract?

A. Proposal

B. Exchange of value

C. Performance

D. Agreement

Question 27 - Mock Test 2

Each party is obliged to a certain date for performance if a real estate sales contract includes:

A. A due-on-sale requirement

B. A provision that time is of the essence

C. A celebratory acknowledgment

D. A deadline for mortgage approval

Question 28 - Mock Test 2

If a buyer retracts an offer before the seller accepts it:

A. The broker can demand the buyer complete the purchase

B. The seller can successfully demand contract completion

C. The seller keeps half the earnest money

D. The buyer is entitled to a refund of the earnest money deposit

Question 29 - Mock Test 2

The legal principle requiring real estate contracts to be in writing is the:

A. Statute of frauds

B. Time-limit statute

C. Spoken evidence regulation

D. Inheritance and property law

Question 30 - Mock Test 2

A verbal agreement is made by a tenant to rent a home for six months. The renter informs the owner that he would be moving out the next month because he has discovered a more appealing apartment. The agreement is:

A. Void

B. Invalid due to lack of writing

C. Not legally binding

D. Enforceable

Question 31 - Mock Test 2

Once a purchase contract is signed by both Joe (buyer) and Stephen (seller), what type of title interest does Joe have?

A. Revocable interest

B. Title insurance interest

C. Legal title interest

D. Equitable

Question 32 - Mock Test 2

When an owner gives a life estate to her grandson, specifying that it passes to her son-in-law upon her death, the son-in-law holds:

A. A statutory life estate

B. Remainder interest

C. An interest in reverting

D. A fixed-term estate

Question 33 - Mock Test 2

A fee simple estate is best described as:

A. A fixed-term estate

B. Unrestricted ownership

C. The most interest that one can hold in land

D. A lifetime ownership

Question 34 - Mock Test 2

A vacant lot near a hospital was owned in fee simple. She chose to make the lot accessible to the hospital. Her attorney drafted a deed transferring title of the lot to the hospital "so long as it is used for medical purposes." After the gift is complete, the hospital will own:

A. A fee simple defeasible estate

B. A fixed-term lease

C. A perpetual care estate

D. A renewable lease

Question 35 - Mock Test 2

A municipality's regulatory powers do not extend to:

A. Restrictive covenants
B. Minimum parcel sizes
C. Construction types
D. Building heights

Question 36 - Mock Test 2

Oscar, Andrew, and Douglas are co-tenants who jointly own a piece of property. Douglas tells his old friend Joe that he's interested. Following the transfer, Oscar and Andrew:

A. Jointly include Joe
B. Retain joint tenancy without Douglas
C. Remain joint tenants owning a two-thirds interest
D. Share ownership equally with Joe

Question 37 - Mock Test 2

A specific, involuntary lien refers to:

A. Federal income tax obligations
B. A real estate property tax lien
C. Estate taxes due
D. Court-awarded debt claims

Question 38 - Mock Test 2

Oscar and Susan reside next door. Oscar is told by Susan that he can keep his camper in her yard until she needs the space, which should be a few weeks. Oscar was not charged rent by Susan for

using her yard. Oscar has received what from Susan?

A. License
B. Required access right
C. Land use right
D. Temporary use permission

Question 39 - Mock Test 2

Which item is not traditionally considered an appurtenance?

A. A built-in swimming facility
B. Trade Fixture
C. A right-of-way agreement
D. Natural features like trees

Question 40 - Mock Test 2

If one has a permanent right to access their home through another's property, their property is:

A. Individually burdened
B. A dominant tenement
C. Temporarily permitted
D. Burdened by the easement

Question 41 - Mock Test 2

When evaluating a/an, _____ the income capitalization method to value would be the most crucial.

A. office building
B. vacant residential lot
C. condominium
D. single-family residence

Question 42 - Mock Test 2

When there is a decline in supply and no change in demand, _____.

A. demand tends to decline

B. price tends to decline

C. price tends to rise

D. demand tends to rise

Question 43 - Mock Test 2

Susan recently found out that the city wants to demolish three houses across the street and replace them with a brand-new, multi-unit apartment complex. She wishes to get rid of her house quickly to avoid a drop in value. Here's an illustration of:

A. Anticipation

B. Participation

C. Conformance

D. Rivalry

Question 44 - Mock Test 2

The appraiser uses the following when applying the cost approach to value:

A. Prices paid for comparable local buildings

B. The building's estimated current replacement cost

C. Evaluated building value

D. The building's initial cost to the owner

Question 45 - Mock Test 2

A home with four bedrooms and a single-car garage would be an example of:

A. Functional obsolescence

B. Financial obsolescence

C. Environmental obsolescence

D. Physical degradation

Question 46 - Mock Test 2

An owner was building a home for himself. He chose not to add a bathtub out of personal taste. This could lead to:

A. Physical Deterioration

B. Functional Obsolescence

C. Social Obsolescence

D. External Obsolescence

Question 47 - Mock Test 2

How many acres may be found in a lot measuring 1/4 mile broad by 1/4 mile long?

A. 50 acres

B. 100 acres

C. 120 acres

D. 40 acres

Question 48 - Mock Test 2

The primary cause of loss of value in real property is:

A. Wear and tear

B. Deferred maintenance

C. Obsolescence

D. Old age

Question 49 - Mock Test 2

What is the purpose of an appraisal?

A. Calculate the estimated revenue of a property

B. Determine the market price of a property

C. Determine the amount of earnest money the seller should accept from a buyer

D. Estimate the market value of a property

Question 50 - Mock Test 2

The definitions of market value are least concerned with:

A. Market cost

B. Value in exchange

C. Open Market

D. Objective value

Question 51 - Mock Test 2

A quitclaim deed to a parcel of real property conveys just the current interest, right, and title of:

A. Occupant

B. Grantee

C. Landlord

D. Grantor

Question 52 - Mock Test 2

For a deed to be considered valid, it must include:

A. The possibility of eviction any day except Sundays

B. Formal acknowledgment by a notary or official

C. The phrase "to have and to hold" within its text

D. Legal property description

Question 53 - Mock Test 2

To alienate the title of property, one:

A. Conveys title

B. Clouds the title

C. Records a homestead

D. Encumbers the title

Question 54 - Mock Test 2

If Joe dies without leaving a will, it is claimed to be:

A. Intestate

B. A Testator

C. In Probate

D. A Testate

Question 55 - Mock Test 2

In real estate, "tax shelter" refers to:

A. Income tax

B. Net earnings from investments

C. Taxes levied on real estate

D. Principal amounts paid on loans

Question 56 - Mock Test 2

What happens to a lease under an "estate for years" agreement when the leased real estate is sold?

A. The lease can be ended with appropriate notice

B. The lease concludes upon the property's sale

C. The lease remains valid but cannot be enforced

D. It binds the new owner

Question 57 - Mock Test 2

Which of the following is not typically taxable?

A. Patents and trademarks

B. Watercraft

C. Earned income

D. Residential property

Question 58 - Mock Test 2

In a sale/leaseback transaction for a commercial building, the buyer's least concern is:

A. The building's physical state

B. The depreciated book value of the building

C. The property's location within the broader community

D. The financial credibility of the seller

Question 59 - Mock Test 2

Once a judgment has been properly recorded, those who buy the property later or those unaware of the judgment have received:

A. Indirect notice

B. Constructive notice

C. Direct legal notice

D. First-hand notice

Question 60 - Mock Test 2

A bill of sale is utilized to transfer ownership of:

A. Fixtures

B. Personal property

C. Real property

D. Appurtenances

Question 61 - Mock Test 2

When a market experiences a significant lack of homes, leading to increased construction, this scenario illustrates:

A. Supply surpassing demand

B. Demand surpassing the market value

C. Consumer confidence

D. The market moving toward a state of equilibrium

Question 62 - Mock Test 2

In a burgeoning town where all prime vacant lots are already developed, the expectation for the prices of existing homes in that premium area is that they:

A. Will stabilize due to inevitable population stabilization
B. Are likely to rise
C. Will decrease due to the impossibility of further construction
D. Cannot be predicted with any consistency

Question 63 - Mock Test 2

The four core factors determining the value of a product include:

A. Endurance, practicality, transferability, and geographic setting
B. Desire, utility, scarcity, and purchasing power
C. Public perception, recognition, marketing efforts, and discounts
D. Exchangeability, cost factors, accessibility, and distinctiveness

Question 64 - Mock Test 2

A decrease in vacancies within the real estate sector typically leads to:

A. Increasing prices
B. Decreasing prices
C. Reduced construction activities
D. Lower rates of property being rented or sold

Question 65 - Mock Test 2

"Absorption" in the context of real estate market analysis is defined as:

A. The addition of new space to the market within a certain timeframe
B. The construction of residential units over a specified period
C. The total occupied space at any moment
D. The number of available units that become occupied over a period of time

Question 66 - Mock Test 2

When a property owner merges two adjacent lots into a single, more valuable entity, this value-increasing strategy is known as:

A. Assemblage
B. Natural growth
C. Enhancement through proximity
D. Division for increased value

Question 67 - Mock Test 2

The measurement of a property's gross living area is typically taken:

A. Excluding the footprint of any structures on the property
B. From the exterior dimensions of above-grade spaces, omitting open areas
C. By calculating the total interior living spaces
D. Excluding basements and attics from the total enclosed spaces

Question 68 - Mock Test 2

Real estate stands out as an economic good due to:

A. Its standardized nature

B. Its diversity

C. Each property's uniqueness

D. Its propensity for value appreciation over time

Question 69 - Mock Test 2

When a market reaches equilibrium, it means that:

A. New competitors will lower the price by entering the market

B. Demand will gradually decrease, reducing prices

C. Unfulfilled demand shifts towards alternative products

D. Supply matches demand, stabilizing prices and values equally

Question 70 - Mock Test 2

An increase in the price of a product typically indicates that:

A. Demand for the product is falling relative to its supply

B. Demand for the product is increasing in relation to supply of the product

C. There is more of the product available

D. Both the product's demand and supply are rising

Question 71 - Mock Test 2

After purchasing their home, the Jacksons discovered a leaky roof during rainstorms. The seller had informed Bankers Agency's broker of the issue, but Bankers claims the Jacksons didn't inquire about it. What is the Jacksons' recourse?

A. They can initiate legal action against the broker for non-disclosure

B. They have no recourse as the inspection should have identified the leak

C. They cannot pursue legal action against the broker according to license law

D. They have the option to sue the seller under license law provisions

Question 72 - Mock Test 2

The typical lease format for an apartment in a residential complex is:

A. A net lease

B. A lease based on a percentage of sales

C. A gross lease

D. A lease concerning the land itself

Question 73 - Mock Test 2

Redlining is defined as:

A. Denying loans based strictly on sound economic reasons

B. The refusal to offer loans or insurance in certain areas, not based on applicants' financial reliability

C. The absence of financial institutions in neighborhoods solely due to non-economic considerations

D. Invalidating mortgage documents through selective editing

Question 74 - Mock Test 2

What is RESPA?

A. A law aimed at preventing discrimination

B. A set of regulations for accommodating disabilities

C. A standard for closing procedures

D. A program designed to assist low-income housing

Question 75 - Mock Test 2

In which scenario should an agent NOT suggest hiring an external inspector?

A. When noticing a toilet with slow drainage

B. When a door hinge is detached

C. Observing sawdust in kitchen cabinets

D. Detecting a gas smell in the basement

Question 76 - Mock Test 2

When presenting offers to sellers, agents should always be:

A. Suspicious and confrontational

B. Enthusiastic and straightforward

C. Careful and responsible

D. Aggressive and combative

Question 77 - Mock Test 2

Which action could lead to a salesperson's license being revoked by the real estate commission?

A. Signing an exclusive listing agreement with a seller

B. Showing a property listed by an unaffiliated broker

C. Attempting to act on behalf of a buyer

D. Depositing a buyer's earnest money into a personal account

Question 78 - Mock Test 2

What does it mean if a licensee claims a property near a large park is "in the best part of town"?

A. Puffing

B. Overstating

C. Misrepresenting

D. Committing fraud

Question 79 - Mock Test 2

How long does an individual have to file a Fair Housing complaint with the Department of Housing and Urban Development after an alleged violation?

A. 6 months

B. 2 years

C. 1 year

D. 5 years

Question 80 - Mock Test 2

The permission to perform specific acts on another's land without holding any estate therein is defined as:

A. A license

B. An option

C. An encroachment

D. An easement

Question 81 - Mock Test 2

The trust and obligation the broker holds as an agent for the client is best described as:

A. A trustor bond

B. A trustee association

C. A confidential connection

D. A fiduciary relationship

Question 82 - Mock Test 2

In an exclusive right-to-sell listing, the broker's commitment to diligently seek a buyer:

A. Does not match any of the other given options

B. Establishes the listing as a bilateral contract

C. Renders the contract cancellable by the owner

D. Forms a unilateral contract

Question 83 - Mock Test 2

Termination of a power of attorney can occur due to:

A. The incapacity of the represented party

B. The principal revoking the authority

C. The death of the attorney-in-fact

D. Any of the listed reasons

Question 84 - Mock Test 2

An agency relationship cannot be established by:

A. A verbal agreement

B. Subornation

C. A need or urgent circumstance

D. Ratification after the fact

Question 85 - Mock Test 2

If a broker represents a seller, the broker's duty to the buyer involves:

A. Only disclosing facts that directly impact the sale price

B. Equally fiduciary responsibilities

C. Merely answering questions truthfully

D. Conducting fair and honest dealings

Question 86 - Mock Test 2

A real estate agent entrusted with loyalty, trust, and confidence by a client is a(n):

A. Agent representing both parties

B. Independent contractor

C. Fiduciary

D. Principal

Question 87 - Mock Test 2

A broker who initiated a series of events leading to a property's sale is termed the:

A. Initial catalyst

B. Procuring cause

C. Justifiable reason for compensation

D. Accountable entity

Question 88 - Mock Test 2

An agent solely representing the buyer is authorized to:

A. Quickly relay offers to the seller

B. Only approach the seller with proposals

C. Disclose their representation but exclusively approach the seller

D. Submit offers directly to the seller or the seller's agent

Question 89 - Mock Test 2

Upon issuing a new counter-offer:

A. The offer terms remain unchanged

B. The counter-offeror becomes the counter-offeree

C. None of the other statements are accurate

D. The offeror may unilaterally alter the offer's conditions

Question 90 - Mock Test 2

An agency relationship cannot be established through:

A. A verbal agreement

B. A documented agreement

C. An implied agreement

D. A voluntary offer by the agent

Question 91 - Mock Test 2

A homeowner purchased a house for $200,000 five years ago. Today, the house sells for $260,000. How much has the property appreciated?

A. 30%

B. 23%

C. 60%

D. 77%

Question 92 - Mock Test 2

Agent Lisa receives an offer of $270,000 on a property she listed at $285,000. How much is the offer as a percent of the listing price?

A. 92%
B. 91%
C. 95%
D. 97%

Question 93 - Mock Test 2

A property is being appraised using the income capitalization approach. Annually, it has potential gross income of $50,000, vacancy and credit losses of $2,000, and operating expenses of $15,000. Using a capitalization rate of 8%, what is the indicated value (to the nearest $1,000)?

A. $412,500
B. $408,000
C. $416,000
D. $400,000

Question 94 - Mock Test 2

If the gross income on a property is $90,000, the net income is $36,000, and the capitalization rate is 9%, what is the value of the property using the income capitalization method?

A. $400,000
B. $444,444
C. $600,000
D. $333,333

Question 95 - Mock Test 2

The roof of a property cost $24,000. The economic life of the roof is 30 years. Assuming the straight-line method of depreciation, what is the depreciated value of the roof after 5 years?

A. $20,000
B. $24,000
C. $16,000
D. $19,200

Question 96 - Mock Test 2

Chris had to report his home office depreciation for the tax year. He has a 3,000 SF home and a 600 SF office area. Chris paid $300,000 for his home, and he figures the land portion carries about 25% of that value. If Chris depreciates on a 39-year basis, how much can he write off for his home office depreciation per year?

A. $1,154
B. $1,538
C. $5,769
D. $2,308

Question 97 - Mock Test 2

A property is being appraised using the cost approach. The appraiser estimates that the land is worth $100,000, and the replacement cost of the improvements is $450,000. Total depreciation from all causes is $75,000. What is the indicated value of the property?

A. $575,000
B. $525,000
C. $375,000
D. $475,000

Question 98 - Mock Test 2

An apartment owner purchased her complex for $600,000 six years ago. At that time, an appraiser valued the land at $150,000, but the land has appreciated 20% over this period. The investor has used a 30-year straight-line depreciation method for the property improvements. What is its current value using the cost approach?

A. $650,000
B. $540,000
C. $610,000
D. $560,000

Question 99 - Mock Test 2

An apartment building recently sold for $360,000 and had monthly gross rent receipts of $3,000. What is its monthly gross rent multiplier?

A. 80
B. 100
C. 120
D. 110

Question 100 - Mock Test 2

A rental home has a monthly gross income of $4,000. A suitable gross income multiplier derived from market data is 15. What estimated sale price (to the nearest $1,000) is indicated?

A. $700,000
B. $720,000
C. $680,000
D. $750,000

Mock Test 3

Question 1 - Mock Test 3

What type of lease is based on a fraction of the gross or net sales from a business, typically a retail property, and often includes a set minimum rent to cover periods of low sales?

A. Net Lease

B. Percentage Lease

C. Gross Lease

D. Sandwich Lease

Question 2 - Mock Test 3

Which appraisal report offers the most comprehensive analysis, including a thorough explanation and support for the appraiser's conclusions?

A. Narrative Form Appraisal Report

B. Letter Form Appraisal Report

C. Short Form Appraisal Report

D. Grand Form Appraisal Report

Question 3 - Mock Test 3

What term describes a summarized record of all pertinent legal documents that affect a property's title?

A. Deed

B. Variance

C. Chain of Title

D. Abstract of Title

Question 4 - Mock Test 3

Which term encompasses the complete set of legal privileges that come with property ownership, such as control, enjoyment, and the right to sell?

A. Facts of Transference

B. Littoral Rights

C. Rights of Estatehood

D. Bundle of Rights

Question 5 - Mock Test 3

What is the term for the rapid and significant removal of land by water, distinguished from slower geological processes like erosion?

A. Avulsion

B. Accretion

C. Reliction

D. Accession

Question 6 - Mock Test 3

What represents the ultimate type of ownership in real estate, providing the owner with the greatest control and rights over the property?

A. Fee Simple Estate

B. Estate at Will

C. Estate for Years

D. Life Estate

Question 7 - Mock Test 3

What type of real estate ownership is established under conditions set by the grantor, and could be nullified upon the occurrence of a specific event?

A. Defeasible Estate

B. Life Estate

C. Fee Simple Estate

D. Estate at Will

Question 8 - Mock Test 3

What financial term describes the process of reducing debt through regular payments that cover both principal and interest?

A. Liquidation

B. Refinance

C. Usury

D. Amortization

Question 9 - Mock Test 3

What is the process called where private property is taken for public use without the owner's consent, though fair compensation must be provided?

A. Escheat

B. Inverse Condemnation

C. Waiver

D. Condemnation

Question 10 - Mock Test 3

Identify the practice where financial institutions refuse to offer loans or mortgages in certain neighborhoods based on demographic factors, regardless of an individual's qualifications.

A. Panic Selling

B. Redlining

C. Steering

D. Blockbusting

Question 11 - Mock Test 3

What is the total balance due on a mortgage loan?

A. Principal

B. Rate of Return

C. Equity

D. Interest

Question 12 - Mock Test 3

Which of the following is prohibited under the Equal Credit Opportunity Act?

A. Discriminating based on marital status, family planning, or property condition

B. Discriminating based on marital status, family planning, or applicant's gender

C. Discriminating based on marital status, family planning, or first-time buyers' down payment

D. Discriminating based on marital status, family planning, or poor credit history

Question 13 - Mock Test 3

What is the term for a mortgage loan that is secured by real estate but not insured or guaranteed by the government?

A. Standby Loan
B. Conventional Loan
C. Budget Mortgage
D. Bancroft Bond

Question 14 - Mock Test 3

Identify the item that is not considered a "finance charge" under Truth-in-Lending regulations.

A. Loan Finder's Fees
B. Borrower's Attorney Fees
C. Loan Fees
D. Service Charges

Question 15 - Mock Test 3

Which statement about conventional loans is incorrect?

A. The loan is based on the borrower's creditworthiness and property collateral
B. It is not insured or guaranteed by any public agency
C. Loan-to-value ratio generally cannot exceed 80% without private mortgage insurance
D. It is never insured by private agencies

Question 16 - Mock Test 3

Which law mandates that finance charges must be presented as an annual percentage rate?

A. Truth in Lending Act
B. Federal Fair Housing Act
C. Real Estate Settlement Procedures Act (RESPA)
D. Equal Credit Opportunity Act (ECOA)

Question 17 - Mock Test 3

What characteristic is typically associated with a second mortgage?

A. It cannot be used as a security instrument
B. It is not negotiable
C. It is usually issued at a higher rate of interest
D. It has priority over a first mortgage

Question 18 - Mock Test 3

Which entity is responsible for enforcing the Truth-in-Lending Act?

A. Real Estate Commissioner
B. Federal Trade Commission
C. Secretary of State
D. Real Estate Settlement Procedures Act

Question 19 - Mock Test 3

What is true about typical land sale contracts?

A. They provide minimal security for buyers as the seller retains title

B. The buyer is guaranteed title upon fulfilling the contract

C. The buyer is not responsible for property taxes until receiving the deed

D. It resembles a lease, granting possession but no title rights

Question 20 - Mock Test 3

What term in accounting refers to an amount that is owed?

A. Debit

B. Credit

C. Pledge

D. Waiver

Question 21 - Mock Test 3

What term refers to pre-agreed monetary compensation for a breach of contract outlined within the contract itself?

A. Consideration

B. Earnest Money

C. Liquidated Damages

D. Performance Guarantees

Question 22 - Mock Test 3

Jones has an accepted offer on Brown's house, yet the sale will only complete in three months. How is their agreement classified currently?

A. Executory

B. Conditional

C. Voided

D. Voidable

Question 23 - Mock Test 3

If a contract is formed under pressure or undue influence, how is its enforceability affected?

A. Unenforceable

B. Invalid

C. Voidable

D. Void

Question 24 - Mock Test 3

What is a primary benefit of engaging in a sale-leaseback transaction?

A. The seller deducting future rent payments as business expenses

B. Option for the purchaser to lease back the property after the lease ends

C. Ability to maintain book value by the new buyer

D. Purchaser can retrieve the deposit without objections

Question 25 - Mock Test 3

What type of lease arrangement is a month-to-month lease?

A. Estate for Years

B. Periodic Tenancy

C. Estate at Sufferance

D. Life Estate

Question 26 - Mock Test 3

What document typically includes a safety clause?

A. Loan broker's statement

B. Lease

C. Deposit receipt

D. Listing agreement

Question 27 - Mock Test 3

Which listing agreement obligates the owner to pay a commission even if they sell the property themselves?

A. Net Listing

B. Exclusive Right to Sell Listing

C. Exclusive Agency Listing

D. Open Listing

Question 28 - Mock Test 3

A buyer paid $2,800 for a 90-day option to acquire a property for $450,000. Within a month, the buyer made an offer to acquire the property right away for $425,000. Which of the following is true in this case?

A. The owner may accept the $425,000 offer

B. Both parties are in violation of contract law

C. The buyer is in default of the option agreement

D. The option money is forfeited

Question 29 - Mock Test 3

What is the role of earnest money in establishing a purchase contract?

A. It is essential for a valid contract

B. It must be held by the seller in escrow

C. It is usually 7.5% of the purchase price

D. It is required by federal law

Question 30 - Mock Test 3

Which type of listing agreement does not require the broker to be the "procuring cause" of the sale to earn a commission?

A. An exclusive right to sell listing

B. There are no exceptions; all listings require proven procuring cause

C. An open listing

D. An exclusive listing

NATIONAL REAL ESTATE LICENSE EXAM PREP

Question 31 - Mock Test 3

A property owner agreed to have a swimming pool put on her land. When the pool was finished, she refused to pay for the upgrade, so the contractor filed a lien for nonpayment. This lien was most likely a:

A. Voluntary lien
B. General lien
C. Judgment lien
D. Mechanic's lien

Question 32 - Mock Test 3

Sally transfers a life estate to Scott for his lifetime and names Bill as the person to whom the property will pass after the life estate expires. When Scott dies, what happens to the property?

A. Sally must designate a new remainderman
B. Bill automatically becomes the fee simple owner of the property
C. The property reverts back to the original property owner
D. The property passes to Scott's heirs

Question 33 - Mock Test 3

What does 'ad valorem' mean?

A. Added value
B. Fixed value
C. At replacement value
D. According to value

Question 34 - Mock Test 3

What is the term for combining two or more contiguous properties under common ownership to increase their value?

A. Terminus ownership
B. Plottage
C. Severalty ownership
D. Disassemblage

Question 35 - Mock Test 3

When two friends (women) own a store as joint tenants and one dies, how does the surviving owner now hold the property?

A. In trust
B. As a tenant in common with the deceased's heirs
C. As a joint tenant with rights of survivorship
D. In severalty

Question 36 - Mock Test 3

What legal right does the purchase of a ticket for a professional sporting event grant the holder?

A. A license to enter and claim a seat for the duration of the game
B. An easement in gross interest in the professional sporting team
C. An easement right to park his car
D. A license to sell food and beverages at the sporting event

Question 37 - Mock Test 3

What type of area is a wooded space with trails between old mills and a housing development considered?

A. A variance to the existing zoning

B. A buffer zone

C. A nonconforming use

D. A utility easement

Question 38 - Mock Test 3

What type of tenancy exists when a tenant stays without a lease and without the landlord's permission after the lease has expired?

A. Tenancy at sufferance

B. Tenancy at will

C. An estate for years

D. An estate from year to year

Question 39 - Mock Test 3

Which of the following best describes an owner's "bundle of rights"?

A. The right to build a structure to whatever height is necessary for the use and purpose of the building

B. The right of ownership including air rights, subjacent support, and mineral rights below the surface

C. The right to build using the zoning laws when the property was purchased not current zoning laws

D. None of the other answers are correct

Question 40 - Mock Test 3

What legal action is used to determine or confirm property ownership?

A. Declaratory relief

B. Quiet title action

C. None of the other options are correct

D. Partition action

Question 41 - Mock Test 3

What is a real estate appraisal based on?

A. Derived from income data covering at least the preceding six months

B. Derived from average tax assessments covering the past five years

C. Based upon analysis of fact as of a specific date

D. Based upon replacement costs

Question 42 - Mock Test 3

Which appraisal approach would be most relied upon for a property converted into an insurance company office?

A. Sales comparison approach

B. Gross rent multiplier approach

C. Income approach

D. Replacement cost approach

Question 43 - Mock Test 3

Under what circumstances is the market data approach considered unreliable?

A. When the market is inactive

B. During times of rapid economic change

C. When there is nothing similar to the subject property

D. All of the other options make this approach unreliable

Question 44 - Mock Test 3

What is the primary responsibility of an appraiser?

A. Computing value

B. Finding value

C. Set value

D. Estimating value

Question 45 - Mock Test 3

How does a homeowner legally acquire new land created by river deposits on their property?

A. Reliction

B. Avulsion

C. Accretion

D. Succession

Question 46 - Mock Test 3

How should an appraiser handle a building on a property that is no longer valuable and needs to be demolished?

A. Deduct the demolition cost from his appraisal

B. Ignore the building in the appraisal

C. Add the salvage value to his appraisal

D. Establish the value by use of the cost approach

Question 47 - Mock Test 3

Which document determines the actual lot size in a real estate transaction if there's a discrepancy?

A. Survey

B. Deed

C. MLS listing

D. Listing contract

Question 48 - Mock Test 3

What is the best method to appraise the land value of a property?

A. Residual

B. Allocation

C. Income

D. Capitalization

Question 49 - Mock Test 3

What type of depreciation does a house with outdated plumbing suffer from?

A. Functional obsolescence

B. Incurable physical deterioration

C. External depreciation

D. Curable physical deterioration

Question 50 - Mock Test 3

How is depreciation commonly defined in real estate?

A. Depreciation

B. Adverse leverage

C. Principle of contribution

D. Economic obsolescence

Question 51 - Mock Test 3

Stephen, his nephew, and niece are joint tenants. Stephen sells his investment to his sister, and his nephew dies. As a result, which of these statements is true?

A. The nephew's heirs are joint tenants with Stephen and his sister

B. Stephen's niece and sister are tenants in common

C. The nephew's heirs and Stephen are joint tenants, but the sister is a tenant in common

D. Stephen's niece and sister are joint tenants

Question 52 - Mock Test 3

How does an assessor typically determine property taxes on a residence?

A. Total all land and improvements and assess them together, then multiply each by the different tax rates for land and improvements

B. Total all land and improvements and assess them together, then multiply by one tax rate

C. Assess land and improvements separately, then multiply each by the different tax rates for land and improvements

D. Assess land and improvements separately, then multiply the total by one tax rate

Question 53 - Mock Test 3

Which option provides a buyer with the best assurance of clear, marketable title?

A. Title insurance

B. Certificate of title

C. Abstract of title

D. General warranty deed

Question 54 - Mock Test 3

In federal income tax law, what is the "basis" of real property typically defined as?

A. Fair market value

B. Assessed value prior to sale

C. Purchase price minus any existing assumed loans

D. Cost

Question 55 - Mock Test 3

What scenario would likely involve considering "boot" in a transaction?

A. Depreciation area

B. Leasehold estate

C. Secondary market

D. Exchange

Question 56 - Mock Test 3

What is the term for the mortgagor's right to regain property after paying the debt following a foreclosure sale in most states?

A. Owner's right of redemption
B. Equitable right of redemption
C. Statutory right of redemption
D. Vendee's right of redemption

Question 57 - Mock Test 3

What is the holder of a life estate not permitted to do with their estate?

A. Rent it
B. Mortgage it
C. Sell it
D. Devise it

Question 58 - Mock Test 3

How can a defect or a cloud on title to property typically be cured?

A. Paying cash for the property at the settlement
B. Obtaining proof of satisfaction from all appropriate parties
C. Bringing an action to register the title
D. Bringing an action to repudiate the title

Question 59 - Mock Test 3

Which feature is covered under an extended coverage policy of title insurance, but not under a standard coverage policy?

A. The lack of capacity of one of the parties to any transaction involving title to the land
B. Detrimental zoning ordinances
C. The results of a forged deed in the chain title
D. The possibility that some improvements on the insured property are located on adjoining land

Question 60 - Mock Test 3

A riparian owner owns land that borders on which of the following?

A. The ocean
B. Any body of water
C. A lake
D. A stream

Question 61 - Mock Test 3

Which description best fits the sales comparison approach in property appraisal?

A. Identify the median sale price of similar properties recently sold and adjust for differences in features compared to the subject property

B. Adjust the sale prices of comparable properties to reflect differences with the subject property

C. Choose at least three similar properties currently for sale and adjust their list prices to reflect differences with the subject property

D. Increase the last sold price of the subject property by an appreciation factor, then adjust for differences with comparable properties currently for sale

Question 62 - Mock Test 3

What is a key advantage of using the sales comparison approach?

A. It considers the investment potential of the subject property

B. It uncovers the profit margins of the developers of the subject property

C. It determines the intrinsic value of the subject property, independent of competing properties

D. It evaluates the impact of specific features of the subject property in the competitive market

Question 63 - Mock Test 3

In the sales comparison approach, when making dollar adjustments, the appraiser should:

A. Increase the value of a comparable if it lacks features found in the subject property

B. Increase the value of the subject property if it lacks features found in a comparable

C. Decrease the value of a comparable if it lacks features found in the subject property

D. Decrease the value of the subject property if it surpasses a comparable in features

Question 64 - Mock Test 3

The most suitable comparable property for the sales comparison approach is one that:

A. Requires extensive and significant adjustments

B. Needs minimal and small adjustments

C. Was sold recently at the highest price

D. Is geographically nearest to the subject property

Question 65 - Mock Test 3

Using the sales comparison approach, if an appraiser is evaluating a house with three bedrooms, two bathrooms, and a patio, and compares it to a similar house sold for $400,000 with three bedrooms, three bathrooms, and no patio, what is the adjusted value?

A. $402,000

B. $407,000

C. $395,000

D. $405,000

Question 66 - Mock Test 3

Which statement accurately describes the core methodology of the cost approach to appraisal?

A. Deduct a depreciation factor from the total cost incurred in acquiring and improving the subject property

B. Calculate the cost of constructing improvements on the subject property from scratch

C. Combine the estimated land value with the actual improvement costs, adjusting for differences with similar properties

D. Sum the estimated land value and the cost of improvements, then subtract the accumulated depreciation.

Question 67 - Mock Test 3

A significant benefit of the cost approach is that it:

A. Accounts for the expenditure required to develop a similar property

B. Is highly precise for properties with new developments that are the optimal use of the site

C. Delivers a concrete sale price rather than an estimated valuation

D. Exposes the return on investment from the development costs incurred by the owner

Question 68 - Mock Test 3

The principle of depreciation from physical deterioration assumes that:

A. A property will eventually become worthless

B. Each year, a property loses a portion of its value due to economic obsolescence

C. The property depreciates uniformly over its economic lifespan

D. The depreciation incurred is permanent and cannot be recovered

Question 69 - Mock Test 3

For a property assessed using the cost approach, if the land is valued at $150,000 and the replacement cost of the improvements is $475,000 with a total depreciation of $50,000, what is the indicated property value?

A. $675,000

B. $650,000

C. $625,000

D. $575,000

Question 70 - Mock Test 3

What describes the application of the income capitalization approach in real estate appraisal?

A. Apply a desired rate of return to the purchase price of an income-generating property

B. Divide the property's income by a desired rate of return

C. Determine the necessary income for a property to recover the capital invested

D. Calculate the rate of return a property owner gets from the property's income.

Question 71 - Mock Test 3

What is the illegal practice of directing minority buyers to areas populated by the same race or religion known as?

A. Blockbusting

B. Panic peddling

C. Steering

D. Redlining

Question 72 - Mock Test 3

In a sales meeting, broker Elizabeth Johnson made statements about (1) soliciting listings in a neighborhood because of minority buyers and (2) advertising those listings only to minority buyers. Which statements are correct?

A. #1 is legal, but #2 is illegal

B. Both #1 and #2 are legal if part of a conversations kept within the firm and not discussed publicly

C. #1 is illegal, but #2 is legal

D. Both #1 and #2 are illegal

Question 73 - Mock Test 3

Under what circumstances can a landlord evict a blind or otherwise disabled tenant?

A. If the tenant makes modifications to the unit at his own expense

B. If the tenant insists on a handicapped parking place

C. If the tenant has loud parties and makes too much noise

D. If the tenant gets a service dog and the apartment policy does not allow pets

Question 74 - Mock Test 3

Salesperson Andrew receives a purchase offer that includes a $2,000 earnest money deposit in the form of a personal note. Which holds true in this case?

A. Andrew should return the note and ask the purchaser to give him a check for the same amount

B. The offer should indicate that the deposit is in the form of a note

C. The resulting contract will be voidable at the seller's option

D. Andrew has breached his agent's duty to the seller

Question 75 - Mock Test 3

What must all exclusive listings include to be valid?

- A. An automatic renewal clause
- B. A definite date of expiration
- C. Permission for the listing broker to appoint subagents
- D. A dragnet clause

Question 76 - Mock Test 3

Which of the following is the best example of 'puffing'?

- A. A licensee exaggerates certain features or benefits of a property
- B. A licensee implies that he is well connected, and knows many influential people in the area
- C. A licensee misrepresents material facts concerning a property
- D. A licensee communicates his opinions about a property as material facts

Question 77 - Mock Test 3

What does the phrase 'company dollar' mean when running a real estate office?

- A. The money the company initially invested to open the office
- B. The net income of a broker after all expenses are subtracted
- C. The income of an office after all commissions are paid to the salespeople
- D. The income after all salaries are paid to others

Question 78 - Mock Test 3

A percentage lease is calculated on a percentage of which of the following?

- A. Gross profit
- B. Net monthly income
- C. Annual net income
- D. Gross sales

Question 79 - Mock Test 3

The Civil Rights Act of 1866 prohibits discrimination based on what?

- A. Discrimination against intellectually disabled persons
- B. Discrimination against intellectually disabled persons, specific religious groups, and race
- C. Discrimination against specific religious groups
- D. Discrimination based on race

Question 80 - Mock Test 3

Under which act is discrimination prohibited in lending practices?

- A. Equal Credit Opportunity Act (ECOA)
- B. Real Estate Settlement Procedures Act (RESPA)
- C. Truth in Lending Act (TILA)
- D. Fannie Mae (FNMA)

Question 81 - Mock Test 3

How can an agency relationship be created?

A. Ratification

B. Agreement

C. Estoppel

D. All of the other options are correct

Question 82 - Mock Test 3

What should a broker advise a salesperson if the listing doesn't authorize the broker to accept a deposit from a potential buyer?

A. The broker will not be able to accept a deposit from the offeror

B. It is the broker's implied right to accept a deposit on behalf of the seller for any offer

C. A deposit can be accepted and retained by the broker from the offeror, but only as an agent of the offeror for that one act

D. It is the broker's implied right to deny the deposit for legal liability

Question 83 - Mock Test 3

Under what condition can a listing broker legally refuse to present a proper offer on the property to the seller?

A. The seller has already accepted a backup offer

B. Acting on the express instructions from the seller

C. The broker plans to purchase the property himself

D. The broker is acting as a gratuitous agent

Question 84 - Mock Test 3

Jones lists his house and informs his listing agent, Brown, "I'm listing it for $480,000, but I might take less." Brown may properly:

A. Share Jones' statement only with the buyer's broker

B. Explain Jones' position to prospective buyers in an effort to obtain an offer

C. Advertise the property for "$480,000 or less"

D. Keep the information to himself

Question 85 - Mock Test 3

What type of agency relationship is created when Seller "A" lets buyer "B" assume that Broker "C" was his agent?

A. None of the other options are correct

B. Agency by ratification

C. Agency by assumption

D. Ostensible authority

Question 86 - Mock Test 3

Who is considered the principal in a typical agency relationship in real estate?

A. Client

B. Subagent

C. Customer

D. Fiduciary

NATIONAL REAL ESTATE LICENSE EXAM PREP

Question 87 - Mock Test 3

Who qualifies for a commission in a real estate transaction?

A. The broker who received the offer from the buyer
B. The broker who communicated the acceptance to the buyer
C. The broker who received the acceptance of an offer
D. The broker who gave the offer to the seller

Question 88 - Mock Test 3

How is a broker's commission typically determined in a real estate transaction?

A. The local real estate board
B. Minimums based on the property type
C. Mutual agreement
D. State law

Question 89 - Mock Test 3

What should a selling broker do if a listing broker verbally agrees to split a commission but later refuses?

A. Do nothing since the agreement was verbal
B. Notify the Bureau of Real Estate
C. Sue the listing broker
D. Contact the MLS

Question 90 - Mock Test 3

Which of the following practices is NOT prohibited by antitrust laws?

A. Competing property management companies agreeing to standardized management fees
B. Competing brokers allocating market shares based on the value of homes
C. Two real estate firms agreeing to not cooperate with another brokerage because of their low fees
D. A broker setting a company-wide commission schedule

Question 91 - Mock Test 3

Michael obtains a 70% LTV loan on his new $500,000 home with an annual interest rate of 5%. What is the first month's interest payment?

A. $1,458.33
B. $1,500.00
C. $1,750.00
D. $2,000.00

Question 92 - Mock Test 3

James has an interest-only home equity loan at an annual interest rate of 6%. If his monthly payment is $1,800, how much is the loan's principal balance (to the nearest $1,000)?

A. $360,000

B. $300,000

C. $180,000

D. $216,000

Question 93 - Mock Test 3

The loan officer at Maple Bank tells David he can afford a monthly payment of $1,200 on his new home loan. Assuming this is an interest-only loan, and the principal balance is $288,000, what interest rate is David getting?

A. 4.50%

B. 5.00%

C. 6.00%

D. 5.25%

Question 94 - Mock Test 3

The Thompsons obtain a fixed-rate amortized 30-year loan for $320,000 at 5.75% interest. If the monthly payments are $1,868, how much interest do the Thompsons pay in the second month of the loan?

A. $1,533.33

B. $1,531.88

C. $1,868.00

D. $1,530.00

Question 95 - Mock Test 3

A lender offers the Millers two alternative loan packages for their $100,000 home equity application. One option is an interest-only loan for 5 years at 5.5% interest with no points, and the second is a 5.25% interest-only loan for 5 years with 1 point to be paid at closing. Which loan will cost the Millers less total interest, and by how much?

A. The first option, by $250

B. The second option, by $250

C. The second option, by $1,250

D. Both options charge the same amount of interest

Question 96 - Mock Test 3

Sarah recently obtained an 85% loan on her $360,000 home, and she had to pay $6,120 for points. How many points did she pay?

A. 1.5 points

B. 2.5 points

C. 3 points

D. 2 points

Question 97 - Mock Test 3

Taylor is buying Alex's house for $600,000. Taylor's loan amount is $360,000. She has agreed to pay 2 points at closing. How much will Taylor pay for points?

A. $7,200
B. $3,600
C. $4,500
D. $6,000

Question 98 - Mock Test 3

A lender determines that a homebuyer can afford to borrow $450,000 on a mortgage loan. The lender requires a 75% loan-to-value (LTV) ratio. How much can the borrower pay for a property and still qualify for this loan amount?

A. $337,500
B. $562,500
C. $600,000
D. $525,000

Question 99 - Mock Test 3

Home buyer Michael pays $2,000 per month for the interest-only loan on his new house. The loan's interest rate is 5.5%. If he obtained an 80% loan, what was the purchase price?:

A. $550,000
B. $436,364
C. $545,455
D. $490,000

Question 100 - Mock Test 3

Loan applicant Jordan has an annual gross income of $84,000. How much will a lender allow Jordan to pay for monthly housing expenses to qualify for a loan if the lender uses an income ratio of 28%?

A. $2,100
B. $1,960
C. $2,333
D. $2,240

Mock Test 4

Question 1 - Mock Test 4

What term refers to the intentional relinquishment of ownership rights or interests, such as in the case of property or easements?

A. Accession

B. Abandonment

C. Novation

D. Affirmation

Question 2 - Mock Test 4

What document summarizes the history of ownership transfers and encumbrances affecting a specific piece of real estate?

A. Accession

B. Plottage

C. Abstract

D. Lien

Question 3 - Mock Test 4

What are the rules called that govern land use in different areas within a community?

A. Building Codes

B. Escheat

C. Eminent Domain

D. Zoning

Question 4 - Mock Test 4

This document provides a summarized history of all transactions and legal activities affecting a particular property. What is it called?

A. Certificate of Title

B. Evidence of Title

C. Chain of Title

D. Abstract of Title

Question 5 - Mock Test 4

What term describes the financial return on an investment as a proportion of its cost over a specified time?

A. Interest

B. Yield

C. Lien

D. Amortization

Question 6 - Mock Test 4

What type of property is generally considered movable and not permanently attached to real estate?

A. Real Property

B. Ad Valorem

C. Ibid Santurum

D. Personal Property

Question 7 - Mock Test 4

What legal action can a buyer pursue when financial compensation isn't adequate to resolve a breach of contract in real estate transactions?

A. Writ of Execution

B. Commingling

C. Conversion

D. Specific Performance

Question 8 - Mock Test 4

Under what type of real estate listing does the agent receive any excess amount over a preset net price to the seller?

A. Open Listing

B. Exclusive Listing

C. Net Listing

D. Non-Exclusive Listing

Question 9 - Mock Test 4

What term is used for any legal liability or interest on real property that might reduce its value but doesn't hinder its transfer?

A. Fixture

B. Lien

C. Encumbrance

D. Easement

Question 10 - Mock Test 4

What is the term for a land measurement unit in the U.S. Federal Survey System that is six miles by six miles and contains thirty-six one-mile square sections?

A. Acre

B. Section

C. Plot

D. Township

Question 11 - Mock Test 4

When is a mortgage payment legally considered overdue by statute?

A. More than 10 days after the due date

B. 3 days after the due date

C. 10 days after the due date

D. 5 days after the due date

Question 12 - Mock Test 4

Which of the following is NOT stated by the Consumer Financial Protection Bureau (CFPB) for residential loans?

A. Borrowers must be informed about settlement charges

B. A new closing disclosure must be used at loan closings

C. Borrowers can cancel the first home purchase loan transaction within three days after settlement

D. Lenders must give borrowers a new estimate of closing costs early in the loan application process

Question 13 - Mock Test 4

What is the term for a legal document used in some states in place of a traditional mortgage?

A. Promissory Note
B. Negotiable Instrument
C. Release Deed
D. Deed of Trust

Question 14 - Mock Test 4

Jones has three pieces of property: a house, a lakeside cottage, and a plot of land. Which of the following expenses can be deducted for all three properties on the Jones' income tax return?

A. Mortgage Interest
B. Both Mortgage Interest and Property Taxes
C. Insurance Premiums
D. Property Taxes

Question 15 - Mock Test 4

In commercial real estate appraisal, what is the primary concern for appraisers?

A. Sales prices of comparable properties
B. Income generated by the property
C. Total debt service on the property
D. Accrued depreciation on the property

Question 16 - Mock Test 4

What is defined as the value of a property minus all liens against it?

A. Collateral
B. Equity
C. Actual Cash Value
D. Down Payment

Question 17 - Mock Test 4

From where are conventional loans typically sourced?

A. Private sources
B. Fannie Mae' funds
C. FHA funds
D. Home Owners Loan Corporation

Question 18 - Mock Test 4

Which statement about the Real Estate Settlement Procedures Act (RESPA) is incorrect?

A. Real estate brokers may not split a commission with cooperating MLS members
B. Anyone getting a federally regulated mortgage for a single-family home must receive the Home Loan Toolkit
C. A lender may not receive a referral fee for directing a seller to a specific title insurance company
D. RESPA applies to all sales of one-to-four family residences when obtaining a federally related mortgage

Question 19 - Mock Test 4

Which statement about obtaining a home loan is not true?

A. A promissory note acts as security for the loan

B. A promissory note is a written commitment to repay the loan

C. A promissory note is unnecessary if the borrower puts more than 30% down

D. A promissory note must accompany the mortgage for the loan to be funded

Question 20 - Mock Test 4

How is a trust deed officially removed from property records?

A. Recording a reconveyance deed

B. A title report

C. Payment in full

D. Recording the note

Question 21 - Mock Test 4

When altering a contract, what must be done for the changes to be valid?

A. Each party must initial the change in the margin

B. The party who did not make the changes becomes responsible for the deal

C. The document must be retyped

D. The whole contract becomes void

Question 22 - Mock Test 4

Which statement is true about the relationship between a promissory note and a deed of trust?

A. Promissory note isn't part of a deed of trust

B. A grant deed secures a promissory note

C. A deed of trust secures a promissory note

D. A promissory note secures a deed of trust

Question 23 - Mock Test 4

According to the statute of frauds, real estate contracts must be:

A. Drafted by a lawyer

B. On a government-approved form

C. In writing

D. A unilateral agreement

Question 24 - Mock Test 4

Which of the following is NOT necessarily a requirement for all contracts to be valid?

A. In writing

B. Capable parties

C. Mutual consent

D. None are correct

Question 25 - Mock Test 4

What is the status of a contract based on illegal consideration?

A. Valid

B. Voidable

C. Enforceable

D. Void

Question 26 - Mock Test 4

Beth, the salesperson, delivered her buyer's purchase offer to the listing agent, broker Smith. The buyer provided a $1,000.00 promissory note as the earnest money deposit. Broker Smith should do which of the following after receiving the offer?

A. Tell Beth the note is not sufficient without a deed

B. Tell Beth that a promissory note can be acceptable for the deposit and present the offer to his seller

C. Tell Beth that he cannot accept the offer without cash or a check for the deposit

D. Tell Beth he won't present the offer as written to the seller

Question 27 - Mock Test 4

Which circumstance does NOT make a contract voidable?

A. Duress

B. Illegal purpose

C. Fraud

D. Undue influence

Question 28 - Mock Test 4

What does it mean when a contract states that "time is of the essence"?

A. The contract must be delivered and presented as soon as possible

B. The contract must be delivered within twenty-four hours

C. The contract must be delivered within two business days

D. The contract must be delivered within forty-eight hours

Question 29 - Mock Test 4

A broker receives a full-price bid on a house he has listed in compliance with the listing agreement. Before he can deliver the offer, another broker comes in with a little better deal, but for $500 less. What should the listing broker do?

A. Tell the other broker the property has been sold

B. Present both offers at the same time

C. Refuse to accept the second offer

D. Wait until the seller makes a decision on the first offer before presenting the second

Question 30 - Mock Test 4

If a buyer defaults on a contract of sale and no liquidated damages are specified, what can the seller legally pursue?

A. Arrange for criminal proceedings against the buyer

B. Require the buyer to find a substitute purchaser

C. Sue the buyer for compensatory damages

D. Obtain a court order preventing the buyer from purchasing another property

Question 31 - Mock Test 4

What is the nature of ownership when four persons hold title to real property as tenants in common?

- A. They would be unable to determine which portion of the land is theirs
- B. They could not transfer their interest without the consent of the others
- C. They must each own a one-quarter interest
- D. They would have the right of survivorship

Question 32 - Mock Test 4

Which of the following is NOT included in the bundle of legal rights associated with property ownership?

- A. Right of control of the property
- B. Right of survivorship
- C. Right of enjoyment
- D. Right of exclusion

Question 33 - Mock Test 4

When a husband and wife own property as tenants in common, what characteristic does this form of ownership allow?

- A. Title in severalty
- B. The option of unequal shares of ownership
- C. Everything to be equal as per ownership of the property
- D. The right of survivorship

Question 34 - Mock Test 4

What legal power allows a city to acquire private property for public use if the owner refuses to sell?

- A. Descent and distribution
- B. Confiscation
- C. Eminent domain
- D. Escheat

Question 35 - Mock Test 4

Which of the following would be considered real property?

- A. Diamonds which have been mined
- B. Trade fixtures
- C. A cell phone
- D. Bearing wall

Question 36 - Mock Test 4

Which of the following is considered real property?

- A. Appurtenances, rights that belong to the land, and attached personal property
- B. Appurtenances, rights that belong to the land, and harvested crops
- C. Appurtenances, rights belonging to the land, and trade fixtures
- D. Appurtenances, rights that belong to the land, and all personal property

Question 37 - Mock Test 4

A woman transfers ownership of an office building to a nursing home. The nursing home agrees that the rental income will cover the cost of caring for the woman's parents. When the woman's parents die, she inherits ownership of the office building. The nursing home's estate is:

A. Legal life estate

B. Temporary leasehold estate

C. Remainder life estate

D. Life estate pur autre vie

Question 38 - Mock Test 4

An individual sold her house and relocated to a shared flat. Under the cooperative form of ownership, individuals will:

A. Not lose her apartment if she pays her share of the expenses

B. Receive a fixed-term lease for her unit

C. Have to take out a new mortgage loan on her unit

D. Become a shareholder in the corporation

Question 39 - Mock Test 4

How can each lot in a subdivision be legally described after a plat is filed?

A. Street address

B. Lot and block system

C. Government survey

D. Metes-and-bounds system

Question 40 - Mock Test 4

What is required of a landlord to obtain possession of a property after an estate for years expires according to the lease terms?

A. Must give the tenant 60 days' notice

B. Must give the tenant 15 days' notice

C. Must give the tenant 30 days' notice

D. Is not required to give the tenant any notice

Question 41 - Mock Test 4

For which type of property is the cost approach most suitable when conducting an appraisal?

A. Middle-aged property

B. Multi-family property

C. New property

D. Old property

Question 42 - Mock Test 4

Which principle is used to determine the value of property amenities like a swimming pool?

A. Progression

B. Conformity

C. Substitution

D. Contribution

Question 43 - Mock Test 4

When an appraiser correlates the three approaches to value into a final estimate, they:

A. Average the estimate

B. Reconcile the differences according to the type of property being appraised and the quantity and quality of data available

C. Accord the greatest weight to the median value

D. Select the estimate nearest that desired by the employer

Question 44 - Mock Test 4

How should an appraiser adjust the sales price of a foreclosed home when used as a comparable?

A. Make a negative adjustment to the value of the subject property

B. Make a positive adjustment to the value of the subject property

C. Make a positive adjustment to the sales price of the foreclosed home

D. Make a negative adjustment to the sales price of the foreclosed home

Question 45 - Mock Test 4

What factor most limits the effectiveness of the market data approach in appraising?

A. The financing terms of comparable property

B. Types of property that are regularly sold

C. The differences in the comparable property

D. Economic conditions that rapidly change

Question 46 - Mock Test 4

In the cost approach, what does an appraiser primarily use to estimate property value?

A. The owner's original cost of construction

B. An estimate of the building's replacement cost

C. The property's assessed value as used for tax purposes

D. Sales prices of similar properties

Question 47 - Mock Test 4

How is appreciation best defined?

A. Increase of value over time

B. Increase of money over time

C. Increase of land over time

D. Increase of wealth over time

Question 48 - Mock Test 4

What does the general term "value" signify?

A. The function of an object

B. The worth, usefulness, or utility of an object to someone for some purpose

C. The average use and function of an object to all people

D. A good buy

D. Certificate of title

Question 49 - Mock Test 4

What is the most challenging aspect of the market data method of appraising?

A. Establishing the unit of comparison
B. Collecting a sufficient volume of sales data
C. Adjusting for differences between the comparable and the subject property
D. Analyzing the volume of sales data

Question 50 - Mock Test 4

What does the capitalization rate represent under the income approach to real estate valuation?

A. Rate of return a property earns as an investment
B. Rate of capital required to keep a property operating most efficiently
C. Maximum rate of return allowed by law on an investment
D. Rate at which a property increases in value

Question 51 - Mock Test 4

What is the list of previous owners from whom the present real estate owner derives their title known as?

A. Chain of title
B. Title insurance policy
C. Abstract of title

Question 52 - Mock Test 4

When Robert refers to tax shelters in discussing properties, what is he primarily referring to?

A. Real property taxes
B. Income taxes
C. Interest income
D. Mortgage relief

Question 53 - Mock Test 4

A person offers to sell their property for $500,000. The buyer pays $150 for a six-month option. Which statement is correct?

A. The seller cannot accept money for the option
B. The buyer must have at least 20% down
C. The $150 is valuable consideration if the seller accepts it
D. The buyer must have at least 5% down as valuable consideration

Question 54 - Mock Test 4

What does it typically mean to rehabilitate real property?

A. The property must be replaced to obtain its highest and best use potential
B. Design changes must be made to the property
C. The use of the property will be changed
D. The property will be restored to a good condition

Question 55 - Mock Test 4

Sam possessed a triplex worth $150,000, with an adjusted basis of $70,000. King possessed a duplex worth $145,000. Both properties were held free and clear. They exchanged properties, with King handing Sam $5,000 in cash. For federal income tax purposes:

A. King has a taxable gain
B. Neither has a taxable gain
C. Sam has a recognized gain
D. Both will be taxed on the difference between the value and the basis

Question 56 - Mock Test 4

What is required if personal property is used as consideration in the purchase of real property?

A. Bill of sale
B. A current appraisal of the personal property
C. Writ of Attachment
D. Title insurance

Question 57 - Mock Test 4

What is an order from a court to sell property to pay a judgment called?

A. A writ of execution
B. A deficiency judgment
C. An attachment
D. A foreclosure

Question 58 - Mock Test 4

What is a lis pendens?

A. May affect title to real property based on the results of the lawsuit
B. Can be recorded no matter what the type of lawsuit is
C. Only affects title to real property if the owner is not a party to the lawsuit
D. Can only be removed from the public records by a court order

Question 59 - Mock Test 4

Who signs a deed to convey property?

A. A notary public only
B. Any authorized public officer
C. The grantor
D. The grantee

Question 60 - Mock Test 4

What is the primary purpose of a deed?

A. Give constructive notice
B. Transfer title rights
C. Prove ownership
D. Prevent adverse possession

Question 61 - Mock Test 4

A strength of the income capitalization approach is that it:

A. Applies a universally required rate of return for all buyers in the market

B. Provides a precise forecast of potential investment returns

C. Is a method used by investors to decide the purchase price for a property

D. Is suitable for any property type across all markets

Question 62 - Mock Test 4

Using the income capitalization approach, if a property generates an estimated annual gross income of $60,000, with $3,000 in losses and $20,000 in operating expenses, and the capitalization rate is 10%, what is the indicated value?

A. $370,000

B. $400,000

C. $570,000

D. $600,000

Question 63 - Mock Test 4

An apartment building sold for $450,000 with monthly gross rents of $3,000. What is its monthly gross rent multiplier?

A. 12.5

B. 0.01

C. 0.08

D. 150

Question 64 - Mock Test 4

A rental house earns $2,400 per month. With a market-derived gross income multiplier of 14.1, what is the indicated sale price?

A. $338,000

B. $204,000

C. $406,000

D. $346,000

Question 65 - Mock Test 4

A certified appraiser is officially recognized by:

A. A recognized real estate school

B. The Appraisal Institute

C. The state where they operate

D. The Appraisal Review Board

Question 66 - Mock Test 4

Which act mandates that federally-related appraisals be conducted by certified appraisers?

A. The Financial Institutions Reform, Recovery and Enforcement Act (FIRREA)

B. The Uniform Standards of Professional Appraisal Practice Act (USPAPA)

C. The Appraisal Foundation Authorization and Reform Act (AFAR)

D. The Federal Institution for Regulation and Enforcement of Appraisal Act (FIREAA)

Question 67 - Mock Test 4

The principle of substitution in real estate valuation states that:

A. A buyer will opt for the less expensive of two comparable properties

B. If one home is pricier, the value of a neighboring home will likely increase

C. If a market is oversaturated with properties, prices will generally decrease

D. A buyer will switch homes if the alternate offers equal value

Question 68 - Mock Test 4

The highest and best use of a property is defined as the use that is:

A. Physically possible, financially viable, legally permissible, and yields the highest productivity

B. Legal, feasible, and deemed most appropriate by zoning authorities

C. Includes the largest possible building allowed under zoning laws

D. Matches the usage patterns of surrounding properties

Question 69 - Mock Test 4

Lynne bought a house for $375,000, which was less than the asking price of $390,000. Another party offered $370,000, which was rejected. After purchasing, she receives an offer of $380,000, and an appraiser values the house at $400,000. What is the market value?

A. $375,000

B. $380,000

C. $390,000

D. $400,000

Question 70 - Mock Test 4

A notable limitation of the sales comparison approach is that:

A. The market might lack current sales data

B. It does not adhere to the principle of substitution

C. It is only accurate for unique or special-purpose properties

D. Comparisons are challenging as each property is unique

Question 71 - Mock Test 4

A tenant complained to HUD about his landlord's discriminatory actions in his or her building. A week later, the landlord issued the tenant an eviction notice. Which of the following situations would violate the Federal Fair Housing Act?

A. When the tenant is two months behind in his/her rent

B. When the tenant has damaged the premises

C. When the tenant is conducting an illegal use on the premises

D. When the landlord evicts the tenant for reporting him to HUD

Question 72 - Mock Test 4

A broker prepared an offer for a buyer that included a 10-day acceptance clause and a $2,000 deposit. On the fifth day, the buyer contacted the broker that he wished to withdraw the contract and receive his deposit check of $2000. Which of the following assertions is accurate regarding the situation?

A. The buyer must wait until the seller acknowledges the offer, then the buyer can terminate the offer with a counteroffer

B. The buyer must wait until the preliminary title report has been delivered, then terminate the offer and ask for the $2000 deposit to be returned

C. The buyer must wait until the 10-day acceptance clause has ended before revoking the offer

D. The buyer can revoke the offer immediately, provided the seller has not responded to the buyer's offer

Question 73 - Mock Test 4

Under the Federal Truth-in-Lending Act, which two critical facts must be disclosed to borrowers?

A. The duration of the contract and discount rate

B. The carrying charge and advertising expense

C. The finance charge and annual percentage rate

D. The installment payments and cancellation rights

Question 74 - Mock Test 4

Which form of listing agreement provides the most benefit and protection to a broker?

A. Exclusive agency listing

B. Exclusive right to sell listing

C. Open listing

D. Multiple listing

Question 75 - Mock Test 4

Which of the following is a violation of fair housing laws?

A. The landlord requires every tenant have a good credit rating and a steady source of income

B. A landlord that requires all tenants pay first, and last month's rent in advance

C. The landlord requires all tenants to furnish references from their previous landlords

D. The landlord requires a co-signer exclusively for tenants who are single

Question 76 - Mock Test 4

What violation is a real estate salesperson guilty of when telling homeowners to sell because minorities are moving into the neighborhood?

A. Redlining

B. Steering

C. Panic peddling and/or Blockbusting

D. ADA "reasonable accommodations" law

Question 77 - Mock Test 4

What is the right called that allows a mortgagor to regain the property by paying the debt after a foreclosure sale in most states?

A. Vendee's right of redemption

B. Equitable right of redemption

C. Statutory right of redemption

D. Owner's right of redemption

Question 78 - Mock Test 4

What can a buyer's earnest money deposit be?

A. A dated check

B. A promissory note

C. Anything of value

D. Paid by credit card

Question 79 - Mock Test 4

What can Ms. Lee legally do when asked to specify her marital status and ethnic background on a loan application?

A. Not decline to answer those questions if she wants the loan

B. Sue the lender and the real estate broker for discrimination

C. Be denied the loan if she refuses to answer those questions

D. Refuse to fill out that portion of the loan application

Question 80 - Mock Test 4

Which act requires that "reasonable accommodation" be made in public accommodations?

A. Fair Housing Act

B. Equal Opportunity Act

C. Americans with Disabilities Act

D. Civil Rights Act

Question 81 - Mock Test 4

What type of agent is a real estate broker representing a seller usually considered?

A. A special agent

B. A general agent

C. An ostensible agent

D. A factor agent

Question 82 - Mock Test 4

What has a broker breached if negligent in preparing a sales contract, allowing the purchaser to void the agreement?

A. Personal performance

B. Honesty

C. Due care

D. Accuracy

Question 83 - Mock Test 4

What is the name of the clause in an agency agreement that binds the buyer to pay the broker's fee if the buyer purchases a property shown during the agency period?

A. Automatic extension clause

B. Buyer liability clause

C. Limited coverage clause

D. Broker protection clause

Question 84 - Mock Test 4

If Arthur, a licensed principal real estate broker, is sued for conversion, what is he alleged to have done?

A. Commingled the client's trust account funds with his own

B. Misappropriated his client's funds

C. Failed to reconcile his clients' trust account in a timely manner

D. Failed to maintain a positive balance in his clients' trust account

Question 85 - Mock Test 4

What happens if the owner sells the property themselves under an exclusive agency listing?

A. The broker is entitled to 25 percent commission

B. The broker is entitled to 50 percent of his commission

C. No commission is owed

D. The broker is entitled to full commission

Question 86 - Mock Test 4

What is CORRECT about the law of agency?

A. It establishes a fiduciary relationship

B. It refers specifically to insurance

C. There is no employment relationship

D. It does not require a high degree of loyalty and fidelity from an agent

Question 87 - Mock Test 4

Which of the following is a requirement for a valid agency relationship?

A. Written agreement

B. Compensation

C. Mutual consent

D. Brokerage license

Question 88 - Mock Test 4

What is true for both the lessee of an apartment and the owner of a condominium?

A. They each hold a fee interest

B. They each hold an estate in real property

C. They each hold an estate of inheritance

D. They each hold a less than freehold estate

Question 89 - Mock Test 4

What is the status of a contract signed under duress?

A. Unenforceable

B. Voidable

C. Void

D. Illegal

Question 90 - Mock Test 4

Who is considered a "client" in a real estate transaction?

A. Any person who signs an agreement for the sale or purchase of a property with a licensee

B. Any person who expresses interest in working with an individual firm or licensee

C. Any person who views property in the company of a licensed salesperson or broker

D. Any person who phones or visits a company seeking more information about specific properties

Question 91 - Mock Test 4

Investor Linda paid $90,000 for a lot and $540,000 to have an apartment building constructed on it. She has depreciated the property for the past 10 years on a 39-year straight-line schedule. If she sells the property this year and realizes $750,000, what is her capital gain?

A. $258,462

B. $274,000

C. $250,000

D. $179,000

Question 92 - Mock Test 4

Homeowner Karen bought a house five years ago for $300,000. Since then, Karen has spent $3,000 to build a screened porch and has added a central air-conditioning system at a cost of $7,500. What is Karen's adjusted basis if the house is sold today?

A. $310,000

B. $310,500

C. $305,000

D. $312,500

Question 93 - Mock Test 4

Homeowner Linda sold her house and had net proceeds of $300,000. Her adjusted basis in the home was $250,000. She immediately bought another house for $350,000. What was her capital gain?

A. $300,000

B. $50,000

C. $60,000

D. None

Question 94 - Mock Test 4

Homeowner Sarah purchased a house for $400,000, making a $80,000 down payment and securing a mortgage loan of $320,000. Two years later, she installed a new deck at a cost of $20,000. What is Sarah's adjusted basis in the house if she decides to sell it today?

A. $400,000

B. $340,000

C. $420,000

D. $360,000

Question 95 - Mock Test 4

Investor Emma desires a 10% return on investment from any real estate investment. A property priced at $500,000 has gross income of $80,000 and expenses of $25,000. Approximately how much too high or too low is the price of this property for the investor to obtain her desired return exactly?

A. $2,000 overpriced

B. $8,000 underpriced

C. $10,000 overpriced

D. $12,000 underpriced

Question 96 - Mock Test 4

Investor Mark sees a listing of an office building priced at $3,000,000. He loves the property, but he knows he needs to make a return of at least 9% to satisfy his partners. If the building is 30,000 SF, rents for $12.75/SF per year, has 5%

vacancy, and annual expenses of $80,000, should he buy it? What is his return?

A. No, since he will yield 7.50%

B. Yes, since he will yield 9.375%

C. Yes, since he will yield 9%

D. Yes, since he will yield 10.00%

Question 97 - Mock Test 4

Homeowner Jessica sold her house and had net proceeds of $500,000. Her adjusted basis in the home was $430,000. She immediately bought another house for $480,000. What was her capital gain?

A. $60,000

B. $70,000

C. $80,000

D. None

Question 98 - Mock Test 4

Investor Lily owns a small commercial property that has a net income of $140,000, interest payments of $100,000, principal payments of $25,000, and annual cost recovery of $2,000. The property's tax rate is 28%. What is the property's annual tax on income?

A. $10,640

B. $14,000

C. $8,400

D. $12,600

Question 99 - Mock Test 4

Investor Sam purchased 5 oversized lots for $800,000 to subdivide. After subdividing, he sold each lot for $250,000. Excluding commissions and closing costs, what percent profit did the investor realize?

A. 0%

B. 45%

C. 23.90%

D. 56.25%

Question 100 - Mock Test 4

The Greenwood County has a tax rate of 15 mills. The county's required revenue from taxes is $12,000,000. What is the tax base of the area?

A. $12,000,000

B. $80,000,000

C. $800,000,000

D. $120,000,000,000

Mock Test 5

A. Grantus

B. Grantor

C. Gratie

D. Grantee

Question 1 - Mock Test 5

What type of lease bases the rental fee on a portion of the tenant's business income?

A. Sandwich Lease

B. Percentage Lease

C. Net Lease

D. Gross Lease

Question 5 - Mock Test 5

What term describes the legal situation where a person passes away without a valid will?

A. Testate

B. Intestate

C. A Writ of Execution

D. Injunction

Question 2 - Mock Test 5

What term is used for crops that are produced annually for sale, grown by a tenant on leased land?

A. Adobes

B. Easements

C. Emblements

D. Appurtenance

Question 6 - Mock Test 5

What is the process called where property value is estimated for taxation purposes?

A. Hypothecation

B. Novation

C. Assessment

D. Appraisal

Question 3 - Mock Test 5

Which document is typically used to evidence a financial obligation or debt?

A. Title

B. Mortgages

C. Promissory Notes

D. Deeds

Question 7 - Mock Test 5

What is the term for a transaction that allows property owners to delay taxes on gains by reinvesting in similar property?

A. A Writ of Execution

B. Tax Deferred Exchange

C. Sheltering Cost

D. Quiet Title Action

Question 4 - Mock Test 5

Who is the person that transfers property or property rights?

Question 8 - Mock Test 5

What power allows governments at all levels to regulate property use for urban planning?

A. Eminent Domain

B. Taxation

C. Escheat

D. Police Power

Question 9 - Mock Test 5

Which form of property ownership requires unity of time, title, interest, and possession?

A. Tenancy in Common

B. Joint Tenancy

C. Ownership in Severalty

D. Dual Estate

Question 10 - Mock Test 5

What clause in a mortgage allows the borrower to secure additional financing using the same property as collateral?

A. Subordination Clause

B. Release Clause

C. Open-End Clause

D. Pre-Payment Penalty Clause

Question 11 - Mock Test 5

What does "quiet enjoyment and possession" refer to in property terms?

A. Possession without disturbance from owner of paramount title

B. The right to demand silence from neighbors

C. Freedom from all encumbrances

D. Nuisance created by adjacent landowners

Question 12 - Mock Test 5

Which entity does not originate primary loans directly?

A. Savings and Loans

B. Commercial Banks

C. FHA

D. Credit Unions

Question 13 - Mock Test 5

What is a promissory note in the context of a real estate loan?

A. A document unrelated to real estate loans

B. A commitment to perform or refrain from certain acts

C. A guarantee by a government agency

D. The primary evidence of a debt obligation

Question 14 - Mock Test 5

What term describes the valuation assigned to property by a tax assessor for tax purposes?

A. Estimated Value

B. Assessed Value

C. Actual Value

D. Appraised Value

Question 15 - Mock Test 5

What term describes the process where a mortgage company assembles multiple loans to sell to permanent investors?

A. Discounting
B. Blanket Financing
C. Package Financing
D. Warehousing

Question 16 - Mock Test 5

What is the most crucial requirement for a property to qualify for a tax-free exchange?

A. Equal Equities
B. Equal Value
C. Like Kind
D. Residential

Question 17 - Mock Test 5

Which clause in a loan agreement results in periodic increases in payments?

A. Alienation Clause
B. Acceleration Clause
C. Interest Clause
D. Escalation Clause

Question 18 - Mock Test 5

What does RESPA specifically prohibit among the following practices?

A. Blockbusting
B. Steering
C. Paying of Kickbacks
D. Redlining

Question 19 - Mock Test 5

Who primarily enacts laws regulating the maximum interest rates that can be charged on loans?

A. The World Trade Organization
B. The Treasury Department
C. Individual States
D. Congress

Question 20 - Mock Test 5

What is the implication of a lower loan-to-value ratio for a lender?

A. Higher loan amount
B. Greater equity
C. Increased likelihood of default
D. Higher appraised value

Question 21 - Mock Test 5

What type of contract is considered fully performed by all parties involved?

A. Expired contract
B. Executory contract
C. Contingent contract
D. Executed contract

Question 22 - Mock Test 5

Which of the following is NOT typically included in an advance fee contract for real estate or business listings?

A. The date the fee is to be paid

B. A guarantee that the sale, lease, or exchange will be completed

C. The total amount of the advance fee to be charged

D. A detailed description of the services to be performed

Question 23 - Mock Test 5

Which description best defines an "executed contract" in legal terms?

A. A contract in which all parties have fulfilled their promises and performed the contract

B. A contract that is dead in the water

C. A contract that has been terminated by both the listing agent and the homeowner

D. A contract terminated by either party

Question 24 - Mock Test 5

According to the Statute of Frauds, which of the following contracts must be in writing to be enforceable?

A. The employment of a broker to exchange leases on property zoned for retail

B. Any real estate agreement not to be performed within one year

C. A bill of sale on real property

D. The employment of a business opportunity to sell stock

Question 25 - Mock Test 5

When interpreting real estate contracts with pre-printed and written information, which is given precedence?

A. The written parts take precedence over the pre-printed parts

B. The written parts and the pre-printed parts are given equal consideration

C. No changes or amendments to the pre-printed clauses are permitted by law

D. Pre-printed parts take precedence over the written parts

Question 26 - Mock Test 5

If you unknowingly enter into a contract with someone who was judicially declared incompetent, the contract is:

A. Void

B. Enforceable

C. Valid

D. Voidable

Question 27 - Mock Test 5

How is the duration of a listing agreement determined?

A. Whatever is negotiated between the broker and seller

B. Whatever is negotiated between the seller and the buyer

C. 6 months

D. 90 days

Question 28 - Mock Test 5

In a real estate transaction, if a buyer fails to perform, what may the seller retain as specified in the contract?

A. Liquidated damages

B. Compensatory losses

C. An escrow bonus

D. Due compensation

Question 29 - Mock Test 5

Which statement is true about an option contract in real estate?

A. Title acquired by exercising an option usually dates back to the time of the option and cuts off intervening rights acquired with knowledge of the existence of the option

B. The optionee has no interest or estate in the land

C. Only the optionor is bound to a sale

D. All of the other answers are correct

Question 30 - Mock Test 5

What type of lease involves the tenant paying a fixed rent plus all property expenses such as taxes and insurance?

A. Percentage lease

B. Graduated lease

C. Gross lease

D. Net lease

Question 31 - Mock Test 5

A grandfather grants his grandson a life estate and states that upon his death, the title to the land shall transfer to his son-in-law. What is this second estate called?

A. A reversion

B. An estate for years

C. A remainder

D. An estate at sufferance

Question 32 - Mock Test 5

How was property owned between two women if, upon the death of one, the surviving owner now shares the property with the deceased's heirs?

A. As tenants in common

B. As shareholders in their own corporation

C. As joint tenants

D. By entirety

Question 33 - Mock Test 5

What state right protects a homeowner from certain creditor judgments?

A. Prior appropriation rights

B. Homestead rights

C. Littoral rights

D. Fee simple rights

Question 34 - Mock Test 5

What defines a tenancy for years regarding its termination?

A. A 30-day notice is required to terminate the lease

B. The lessee has a freehold estate

C. The term of the lease must be for at least one year

D. The lease will terminate automatically if not renewed

Question 35 - Mock Test 5

Which instrument typically transfers possession but not ownership of real property?

A. An easement

B. A sublease

C. A mortgage

D. A security agreement

Question 36 - Mock Test 5

What legal issue does a fence that extends over a property line without permission create?

A. License

B. Easement by necessity

C. Easement by prescription

D. Encroachment

Question 37 - Mock Test 5

How many acres is a square that measures 1/8 of a mile by 1/8 of a mile?

A. 20 acres

B. 40 acres

C. 10 acres

D. 160 acres

Question 38 - Mock Test 5

Which of these options is a type of leasehold estate?

A. An estate at sufferance

B. A life estate

C. A property lien

D. An estate for years

Question 39 - Mock Test 5

What does the "bundle of rights" refer to in real estate?

A. That is synonymous with the Bill of Rights

B. Guaranteed to citizens by the Statute of Rights

C. Enjoyed by the owner of a property

D. Specified in a deed or land contract

Question 40 - Mock Test 5

To determine if a location can be used as a retail store in the future, which documents should be examined?

A. Zoning ordinances or regulations
B. Building code
C. List of permitted nonconforming uses
D. Housing code

Question 41 - Mock Test 5

What does an appraiser consider when determining the value of a single-family home?

A. Properties located within a 10-mile radius
B. Racial demographics
C. Pending property sales
D. Date sold

Question 42 - Mock Test 5

What is typically not included in an appraiser's narrative appraisal report of a single-family residence?

A. The appraiser's qualifications
B. A buyer's financing
C. The neighborhood amenities
D. A special studies zone map

Question 43 - Mock Test 5

What should be included when land is surveyed?

A. The area contained within the described boundaries expressed in accepted units of measure
B. The corners of the property
C. All of the items listed in the other answers
D. A specific length and direction of the sides of the property

Question 44 - Mock Test 5

Which of the following is NOT included when computing the square footage of a single-family home's gross living area?

A. A laundry room
B. A finished basement
C. An extra bedroom
D. A porch

Question 45 - Mock Test 5

Which scenario would be classified as external depreciation?

A. Convenient access to schools and recreational facilities
B. A leaking roof that needs to be completely replaced
C. A poorly designed floor plan that could be modified
D. Poorly maintained properties in the neighborhood

Question 46 - Mock Test 5

The market value of a parcel of real estate is defined as what?

A. Its value without improvements

B. The most probable price it should bring

C. The amount of money paid for the property

D. An estimate of its future benefits

Question 47 - Mock Test 5

A buyer bought two parcels of land. One piece was a square mile, while the other was 10 acres. If the land cost $2,500 per acre, how much did the land cost?

A. $1,625,000

B. $1,600,000

C. $1,526,000

D. $1,425,000

Question 48 - Mock Test 5

Which type of depreciation is the most difficult to cure?

A. Economic Obsolescence

B. Functional Obsolescence

C. Residential Deterioration

D. Physical Deterioration

Question 49 - Mock Test 5

How would a home with its kitchen next to the master bedroom be considered?

A. Functionally obsolete

B. Economically obsolete

C. Physically obsolete

D. Diminished

Question 50 - Mock Test 5

Which appraisal approach is most commonly used by real estate licensees?

A. Income

B. Cost replacement

C. Residential

D. Market Data

Question 51 - Mock Test 5

What primarily determines the cost of title insurance?

A. The value of a property

B. Statutes of descent and distribution

C. The age of a property

D. Any number of covenants in the warranty deed

Question 52 - Mock Test 5

Which of the following deeds would least likely contain implied covenants by the grantor?

A. Warranty deed

B. Quitclaim deed

C. Grant deed

D. Gift deed

Question 53 - Mock Test 5

How does the IRS define marginal tax rate?

A. The tax rate used for your state income taxes

B. None of the other options are correct

C. The difference between the present tax rate and the past tax rate

D. The tax rate which is used for the next dollar of taxable income

Question 54 - Mock Test 5

What happens in a 1031 Exchange when 'boot' is involved?

A. When taxable income is more than the true value of the property

B. When straight line depreciation is used for an income property

C. When there is a difference between the equity of properties being exchanged

D. When depreciating an income property for tax purposes

Question 55 - Mock Test 5

In a settlement statement, how are prorated prepaid utility charges typically reflected?

A. As a credit to the seller only

B. As a debit to the seller and a credit to the buyer

C. As a debit to the buyer only

D. As a debit to the buyer and a credit to the seller

Question 56 - Mock Test 5

Individuals typically DO NOT have which of the following real property ownership rights?

A. Severance rights

B. Riparian rights

C. Eminent domain rights

D. Reliction rights

Question 57 - Mock Test 5

What do easements and liens have in common?

A. Neither can be done without the consent of the owner

B. Both must be on public record to be valid

C. Both are encumbrances

D. Both are money claims against the property

Question 58 - Mock Test 5

Which of the following is an example of "boot," according to income tax?

A. An increase in deductible depreciation

B. Debt relief from a mortgage in a 1031 exchange

C. A decrease in basis

D. A decrease in real estate property taxes

Question 59 - Mock Test 5

Joe transfers property to Vivian by providing a deed. The deed has six covenants. This is most likely a:

A. Warranty deed

B. Grant deed

C. Deed in trust

D. Quitclaim deed

Question 60 - Mock Test 5

Which among the following is an example of involuntary alienation of property?

A. Quitclaim

B. Inheritance

C. Condemnation

D. Gifting

Question 61 - Mock Test 5

In the market data approach, an appraiser usually:

A. Selects nearby properties, makes adjustments for differences, and estimates the property's value

B. Collects relevant pricing data, applies this data to the subject property, and calculates its value

C. Chooses similar properties, adjusts for differences, and computes the estimated value

D. Notes the historical purchase price, applies an appreciation rate, and computes the estimated value

Question 62 - Mock Test 5

In the sales comparison approach, an adjustment is necessary when:

A. The property is purchased with standard financing

B. The seller provides financing below market rates

C. A comparable property is in a different but similar neighborhood

D. The properties differ in roof style, such as one having a hip roof and the other a gabled roof

Question 63 - Mock Test 5

To finalize the sales comparison approach, the appraiser should:

A. Average the values of the comparables

B. Assign weights to the values of the comparables

C. Determine the subject's value based on the median value of the comparables

D. Align the subject's value with the closest comparable's value

Question 64 - Mock Test 5

A limitation of the cost approach in appraising market value is that:

A. Contractors may not pay market rates for materials or labor
B. The market value may differ from the actual construction cost
C. Comparables might not match in construction quality
D. New constructions have unpredictable costs and depreciation rates

Question 65 - Mock Test 5

The cost to construct a functional equivalent of a property is called the:

A. Reproduction cost
B. Replacement cost
C. Restitution cost
D. Reconstruction cost

Question 66 - Mock Test 5

An office building without modern fiber optic cabling exhibits:

A. Physical deterioration
B. Economic obsolescence
C. Incurable depreciation
D. Functional obsolescence

Question 67 - Mock Test 5

A home in a poorly maintained neighborhood exemplifies:

A. Curable external obsolescence
B. Incurable economic obsolescence
C. Functional obsolescence
D. Physical deterioration

Question 68 - Mock Test 5

In appraisal, the general loss of property value from any source is termed:

A. Deterioration
B. Obsolescence
C. Depreciation
D. Deflation

Question 69 - Mock Test 5

In the cost approach, after evaluating the value of the land and the cost of renovations, the appraiser:

A. Calculates and subtracts depreciation from the cost, then adds the land value
B. Deducts physical deterioration from the cost, evaluates land depreciation, and sums these values
C. Assesses total depreciation of the land and improvements, then subtracts from the initial cost
D. Determines obsolescence and subtracts it from the combined cost of land and improvements

NATIONAL REAL ESTATE LICENSE EXAM PREP

Question 70 - Mock Test 5

Which entity or code sets standards for an appraiser's practices, including methods, reporting, and disclosures?

A. Financial Institutions Reform, Recovery, and Enforcement Act (FIRREA)

B. Uniform Standards of Professional Appraisal Practice (USPAP)

C. National Association of Realtors®' Code of Ethics

D. Federal Appraisal Regulation and Licensing Board

Question 71 - Mock Test 5

A prospective minority buyer requests to be shown properties but does not indicate whether he wishes to live in a community with other minorities or not. How should a licensee determine which properties to show him?

A. The licensee does not need to provide service for the prospect at all

B. The licensee has no obligation to show homes in non-minority neighborhoods to the prospect

C. The licensee could assume that the prospective buyer is not interested in such homes

D. The licensee may select homes for showing as he would for any other prospect

Question 72 - Mock Test 5

The Civil Rights Act of 1866 prohibits discrimination in real estate based on what factor?

A. Handicap and country of origin

B. Gender and religion

C. Race

D. Race and gender

Question 73 - Mock Test 5

The personal, revocable, and unassignable permission of authority to perform one or more acts on the territory of another without owning any stake therein is defined as:

A. A license

B. An option

C. An easement

D. An encroachment

Question 74 - Mock Test 5

What is steering in the context of real estate?

A. The practice of guiding a prospective home buyer to look at homes within his or her price range

B. Channeling of prospective homebuyers to or away from particular neighborhoods, thereby limiting their choices

C. All of the other options are correct

D. The practice of driving prospective home buyers to see homes for sale

Question 75 - Mock Test 5

What is the main purpose of RESPA (Real Estate Settlement Procedures Act)?

A. Place a fixed limit on settlement costs in all real estate transactions

B. Place a fixed limit on settlement costs on residential property of four units or less

C. Provide consumers with enough information to enable them to shop for settlement services

D. Standardize settlement services throughout the United States

Question 76 - Mock Test 5

Repairing or remodeling a property often increases its value. In recognition of the role contractors and suppliers play in boosting the value of a property, many states guarantee payment for their goods and services by allowing them to file a:

A. Complaint with the federal government

B. Declaratory judgment against the owner

C. Mechanic's lien against the property

D. Lis pendens against the owner

Question 77 - Mock Test 5

How does the sale of a leased property affect the tenant?

A. The tenant is protected by the lease, so the new owner must honor the current terms and conditions of the lease

B. The tenant must move or renegotiate his lease within 30 days

C. That tenant is protected only if the lease has been recorded in the recorder's office

D. The tenant must be sure to obtain the return of his security deposit from the seller

Question 78 - Mock Test 5

A broker having a valid listing on a property posts a classified ad with only the following information: "For Sale - 3 bedroom, 3 bath home with swimming pool." Asking price: $175,000. Call 555-8298". This sort of advertisement is an example of:

A. Silent ad

B. Display ad

C. Qualified ad

D. Blind ad

Question 79 - Mock Test 5

Under what condition can a real estate licensee lawfully refuse to show a home to a minority prospect?

A. When the licensee sincerely believes that showing the property to minorities would cause panic in the neighborhood

B. When the owner is exempt under the 1968 Fair Housing law and has stated that his single-family home is not available to minority persons

C. When the owner is out of town and has instructed the licensee that no showing may be made in his absence

D. The agent may not refuse to show any home to a minority person at any time

Question 80 - Mock Test 5

Which act requires that public accommodations be accessible to all people?

A. The Americans with Disabilities Act

B. The Federal Depositors Insurance Act

C. The Fair Housing Accommodations Act

D. The Labor Standards Act

Question 81 - Mock Test 5

To whom are fiduciary duties owed in a real estate transaction?

A. Broker

B. Principal

C. Agent

D. Customer

Question 82 - Mock Test 5

What type of listing agreement allows the owner to have an exclusive agent while retaining the right to sell the property themselves without owing a commission?

A. Multiple listing

B. Open listing

C. Exclusive right to sell

D. Exclusive agency

Question 83 - Mock Test 5

Ivonne represents the Sparks, who are selling their property. Which of the following activities must Ivonne take when prospective buyers request to inspect the property?

A. Inform them that she represents the seller's interests

B. Inform them, either orally or in writing, that she represents a certain brokerage

C. She may show them the property without any required disclosures or agreements

D. Inform them that they must complete a buyer representation agreement

Question 84 - Mock Test 5

What is required before placing a "For Sale" sign on a listed property?

A. All of the other options are correct

B. Get the neighbor's permission

C. List the property

D. Obtain the property owner's consent

Question 85 - Mock Test 5

Under what circumstances is it acceptable for a broker to collect a commission from both the buyer and the seller?

A. Only with approval from the state licensing authorities

B. If both parties give informed consent

C. If doing so does not violate company policy

D. Under no circumstances

Question 86 - Mock Test 5

A seller lists her home with a broker for $90,000, and the broker advises a potential buyer to make a low offer because the seller is desperate to sell. The buyer offers $85,000, which the seller accepts. In this scenario:

A. Any broker is authorized to encourage such bids for the property

B. The broker was unethical, but the seller did get to sell her property

C. The broker has violated his agency relationship with the seller

D. The broker acted properly to obtain a quick offer on the property

Question 87 - Mock Test 5

What type of fraud occurs when an agent makes unrealistic promises without intent to fulfill them?

A. Constructive fraud

B. Illusory fraud

C. Deliberate fraud

D. Actual fraud

Question 88 - Mock Test 5

What is the relationship between two brokers from different firms, one representing a seller and the other a buyer?

A. Dual agency

B. Customer

C. Agency relationship

D. There is no relationship; each represents different clients separately

Question 89 - Mock Test 5

Which type of lease involves the lessee paying a flat rent, while the lessor covers other expenses?

A. Percentage lease

B. Sandwich lease

C. Net lease

D. Gross lease

Question 90 - Mock Test 5

What characterizes a listing that does not obligate a broker to diligently seek a purchaser?

    A. Void
    B. Not an exclusive listing
    C. A bilateral contract
    D. Illegal

Question 91 - Mock Test 5

Homeowner Emily has a residence with an assessed valuation of $300,000, and a market value of $380,000. The homestead exemption is $50,000. Tax rates for the property are 6 mills for schools; 2 mills for the city; 2 mills for the county; and 1 mill for the local community college. What is Emily's tax bill?

    A. $2,750
    B. $3,500
    C. $1,650
    D. $4,420

Question 92 - Mock Test 5

The town of Lakeview has an annual budget requirement of $9,000,000 to be funded by property taxes. Assessed valuations are $450,000,000, and exemptions total $30,000,000. What must the tax rate be to finance the budget?

    A. 2.00%
    B. 2.14%
    C. 1.50%
    D. 2.25%

Question 93 - Mock Test 5

A property has sold for $750,000. The listing agreement calls for a commission of 6%. The listing broker and selling broker agree to share the commission equally. What will the listing agent receive if the agent is scheduled to get a 35% share from his broker?

    A. $15,750
    B. $12,600
    C. $7,875
    D. $18,900

Question 94 - Mock Test 5

Agent Lily, who works for selling broker Max, sells a house listed by listing broker Johnson. The house sells for $500,000. The co-brokerage split between Max and Johnson is 50-50. Lily is on a 65% commission schedule with Max. If the total commission rate is 6%, what is Lily's commission?

    A. $9,750
    B. $10,500
    C. $8,400
    D. $7,800

Question 95 - Mock Test 5

A sale transaction closes on June 15, the 166th day of the tax year. The day of closing belongs to the seller. Real estate taxes for the year, not yet billed, are expected to be $4,200. According to the 365-day method, what should appear on the closing statement?

A. A debit to the buyer and credit to the seller for $1,912.88

B. A debit to the buyer and credit to the seller for $900.00

C. A credit to the buyer and debit to the seller for $1,912.88

D. A credit to the buyer and debit to the seller for $900.00

Question 96 - Mock Test 5

Homebuyer Megan is purchasing Liam's house. The closing date (day belongs to seller) of the sale transaction is November 1 (day 305 of the year). Her loan has a monthly payment of $600, with $525 going to interest in the first month. At closing, Megan must pre-pay interest for the period of Nov. 2-Nov. 30. Use the 365-day method for prorating. What is her prepaid interest amount?

A. $507.50

B. $525.00

C. $543.10

D. $558.58

Question 97 - Mock Test 5

Homeowner Chad is selling a rental property. The sale transaction closes on December 16 (day 350 of the year). The landlord received the December rent of $1,380 on December 1. Assuming the closing day is the buyer's, and that the 365-day method is used for prorating, which of the following entries would appear on the settlement statement?

A. Debit seller $667.74

B. Credit seller $1,380.00

C. Debit buyer $712.26

D. Credit buyer $712.26

Question 98 - Mock Test 5

A property has sold for $322,600 in Primm County. Here, transfer taxes are set at $1.00 per $500 of the sale price. Title insurance runs $450, and the attorney costs $550. The agent's commission is 7%, and the mortgage balance is $210,000. Annual real estate taxes are estimated to be $4,000, half of which will have to be charged to the seller. If the seller pays all of these expenses, what will she net at closing?

A. $86,873

B. $88,371

C. $81,372

D. $86,372

Question 99 - Mock Test 5

A farmer wants to net at least $5,000/acre on the sale of his 300-acre property. If he allows for 10% commissions and closing costs, and to allow for negotiating room, he wants to get 95% of the listing price as the selling price. What should his listing price be per acre?

A. $5,750

B. $5,882

C. $4,250

D. $5,848

Question 100 - Mock Test 5

The Wildes have purchased a $740,000 home. The land is worth 25%, and they insure the improvements at 75% of their replacement value. If the Wildes suffer damage estimated at $500,000, and they have an 80% co-insurance clause, what will their recovery be from the policy?

A. Zero

B. $531,915

C. $500,000

D. $468,750

Answer Sheet

Mock Test 1

Question 1 - Mock Test 1

(D) Blind Ad. This type of advertisement, often illegal in many states for real estate brokers, omits the identity of the advertising party.

Question 2 - Mock Test 1

(A) Involuntary lien. This lien allows entities to claim a property due to unpaid debts without the owner's consent.

Question 3 - Mock Test 1

(A) Building codes. In order to ensure public safety, building codes set minimum criteria for construction. High standards are typically specified by local building codes, and in cases where they diverge from federal or state norms, the builder is obliged to adhere to the higher level. For instance, you need two hand rails as it is the higher standard, even if municipal laws only call for one and federal law mandates two.

Question 4 - Mock Test 1

(B) Estoppels. This principle prohibits individuals from adopting positions that conflict with their previous actions or statements.

Question 5 - Mock Test 1

(A) Mechanic's lien. It secures payment for those involved in constructing or repairing buildings, attaching to both the land and the improvements. Mechanic's liens are often necessary to secure construction help on a project.

Question 6 - Mock Test 1

(B) Panic peddling. This unethical tactic aims to prompt property sales based on the fear of minority integration into the community. An further unlawful real estate practice is "blockbusting". Agents utilize panic peddling in blockbusting in order to profit financially. Agents can earn commissions from the sale of people's homes and may even be able to represent them when they buy new ones if they can incite panic and convince people to sell. Blockbusting may be the solution if it were a possibility, but it isn't, thus "panic peddling" is the best choice.

Question 7 - Mock Test 1

(B) DEBT-TO-INCOME RATIO. This ratio compares a borrower's monthly financial obligations to their gross monthly income.

Question 8 - Mock Test 1

(B) Cloud on title. This refers to any complication that could obstruct the conveyance of a property's title.

Question 9 - Mock Test 1

(A) Accretion. This natural phenomenon gradually enlarges the land along the water's edge, typically becoming the property of the landowner.

Question 10 - Mock Test 1

(A) Title. In real estate, this term signifies the legal ownership and right to use a property.

Question 11 - Mock Test 1

(A) Simple interest. This method calculates interest by multiplying the principal amount by the rate of interest and the time frame between payments.

Question 12 - Mock Test 1

(C) The property buyer. This disclosure, detailing loan terms and costs, is required within three business days of the loan application and at least seven days before closing.

Question 13 - Mock Test 1

(D) The degree of risk. This is the crucial factor for lenders when deciding on loan approval.

Question 14 - Mock Test 1

(C) Consumer credit. This covers debts incurred through the purchase of goods and services by consumers.

Question 15 - Mock Test 1

(A) Buying Title-II loans to keep the market liquid, thereby supporting the housing finance system.

Question 16 - Mock Test 1

(D) PMI covers conventional loans, while MIP is for FHA loans, indicating their respective insurance policies.

Question 17 - Mock Test 1

(C) Hypothecation. This process allows the borrower to secure a loan with property as collateral without relinquishing possession.

Question 18 - Mock Test 1

(C) Hypothecated the property. This ensures the property serves as security for a debt without loss of possession.

Question 19 - Mock Test 1

(C) Excludes principal repayments until the final payment, with interest paid periodically or at term's end.

Question 20 - Mock Test 1

(D) The monthly payments. Designed for young families expecting income growth, these payments start lower and increase over time to match rising incomes.

Question 21 - Mock Test 1

(D) A counter offer immediately nullifies the original offer, transforming the roles of offeror and offeree.

Question 22 - Mock Test 1

(C) Revoke the agency created by the listing contract, but they might have to compensate the broker for any losses incurred.

Question 23 - Mock Test 1

(A) Percentage lease. The rent is partially determined by the tenant's sales, combining fixed and variable elements.

Question 24 - Mock Test 1

(B) Novation. In contract and business law, novation refers to the act of replacing a duty to fulfill with a new obligation or of replacing a party to an agreement with a new party. Remember that "nova" is Latin meaning "new".

Question 25 - Mock Test 1

(B) Offers must be presented even after the seller has accepted them. Willfully failing to deliver any written purchase offer prior to the closing of the sale constitutes a breach of an agent's fiduciary duty, unless the owner expressly instructs the agent not to present any more offers (or the offer is plainly frivolous). Depending on the conditions of the agreement, the seller may be unable to accept the offer during the escrow period.

Question 26 - Mock Test 1

(C) Upon informing the buyer of the acceptance, as communication of consent is essential for contract validation.

Question 27 - Mock Test 1

(D) An open buyer agency agreement, similar to an open listing from a seller's perspective.

Question 28 - Mock Test 1

(C) Rescind the contract, as undisclosed material facts about the property provide grounds for contract rescission.

Question 29 - Mock Test 1

(D) Assignment, where the tenant's rights and obligations under the lease are fully transferred to another entity.

Question 30 - Mock Test 1

(B) Tenant improvement allowance, where landlords provide financial assistance for tenant-specific modifications.

Question 31 - Mock Test 1

(C) In property law, a reversionary interest denotes the grantor of the trust (or deed) having a right to reclaim transmitted property at a later date or subject to specific requirements. Life estates such as the one in question mean that upon Stephen's death, estate ownership "reverts" to Douglas (or his estate, if he has also passed away). The property usually reverts to the grantor in reversion if the deed contains no language designating a remainderman, such as "to Stephen for life, then to Mary".

Question 32 - Mock Test 1

(D) An encumbrance without being a lien, granting property use rights for a specific purpose without ownership transfer.

Question 33 - Mock Test 1

(D) A judgment is an all-encompassing, involuntary, equitable lien on the debtor's personal and real possessions. Typically, a lien only extends to real estate situated within the county where it was filed. If a creditor wants to expand coverage to a different county, they must submit notices of the lien in that county.

Question 34 - Mock Test 1

(D) The first, and typically most economical, step for someone who provides labor and/or materials to a homeowner to recover money due is to file a mechanic's lien. The homeowner is under pressure from a mechanic's lien to reach a settlement swiftly and without incurring expensive legal fees.

Question 35 - Mock Test 1

(D) A license is the individual, revocable right to use another person's property as long as the owner grants permission. Permission is individual, non-transferable, and subject to revocation at any moment. A property owner who wants to use their property for a particular nonconforming use in a residential area can apply for a conditional use permit from a city or municipality. Owners of land adjacent to a river, stream, or other body of water are granted the privilege of using the water in accordance with local or state regulations. This is known as riparian rights. When a landowner sells a piece of land that has no access to a public way other than

over the seller's remaining land, the court creates an easement by necessity.

Question 36 - Mock Test 1

(C) Time, Title, Interest, and Possession are the four components of a joint tenancy; "TTIP" is an easy acronym to recall for these.

Question 37 - Mock Test 1

(A) When two people live in a joint tenancy, their ownership of a certain property is undivided and, in the event of one member's death, the surviving party instantly becomes the complete owner. "In severalty" does not signify as a sole owner, despite the sound of it.

Question 38 - Mock Test 1

(C) A life estate is a kind of property ownership that is usually created by a deed. It is frequently used to skip probate and give property to an heir, or remainderman, right away when an owner passes away. The future interest that the remainderman receives from the deed is known as the remainder.

Question 39 - Mock Test 1

(A) The heirs may inherit a deceased owner's property in a tenancy in common in accordance with the terms of the will. The property would not have passed in accordance with the will if the dead owner had been a joint tenant, as the property interests would have flowed immediately to the other two friends (co-tenants) in a joint tenancy. The owner who passed away wasn't a tenant by the entirety, which is a position only held by married partners.

Furthermore, since only one person is permitted to hold property under severalty ownership, the deceased owner was not a severalty owner.

Question 40 - Mock Test 1

(C) One person is the owner of property held in severalty. The sole authority to transfer ownership or use of the property to another individual or corporation belongs to the owner. Spouses may possess separate properties in severalty, which is the legal term for when one individual owns two or more distinct properties.

Question 41 - Mock Test 1

(C) Using the meridian (north-south line) and baseline (east-west line) as its points of division, a district is divided into quadrangles of 24 square miles using the Government Rectangular Survey System. The tracts are separated into townships, which are 6-mile-square sections, and sections, which are 36 plots that are 1 mile by 1 mile square.

Question 42 - Mock Test 1

(D) Making adjustments for variances between the two assets being compared is the most challenging part of the Market Data Approach. While certain properties are comparable, two properties are rarely similar in every way, necessitating adjustments. Only modify the comparable properties—never the subject property—when making changes. For instance, to get the expected value of the subject property, deduct the value of the pool from the comparable property when valuing a home without a pool and one with one.

Question 43 - Mock Test 1

(A) The three approaches to value typically produce three different values. An in-depth analysis of these values is required to determine the most valid, logical, and reliable approach to be used to provide the final value estimate. Determining depreciation, a loss of value due to any cause, is part of the process of the cost approach. The highest and best use of a property is the single most profitable use for that property. Determining highest and best use is only one of the factors considered in an appraisal prior to choosing an approach to value and reconciliation.

Question 44 - Mock Test 1

(D) Lack of maintenance and ordinary wear and tear are marks of physical deterioration. Outdated items and outdated technology indicate functional obsolescence in a property. Obsolescence that is economically feasible to correct is curable obsolescence.

Question 45 - Mock Test 1

(C) A bearing wall is a wall that can carry both its own weight and any load in the vertical plane. Since it is the strongest component and can be erected at any angle to windows and doors, it is significant when remodeling.

Question 46 - Mock Test 1

(D) The top bounds of value are defined by the cost (replacement) method. The cost (replacement) approach is a method of valuing a property that involves adding the appraiser's estimate of the building's replacement cost, less depreciation, to the estimated land value.

Question 47 - Mock Test 1

(C) Capitalization is a way of determining the current value of future earnings.

Question 48 - Mock Test 1

(C) Neighborhood analysis is a rigorous method that identifies, measures, and analyzes the factors that influence a neighborhood's vitality and desirability. It is useful for estimating the worth of homes in a certain area.

Question 49 - Mock Test 1

(B) "Functional obsolescence" generally manifests itself in one of two ways: first, through bad initial design, as in this example; and second, when the home's features and design have become outmoded in comparison to competing properties.

Question 50 - Mock Test 1

(B) A trade fixture with a specialized function for a business is the iron oven. Even if it's attached to the rented space, it is still personal property. On or before the last day of the lease, the owner is required to remove the oven. An object that is affixed to a property permanently is called a fixture and is classified as real property. If the proprietor of the restaurant constructs an oven in the area that is difficult to remove, doing so could

seriously harm the area. The oven becomes a permanent fixture and landlord's actual property if it isn't removed.

Question 51 - Mock Test 1

(D) All interests the seller had in the property have been transferred to the buyer, though a quitclaim deed does not guarantee the extent of the seller's interests or that the title is clear of other claims.

Question 52 - Mock Test 1

(B) The person transferring the property lacks legal competence, as legal capacity of the grantor is essential for a deed to validly convey property.

Question 53 - Mock Test 1

(D) The capacity to transfer an interest in real property, including selling, bequeathing, or gifting it.

Question 54 - Mock Test 1

(B) The covenant of seisin, confirming the grantor's ownership and right to convey the property.

Question 55 - Mock Test 1

(D) A tax lien or judgment lien attaches to all personal and real property of a person or corporation (the "lienee"), so constituting a general lien. The attachment of judgment liens to personal property varies by state, although it is recognized nationwide.

Question 56 - Mock Test 1

(A) Delinquent property taxes, which supersede all other claims or liens against the property.

Question 57 - Mock Test 1

(A) A deficiency judgment is an unsecured money judgment against a borrower whose mortgage foreclosure sale did not generate enough funds to pay off the underlying promissory note, or loan in full.

Question 58 - Mock Test 1

(D) Handed over to and accepted by the recipient, signifying the completion of the title transfer process.

Question 59 - Mock Test 1

(B) Title insurance typically does not cover changes in zoning or city regulations.

Question 60 - Mock Test 1

(C) Escheat is the reversion of property to the state in the absence of a private owner. It frequently arises when a property owner dies intestate (without a will) and has no heirs. An individual cannot obtain property through Escheat.

Question 61 - Mock Test 1

(C) Its susceptibility to swings in the local economy, due to the immobility of real estate, making its market value heavily influenced by the local environment rather than broader marketplaces.

Question 62 - Mock Test 1

(D) Residential homeowners and renters value these aspects highly for the welfare and happiness of their families, unlike other sectors with different primary concerns.

Question 63 - Mock Test 1

(B) An increase in vacancies leading to price drops, as the new supply aims to balance out previous demand excesses, impacting market prices and occupancy rates.

Question 64 - Mock Test 1

(C) The migration of significant businesses into or out of the area directly impacts local demand for real estate, affecting market dynamics distinctly from broader economic influences.

Question 65 - Mock Test 1

(A) Local government's intervention in the market due to infrastructure constraints or planning goals, potentially affecting price trends by limiting supply growth.

Question 66 - Mock Test 1

(D) Unoccupied spaces of a specific type at a given moment, often expressed as a percentage of the total inventory, indicating market absorption and demand.

Question 67 - Mock Test 1

(B) Employment numbers in foundational economic sectors, which are crucial for the area's economic health and directly influence real estate demand.

Question 68 - Mock Test 1

(C) Challenges in quickly converting properties into cash, reflecting the complex and time-consuming process of matching properties with suitable buyers at favorable prices.

Question 69 - Mock Test 1

(A) Have been on the rise, indicating a reaction to increased demand not yet met by the existing supply, prompting new development.

Question 70 - Mock Test 1

(C) The market is over-supplied, with supply exceeding current demand, leading to reduced rental rates as owners and managers vie to attract tenants.

Question 71 - Mock Test 1

(D) Misappropriately using client funds for personal use, which refers to the unauthorized use of another's property or funds.

Question 72 - Mock Test 1

(A) Restrictions on specific real estate activities, like prohibiting sale signs, to help stabilize the neighborhood.

Question 73 - Mock Test 1

(C) Race, as part of the earliest civil rights legislation, with later laws expanding protections to include religion, sex, and marital status.

Question 74 - Mock Test 1

(D) Racial steering is the practice of encouraging consumers to buy homes in specific neighborhoods depending on their race; the broker "steers" the buyer toward a particular community based on their race. Fair housing laws forbid guiding and other discriminatory actions.

Question 75 - Mock Test 1

(D) Operational costs, which are expenses incurred from maintaining income-generating property, excluding mortgage or interest expenses.

Question 76 - Mock Test 1

(B) Each state determines the maximum interest rate that lenders may charge. Rates higher than that ceiling are considered usurious and illegal. No legitimate lender will charge more than those rates, and those who do are known as loan sharks.

Question 77 - Mock Test 1

(C) Injunctions are court orders that stop or prevent particular actions by specific individuals or corporations. For example, members of a residential neighborhood could seek an injunction to stop someone from burning leaves.

Question 78 - Mock Test 1

(D) Requiring a co-signer only from single tenants, as it discriminates based on marital status.

Question 79 - Mock Test 1

(D) All of the solutions presented are forbidden by anti-discrimination laws.

Question 80 - Mock Test 1

(A) Offering a service that, for compensation, pairs buyers and sellers of real estate, requiring the legal authorization granted by a real estate license.

Question 81 - Mock Test 1

(D) Compensation, as it's the principal's main obligation to compensate the broker according to their agreement.

Question 82 - Mock Test 1

(D) Property owner, who has the final say in determining the asking price for their property, despite the broker's guidance.

Question 83 - Mock Test 1

(D) General agency, where the property manager acts extensively on behalf of the owner in various capacities.

Question 84 - Mock Test 1

(A) Johnson received the commission in accordance with the listing agreement. Remember that listing agreements are between a broker/principal broker and a client, not the salesperson/associate broker who may be assisting the customer. Because the offer was submitted through another broker, a commission split is possible.

Question 85 - Mock Test 1

(C) Financial stewardship, which demands accurate handling and reporting of any funds entrusted to the agent by clients.

Question 86 - Mock Test 1

(B) There are currently no rules governing the commission amount charged by any broker, but it must be disclosed in the employment agreement.

Question 87 - Mock Test 1

(B) Real estate licensees represent the person with whom they have entered into a contract, whether it is the seller or the buyer. The person paying the commission isn't always the principal. Often, a seller may pay a buyer's broker to facilitate the transaction.

Question 88 - Mock Test 1

(C) As a fiduciary, the broker (and salesman) must be loyal to the principal.

Question 89 - Mock Test 1

(A) The listing cannot be terminated solely for the purpose of evading commission payments if the sale proceeds with a buyer introduced by the broker.

Question 90 - Mock Test 1

(C) Ethical procedures involve the use of honesty, integrity, fairness, and responsibility when working with clients, associates, customers, and the general public.

Question 91 - Mock Test 1

(D) Total square footage = 2÷3 × 43,560 = 29,040 SF

Total Commission = 0.07 × $24,000 = $1,680.

Taylor's Share = 0.55 × $1,680 = $924.

Amount per square foot = $924 ÷ 29,040 square feet.

Rounded to three decimal places: $0.032 per square foot.

Question 92 - Mock Test 1

(A) Convert acres to a decimal: 1+(1/2) = 1.5 acres.

Total square footage of the lot: 43,560 SF per acre x 1.5 acres = 65,340 SF

Cost of the land: $0.50 per SF x 65,340 SF = $32,670.

Cost of the home: $125 per SF × 2,600 SF = $325,000.

Determine the total property cost:

Total cost:

$32,670 (land) + $325,000 (home) = $357,670.

Question 93 - Mock Test 1

(B) Lot size = 1/3 acre.

One acre equals 43,560 square feet.

Lot area = 1/3 x 43,560 SF = 14,520 SF.

Tennis court area = 150' × 60' = 9,000 SF.

Remaining area = Lot area - Tennis court area.

Remaining area = 14,520 SF - 9,000 SF = 5,520 SF.

Percentage left over = (Remaining area ÷ Lot area) × 100%.

Percentage left over = (5,520 SF ÷ 14,520 SF) × 100% ≈ 38%.

Question 94 - Mock Test 1

(C) Fraction of area for streets and common areas: 1/3

Area for streets and common areas: 18 acres x (1/3) = 6 acres.

Area available for lots: 18 acres − 6 acres = 12 acres.

1 acre = 43,560 square feet.

Total area in square feet: 12 acres x 43,560 SF per acre = 522,720 SF.

Number of lots: 522,720 SF ÷ 10,000 SF per lot = 52.272 lots.

Since you cannot have a fraction of a lot, the developer can have 52 lots.

Question 95 - Mock Test 1

(A) Area of the two shorter walls: 2 x 15' x 8' = 240 SF

Area of the two longer walls: 2 x 20' x 8' = 320 SF

Total wall area: 240 SF + 320 SF = 560 SF

Each roll measures 2 feet wide and 40 feet long: Area per roll = 2' x 40' = 80 SF

Number of rolls = Total wall area ÷ Area per roll

Equals: 560 SF ÷ 80 SF per roll = 7

Question 96 - Mock Test 1

(B) Original width of the house = 50 feet.

Add mulch area on both sides: 10' + 50' + 10' = 70 feet.

Original length of the house = 35 feet.

Add mulch area on both sides: 10' + 35' + 10' = 55 feet.

Area = Width × Length = 70' × 55' = 3,850 square feet.

Area = Width × Length = 50' × 35' = 1,750 square feet.

Mulched area = Outer rectangle area - House area.

Mulched area = 3,850 SF - 1,750 SF = 2,100 square feet

Question 97 - Mock Test 1

(B) Eastern 1/2 of Section 9: This represents the eastern half of the section

Western 1/2 of the Eastern 1/2: This is the western half of that eastern half.

Southeastern 1/4 of the Western 1/2: This is the southeastern quarter of that western half.

Multiply the fractions sequentially:

(1 ÷ 2) × (1 ÷ 2) × (1 ÷ 4) = 1 ÷ 16.

Total acres in a section: 640 acres.

Acreage of the specified area:

Acreage = 640 acres × (1 ÷ 16).

Acreage = 640 acres ÷ 16.

Acreage = 40 acres

Question 98 - Mock Test 1

(B) Southwestern 1 ÷ 4 of Section 12: This represents the southwestern quarter of the section.

Southeastern 1 ÷ 4 of the Southwestern 1 ÷ 4: This is the southeastern quarter of that southwestern quarter.

Northeastern 1 ÷ 4 of the Southeastern 1 ÷ 4: This is the northeastern quarter of that southeastern quarter.

Multiply the fractions sequentially: 1/4 x 1/4 x 1/4 = 1/64

Total acres in a section: 640 acres.

Acreage = 640 acres × 1/64

Acreage = 640 acres ÷ 64

Acreage = 10 acres

Question 99 - Mock Test 1

(D) Rent per SF per month = $1.40

Total monthly rent = 1,800 SF × $1.40/SF = $2,520

Annual fixed rent = $2,520 × 12 months = $30,240

Percentage rent rate = 1.75%

Average monthly sales = $41,500

Monthly percentage rent = $41,500 × 1.75% = $726.25

Annual percentage rent = $726.25 × 12 months = $8,715

Total annual rent = Annual fixed rent + Annual percentage rent

Total annual rent = $30,240 + $8,715 = $38,955

Question 100 - Mock Test 1

(A) First year appreciation: 1 + 1/4% = 4.25%

Second year appreciation: 5.33%

Third year appreciation: 6.5%

Total appreciation: Add the above three appreciations: 16.0833

Average appreciation: 16.0833/3 = 5.36%.

Mock Test 2

Question 1 - Mock Test 2

(C) PHYSICAL DETERIORATION. This type of depreciation results from regular use and aging, distinct from obsolescence.

Question 2 - Mock Test 2

(B) COMMINGLING. Agents must keep client funds in a designated trust or escrow account to avoid legal issues.

Question 3 - Mock Test 2

(C) PROFIT AND LOSS STATEMENT. It tracks a business's financial activity, showcasing the profit or loss achieved.

Question 4 - Mock Test 2

(B) RIPARIAN RIGHTS. These rights apply to moving water bodies, distinguishing from rights over stationary water like lakes.

Question 5 - Mock Test 2

(B) Trade fixture. These are items that are affixed to the property but are not considered real property because they are related to a business. Trade fixtures are not part of the land; they are personal property. A dentist's chair is a good analogy for this. Although the chair is attached to the ground, it is not real property; rather, it is personal since if the dentist sells his office, the chair will accompany him because it is part of his business. The chair is personal since it belongs to the individual, not the land.

Question 6 - Mock Test 2

(C) Load-bearing wall. It plays a crucial role in distributing the weight from above to the foundation below.

Question 7 - Mock Test 2

(C) Littoral. These rights concern assets that border an ocean or lake rather than a river or stream (riparian). Littoral rights typically deal with the use or pleasure of the coastline. Riparian water rights are a way of allocating water to individuals who own land along its path.

Question 8 - Mock Test 2

(B) NET LEASE. A lease that requires the tenant to cover all costs associated with the leased property, including taxes, insurance, upkeep, etc., in addition to a set rental amount. The terminology "net net," "net net net," "triple net," and similar terms are used in some states.

Question 9 - Mock Test 2

(D) UNEARNED INCREMENT. This increase stems from changes in the surrounding area, not from enhancements to the property.

Question 10 - Mock Test 2

(D) Subordination clause. This clause rearranges the precedence of mortgages, affecting their legal standing.

Question 11 - Mock Test 2

(B) The annual percentage rate (APR) represents the yearly credit cost to borrowers, simplifying comparison across offers.

Question 12 - Mock Test 2

(C) A balloon payment mortgage is one that does not entirely amortize during the life of the note, leaving a debt due at maturity. The final payment is known as a balloon payment due to its huge amount. Balloon payment mortgages are more popular in business than residential real estate.

Question 13 - Mock Test 2

(C) The Federal Housing Administration (FHA) protects lenders against losses in the case of a default. Borrowers with weaker credit scores can qualify for FHA loans, which demand reduced down payments and closing expenses.

Question 14 - Mock Test 2

(C) Minority background. Fair housing laws prohibit discrimination on the basis of ethnic or racial background, ensuring equal treatment in lending.

Question 15 - Mock Test 2

(C) Negative amortization. This scenario, where payments don't cover owed interest, leads to an increase in the loan balance over time.

Question 16 - Mock Test 2

(A) "Acceleration clauses" state that if specific events occur, such as nonpayment, the entire amount of the mortgage may become owing. This is most commonly found in "due on sale" conditions, which demand the mortgage debt to be paid in full when the home is sold.

Question 17 - Mock Test 2

(D) Balloon payment. Mortgages of this type often plan for a future refinance to address the remaining balance.

Question 18 - Mock Test 2

(C) A mortgage given from buyer to seller to secure the purchase price. This seller financing method helps buyers who may not qualify through standard lenders.

Question 19 - Mock Test 2

(D) Decrease loan activity. This action reduces available reserves, consequently decreasing lending activity.

Question 20 - Mock Test 2

(A) A VA Loan typically requires no down payment, but the other forms of loans discussed below would rarely qualify for a loan at 100% of the selling price. VA loans are guaranteed by the United States Department of Veterans Affairs (VA).

Question 21 - Mock Test 2

(A) The final contract price, which is finalized only after an offer is accepted.

Question 22 - Mock Test 2

(B) Unenforceable. A verbal contract is one that is not in writing and is not signed by both parties. It is a valid contract, but it lacks the formal requirement of a memorandum (written instrument) that would make it enforceable in court, rendering it unenforceable. The statute of frauds requires all real property purchases to be in writing in order to be enforceable, so the verbal contract is regarded unenforceable until this real property transaction is completed or a written agreement is entered into.

Question 23 - Mock Test 2

(A) Specific performance is a remedy available in an equity court that requires a defendant to carry out the terms of a contract or agreement. Under certain conditions, a buyer can sue a seller for specified performance; if the buyer wins, the seller is obligated to complete the property sale.

Question 24 - Mock Test 2

(A) Employment contract. Contract of employment between the seller and the broker to procure a buyer. Open listings are considered unilateral because only the seller makes a promise (unless a broker brings a buyer in).

Question 25 - Mock Test 2

(B) An exclusive-right-to-sell listing doesn't require the broker to be the direct cause of the sale for commission entitlement.

Question 26 - Mock Test 2

(C) Performance is not a prerequisite for contract formation but occurs after the contract has been established. The four legal requirements for any contract are: (1) consideration, (2) an offer and acceptance (i.e., a meeting of the minds), (3) a lawful object, and (4) competent parties.

Question 27 - Mock Test 2

(B) When a contract includes a "time is of the essence" clause, the dates and times specified for contract fulfillment are regarded critical and mandatory to the agreement. Failure to act within the term specified may constitute a breach of contract.

Question 28 - Mock Test 2

(D) The buyer is eligible for a full refund of the earnest money since no contract was established.

Question 29 - Mock Test 2

(A) Statute of frauds. Contrary to common assumption, the statute of frauds is not concerned with specific acts of fraud, but rather with the necessity in every state that certain documents, particularly those relating to real estate, be in writing. It is known as the law of frauds because it was first adopted in England in 1677 to prohibit false claims to title.

Question 30 - Mock Test 2

(D) Enforceable as oral leases under one year are generally enforceable.

Question 31 - Mock Test 2

(D) The term "equitable title" in real estate law describes a person's ability to acquire complete ownership of a piece of real land or an interest in it. This is frequently used in opposition to or in combination with "legal title," which refers to the real land ownership. In this instance, Joe acquires an equitable title interest in the property upon signing the purchase contract.

Question 32 - Mock Test 2

(B) The life estate granted to her grandson will terminate at the owner's death, and the son-in-law, who holds the remainder interest, will become the fee simple absolute owner of the land. A leasehold estate that lasts for a set amount of time is called an estate for years. A freehold estate resulting from a provision is called a legal life estate.

Question 33 - Mock Test 2

(C) One kind of freehold estate that is perpetual in nature is the Fee Simple Estate, sometimes known as a "Estate of Inheritance". A fee simple estate has encumbrances and can be sold or inherited.

Question 34 - Mock Test 2

(A) A deed restriction establishes a limited use for a fee simple defeasible estate. If the hospital does not use the land for medical purposes, the previous owner may regain complete ownership. This is known as the reversionary interest. A life estate is a type of freehold estate that is valid for the tenant's entire lifetime. A long-term tenancy is a leasehold property that lasts for a set amount of time, such as months, years, or even days. A less-than-freehold estate known as a periodic tenancy establishes the annual right of possession over real estate.

Question 35 - Mock Test 2

(A) Restrictive covenants are not public, but private property use limitations. A municipality may, in the course of exercising its police duties, control building heights, lot sizes, and structural kinds.

Question 36 - Mock Test 2

(C) Joe becomes a tenant in common with Oscar and Andrew as a result of his passive acquisition of his portion of the property, but Oscar and Andrew remain joint tenants with a two-thirds interest because joint tenancy needs to be disclosed. The right of survivorship provisions is retained in Oscar and Andrew's share but not in Joe's, which is how the two forms differ from one another.

Question 37 - Mock Test 2

(B) A real estate property tax lien is always placed on a particular parcel of real estate; it is an involuntary action taken without the owner's consent. Judgment liens, income tax liens, and estate tax liens are examples of general liens because they can be placed against a debtor's real or personal property and do not supersede other liens.

Question 38 - Mock Test 2

(A) Almost usually, licensing involves allowing someone to use property for a predetermined amount of time and for a particular purpose. Only access—not ownership, usage, or occupancy rights—is granted by easements. Furthermore, the property owner typically uses the access for their own purposes, like upkeep of walkways or utilities.

Question 39 - Mock Test 2

(B) It is stated that appurtenances "Run with the Land" and don't need to be transported separately. In addition to trees and swimming pools, appurtenances also include covenants, minerals, stocks in mutual water companies, and easements. They are regarded as real estate.

Question 40 - Mock Test 2

(B) The dominant estate (or dominant tenement) is the one that benefits from the easement, whereas the servient estate (or servient tenement) is the one that bears the burden or grants the advantage. For instance, parcel A's owner has the right of way to utilize a roadway on parcel B's property in order to access A's residence; in this case, A is the dominant tenement and B is the servient tenement.

Question 41 - Mock Test 2

(A) Investment properties are the only ones where income capitalization matters. It evaluates a property's revenue vs operational expenses before, typically, contrasting the return with alternative investment possibilities given the state of the economy.

Question 42 - Mock Test 2

(C) Under the laws of supply and demand, if supply of a commodity decreases with demand remaining the same or increasing, the price of a commodity increases. Prices tend to drop if the demand for the commodity decreases while the supply remains the same or increases.

Question 43 - Mock Test 2

(A) According to the appraisal concept of anticipation, the value of a property might rise or fall depending on what is anticipated to happen to it in the future—either positively or negatively.

Question 44 - Mock Test 2

(B) The cost approach is a real estate valuation technique that makes the assumption that a property's asking price should be equal to the cost of constructing a structure of similar value. The market value of a property is determined by subtracting depreciation from the total cost of building and land, as determined by a cost approach appraisal.

Question 45 - Mock Test 2

(A) Functional obsolescence, or a decline in property value brought on by a house's floor plan shortcoming, is an appropriate answer. For the four-bedroom house, a single-car garage would not be sufficient.

Question 46 - Mock Test 2

(B) Functional obsolescence can occur from both outmoded features and poor design. For example, an older home with five bedrooms and one bathroom is considered outmoded by today's standards. So is a new home with no bathtubs or bedrooms that can only be entered by passing through another bedroom.

Question 47 - Mock Test 2

(D) To get the square mileage of the land, multiply the sides by 1/4 mile, resulting in 1/16 square mile. To calculate the answer, multiply the square mileage of the land by the number of acres in a square mile (640). 1/16 x 640 = 40.

Question 48 - Mock Test 2

(C) Obsolescence is the leading cause of real property value loss, and it can apply to functional or economic obsolescence. The term obsolescence literally refers to the situation of no longer being usable or useful, or of being obsolete.

Question 49 - Mock Test 2

(D) In an appraisal, An appraiser estimates a property's market value, not its market price, which is the actual sale price and may differ. They may use the income technique to assess projected income. Earnest money and contract considerations do not affect market value.

Question 50 - Mock Test 2

(A) Market value is the present value of one commodity that can be traded on the open market. How much an item costs has no bearing on its worth.

Question 51 - Mock Test 2

(D) The "grantor" is the person transferring the property, therefore they sign the deed. When a title finishes with a "or," it refers to the giver, or the givOR, if you like. A term that ends with "ee," such as "grantee," denotes the recipient because they received the object.

Question 52 - Mock Test 2

(D) Property deeds are used to transfer real property from a grantor (seller) to a grantee (purchaser). For a deed to be legally binding, numerous requirements must be met, including the identity of the grantor and grantee, as well as an acceptable legal description of the property.

Question 53 - Mock Test 2

(A) Alienation of Title refers to the conveyance of title. The reverse is Acquisition of Title (to gain possession of the title).

Question 54 - Mock Test 2

(A) Intestacy refers to the state of a person's estate when they die without leaving a valid will or other legally binding declaration. This may also apply where a will or declaration has been made, but only for a portion of the estate; the remaining estate is referred to as the "intestate estate".

Question 55 - Mock Test 2

(A) Investments in real estate that offer advantages for income tax deduction purposes, such as mortgage interest or property depreciation.

Question 56 - Mock Test 2

(D) Tenancy for years is the most frequent type of rental arrangement, and it generally binds all future owners of the property for the duration of the lease.

Question 57 - Mock Test 2

(A) Intangible personal property is not taxed. Taxation applies to both real property and tangible personal property.

Question 58 - Mock Test 2

(B) In a sale-leaseback arrangement, the seller becomes the new buyer's tenant, allowing him to deduct all future rent payments as business expenditures. In these types of arrangements, the buyer is often more concerned with the seller's company income than with the book value.

Question 59 - Mock Test 2

(B) Constructive notice, implying that the recording of the judgment serves as legal notification to all subsequent parties about its claim on the property.

Question 60 - Mock Test 2

(B) Personal property varies from "real property" in several ways, most notably its portability.

Personal property includes cars, furniture, clothing, paintings, jewelry, appliances, and nearly any other non-food item purchased. A bill of sale is evidence of the transfer of ownership of personal property.

Question 61 - Mock Test 2

(D) The market moving toward a state of equilibrium, as construction efforts aim to address the deficit in supply to meet demand, aligning price, cost, and value closely.

Question 62 - Mock Test 2

(B) Are likely to rise, as the fixed supply faces growing demand, pushing up prices for the available properties.

Question 63 - Mock Test 2

(B) Desire, utility, scarcity, and purchasing power, which dictate the perceived value and the economic principles of a product, including real estate.

Question 64 - Mock Test 2

(A) Increasing prices, as tighter supply relative to demand drives up the cost of leasing or purchasing available spaces.

Question 65 - Mock Test 2

(D) The occupancy of previously available units within a certain timeframe, indicating how much property has been taken up by tenants or buyers recently.

Question 66 - Mock Test 2

(A) Assemblage, which can lead to a combined property worth more than the sum of its parts due to synergistic value or plottage.

Question 67 - Mock Test 2

(B) From the exterior dimensions of above-grade spaces, excluding areas not fully enclosed or below ground level, to capture the usable living space.

Question 68 - Mock Test 2

(C) Each property's uniqueness, making real estate unique among economic products with specific characteristics that affect its value and marketability.

Question 69 - Mock Test 2

(D) A market reaches equilibrium when supply equals demand, and price, cost, and value are equal. Market demand adjusts to meet supply, and supply adjusts to meet demand. If there's a high-demand shortage, suppliers increase production. If there's excess inventory, they reduce production until the surplus is gone.

Question 70 - Mock Test 2

(B) The product is becoming more sought-after compared to its availability, suggesting that demand is outpacing supply, pushing prices upward.

Question 71 - Mock Test 2

(A) The Jacksons have the option to initiate legal action against the broker for nondisclosure, as license law mandates the disclosure of any material facts affecting the value of the property.

Question 72 - Mock Test 2

(C) A gross lease, where tenants pay a fixed rent while the landlord covers property expenses like taxes, insurance, and maintenance.

Question 73 - Mock Test 2

(B) The practice of denying mortgage loans or insurance in specific locales due to factors unrelated to the economic qualifications of applicants.

Question 74 - Mock Test 2

(C) The Real Estate Settlement Procedures Act, which aims to give consumers better disclosures regarding settlement costs and to eliminate unnecessary expenses at closing.

Question 75 - Mock Test 2

(B) Home inspectors are hired to detect serious and frequently hidden property flaws, such as leaking roofs, termites (which leave behind sawdust), foundation cracking, and so on. Hinges and other "wear and tear" items are obvious and not reasons to hire an inspector.

Question 76 - Mock Test 2

(C) Careful and responsible, ensuring they are working in the best interest of facilitating a successful agreement between buyer and seller.

Question 77 - Mock Test 2

(D) A salesperson may not deposit funds into their own bank account. Since salespeople are not permitted to have brokerage trust accounts, the real estate commission has the authority to cancel a salesperson's license for depositing a buyer's earnest money into a personal account.

Question 78 - Mock Test 2

(A) Puffing is defined as making excessive statements about the positive aspects of real estate that are based on opinion rather than fact. Puffing is lawful as long as the remark is not a blatant lie (or a violation of Fair Housing laws, for example).

Question 79 - Mock Test 2

(C) 1 year, after which the option for direct legal action still exists but the formal complaint process through HUD is not available.

Question 80 - Mock Test 2

(A) A license, which grants temporary, revocable permission to use the land for a particular purpose without conveying property rights.

Question 81 - Mock Test 2

(D) A fiduciary relationship, signifying a legal and ethical relationship of trust with the client, where the broker must act in the client's best interests.

Question 82 - Mock Test 2

(B) A bilateral contract is one in which one party agrees to execute an act in exchange for the other party's promise to perform. An exclusive right-to-sell listing is an example of a bilateral contract in which the broker agrees to use his or her best efforts (diligence) to find a ready, willing, and able buyer, and the seller promises to pay the broker a commission if the property is sold.

Question 83 - Mock Test 2

(D) A power of attorney is a written instrument that authorizes a person, the attorney-in-fact, to act as an agent on behalf of another to the extent specified in the instrument. All of the options presented here would lead to the revocation of a power of attorney.

Question 84 - Mock Test 2

(B) Subornation, as suborning someone to act unlawfully does not establish a legitimate agency relationship.

Question 85 - Mock Test 2

(D) Conducting fair and honest dealings, ensuring transparency and integrity in interactions with the buyer.

Question 86 - Mock Test 2

(C) Fiduciary, emphasizing the agent's duty to act in the client's best interest under the legal framework of fiduciary responsibility.

Question 87 - Mock Test 2

(B) Procuring cause, identifying the broker as the key factor in bringing about the sale and therefore entitled to commission.

Question 88 - Mock Test 2

(D) Submit offers directly to the seller or the seller's agent, reflecting the agent's commitment to the buyer's interests.

Question 89 - Mock Test 2

(B) The person making the counter becomes the recipient, essentially switching roles and opening the door for new terms in the negotiation.

Question 90 - Mock Test 2

(D) An agent's offer alone is insufficient to establish an agency relationship; the principal must also provide some permission (implied, written, or oral).

Question 91 - Mock Test 2

(A) Appreciation amount = Current selling price - Original purchase price

Appreciation amount = $260,000 - $200,000 = $60,000

Appreciation percentage = (Appreciation amount / Original purchase price) × 100%

Appreciation percentage = ($60,000 / $200,000) × 100% = 30%

Question 92 - Mock Test 2

(C) Formula: (Offer Price / Listing Price) × 100%

Calculation: ($270,000 / $285,000) × 100% ≈ 94.74%

Rounded Percentage: 95%.

Question 93 - Mock Test 2

(A) EGI = Potential Gross Income - Vacancy and Credit Losses

EGI = $50,000 - $2,000 = $48,000

NOI = EGI - Operating Expenses

NOI = $48,000 - $15,000 = $33,000

Value = NOI / Capitalization Rate

Value = $33,000 / 0.08 = $412,500.

Question 94 - Mock Test 2

(A) Value = Net Income / Capitalization Rate

Value = $36,000 / 0.09

Value = $36,000 / 0.09 = $400,000

Question 95 - Mock Test 2

(A) Annual Depreciation = Cost / Economic Life

Annual Depreciation = $24,000 / 30 years = $800 per year

Total Depreciation = Annual Depreciation × Number of Years

Total Depreciation = $800 per year × 5 years = $4,000

Depreciated Value = Original Cost - Total Depreciation

Depreciated Value = $24,000 - $4,000 = $20,000.

Question 96 - Mock Test 2

(A) Land value: $300,000 × 25% = $75,000

Depreciable basis: $300,000 - $75,000 = $225,000

Annual depreciation: $225,000 ÷ 39 years ≈ $5,769.23

Office area percentage: 600 SF ÷ 3,000 SF = 20%

Home office depreciation: $5,769.23 × 20% = $1,153.85

Therefore, Chris can write off approximately $1,154 per year for his home office depreciation.

Question 97 - Mock Test 2

(D) Value = Land Value + (Replacement Cost of Improvements - Depreciation)

Depreciated Cost = $450,000 (Replacement Cost) - $75,000 (Depreciation) = $375,000

Total Value = $100,000 (Land Value) + $375,000 (Depreciated Improvements) = $475,000

Question 98 - Mock Test 2

(B) Original land value: $150,000

Appreciation amount: $150,000 × 20% = $150,000 × 0.20 = $30,000

Current land value: $150,000 + $30,000 = $180,000

Original cost of improvements: $600,000 (Total cost) - $150,000 (Land value) = $450,000

Annual depreciation: $450,000 ÷ 30 years = $15,000 per year

Total depreciation: $15,000 per year × 6 years = $90,000

Depreciated improvements value: $450,000 - $90,000 = $360,000

Total property value: $180,000 (Current land value) + $360,000 (Depreciated improvements) = $540,000

Question 99 - Mock Test 2

(C) GRM = Sale Price / Monthly Gross Rent

GRM = $360,000 / $3,000

GRM = 120

Question 100 - Mock Test 2

(B) Annual Gross Income = Monthly Gross Income × 12

Annual Gross Income = $4,000 × 12 = $48,000

Sale Price = Gross Income Multiplier × Annual Gross Income

Sale Price = 15 × $48,000 = $720,000

Mock Test 3

Question 1 - Mock Test 3

(B) A percentage lease is a rental that is calculated as a percentage of the monthly or annual gross sales on the property. Percentage leases are frequent in large retail establishments, particularly in shopping malls. The percentage lease is based on the principle that both the landlord and the tenant should benefit from the leased premises' location. There are numerous types of percentage leases, including the straight percentage of gross income with no minimum (uncommon), the fixed minimum rent plus a percentage of the gross, the fixed minimum rent against a percentage of the gross, whichever is greater, and the fixed minimum rent plus a percentage of the gross, with a percentage rental ceiling (among others).

Question 2 - Mock Test 3

(A) There are three types of written assessment reports: narrative reports, short form reports, and letter reports. The narrative evaluation report is the most extensive of the three.

Question 3 - Mock Test 3

(D) An abstract of title is a summary of the title deeds and documentation that prove an owner's right to sell of land, as well as any encumbrances associated with the property.

Question 4 - Mock Test 3

(D) The bundle of rights, also known as bundle of rights theory, is a long-standing idea in real estate ownership. It refers to all of the legal rights that come with owning real property.

Question 5 - Mock Test 3

(A) Avulsion, in real property law, is an abrupt loss or addition of land caused by natural forces (typically water). It varies from accretion. In real estate law, the term accretion refers to an increase in land caused by the deposition of dirt along the coastline of a lake, stream, or sea. While accretion is a gift from Mother Nature to landowners, erosion and avulsion can cause property to shrink in size.

Question 6 - Mock Test 3

(A) A fee simple or fee simple absolute is a land estate that is owned freehold. It is a method of owning real estate and land in common law countries that allows for the maximum possible ownership stake in real property.

Question 7 - Mock Test 3

(A) A defeasible estate is formed when a grantor transfers land on a conditional basis. The transfer may become void or susceptible to annulment if the grantor's stated event or condition occurs.

Question 8 - Mock Test 3

(D) Amortization is the monthly payment plan for your mortgage loan. An amortization schedule shows you how much of your monthly mortgage payment is allocated to interest and how much to principal.

Question 9 - Mock Test 3

(D) Condemnation frequently occurs when a taxpayer owns property or real estate in an area designated for public use or building. Condemnation is the process of taking land, whereas eminent domain refers to the government's right to take land.

Question 10 - Mock Test 3

(B) Redlining is an illegal practice in the housing business whereby mortgage companies prevent minority populations from acquiring house loans to buy homes in neighboring communities while also denying them cash to upgrade their current homes.

Question 11 - Mock Test 3

(A) In finance, the principal refers to the outstanding balance on the original loan amount. The interest is a charge for using the money. The rate of return is the return on investment in a property, which is one way to assess its profitability. An owner's equity is the amount of money left after current liens, including the mortgage, are deducted from the property's current market value.

Question 12 - Mock Test 3

(B) Under the Equal Credit Opportunity Act, lenders may not discriminate against a borrower based on marital status, question about the applicant's plans to start a family, or refuse credit based on the applicant's gender.

Question 13 - Mock Test 3

(B) A conventional loan is a mortgage that does not fall under a specific government program, such as the Federal Housing Administration (FHA), Department of Agriculture (USDA), or Department of Veterans' Affairs (VA).

Question 14 - Mock Test 3

(B) The Truth in Lending Act (TILA) of 1968 is a federal law in the United States that requires disclosures regarding the terms and expenses of consumer credit in order to encourage informed borrowing. TILA standardizes how borrowing expenses are computed and disclosed, including loan fees, loan finder fees, and service charges. TILA does not cover costs linked with the borrower's personal attorney fees.

Question 15 - Mock Test 3

(D) A conventional mortgage is a home loan that is neither guaranteed or insured by the federal government, and is typically insured by private companies. Conventional mortgages that meet the requirements of Fannie Mae and Freddie Mac typically need a 3% down payment.

Question 16 - Mock Test 3

(A) The Truth in Lending Act of 1968 is a federal law in the United States aiming to encourage the informed use of consumer credit by requiring disclosures about its terms and costs, as well as standardizing how borrowing costs are calculated and published.

Question 17 - Mock Test 3

(C) Second mortgages provide a higher risk to lenders because they are "second" in line behind the first mortgage holder. In the event of foreclosure, this means that the first mortgage holder is paid in full before any remaining funds are dispersed. This increased exposure often leads to higher interest rates.

Question 18 - Mock Test 3

(B) The Federal Trade Commission Act of 1914 established the Federal Trade Commission as an independent body of the United States government. Its primary aim is to promote consumer protection while also eliminating and preventing anticompetitive economic practices including coercive monopolies. It enforces and regulates more than 70 laws, including the Truth in Lending Act. The FTC shares this jurisdiction with the Consumer Financial Protection Bureau (which is not an answer but may be right).

Question 19 - Mock Test 3

(A) Land contracts are a type of seller finance. It's similar to a mortgage, but instead of borrowing money from a lender or bank to acquire real estate, the buyer pays the real estate owner, or seller, until the entire purchase price is paid.

Question 20 - Mock Test 3

(A) Debit means an amount owing.

Question 21 - Mock Test 3

(C) Once the contract specifies the sum that will serve as liquidated damages in the event of nonperformance, no higher amount can be sought in court.

Question 22 - Mock Test 3

(A) An executory contract has not yet been conducted; it will be executed following the sale.

Question 23 - Mock Test 3

(C) A voidable contract allows either party to rescind. The contract is valid at the time of its establishment, but it may be invalidated later. Most sales contracts are voidable because they include contingency provisions. Contracts signed under coercion, deceit, or fraud are voidable.

Question 24 - Mock Test 3

(A) In a Sale Leaseback, the seller leases the newly sold property back from the buyer. The seller is now a renter, which allows him to deduct all future rent payments as a business expense.

Question 25 - Mock Test 3

(B) A periodic tenancy is a lease that renews from period to period until one of the parties gives notice of termination. A periodic tenancy has no specific end date.

Question 26 - Mock Test 3

(D) A Protection length Clause (safety clause) in a listing allows a broker to collect a commission for a set length of time after the term of the listing has expired. It is a set amount of time for the licensee to conclude deals with prospects that they have been working with during the listing's term. This is not the time to pursue a fresh opportunity. To earn a commission within the protection time clause, they must submit the prospects' names in writing at the end of the listing period.

Question 27 - Mock Test 3

(B) Exclusive authorization and right to sell. A listing is a contract in which the owner agrees to sell the property in issue via the listing broker. The listing broker is not required to demonstrate that he is the buyer's "procuring cause". They get compensated regardless of who brings the buyer.

Question 28 - Mock Test 3

(A) Either side may attempt to renegotiate the conditions of the agreement. The owner has the right to accept or reject the buyer's offer.

Question 29 - Mock Test 3

(A) A sales contract can be valid even without earnest money. Earnest money's primary purpose is to comfort the seller and demonstrate the buyer's good faith.

Question 30 - Mock Test 3

(A) Under an Exclusive Authorization and Right to Sell Listing, the listing broker is entitled to a commission if the property sells as a result of the broker's or another person's efforts. To be eligible for a commission, the broker does not need to find a buyer or act as the procuring cause.

Question 31 - Mock Test 3

(D) A contractor may file a mechanic's lien if an owner refuses to pay for work done on an upgrade. The lien is a specific, involuntary claim on the property. A general lien covers both personal and real property.

Question 32 - Mock Test 3

(B) The property owner nominated Bill as the remainderman, the person to whom the property would transfer following Scott's death. When Scott dies, the life estate terminates, and the property immediately goes to Bill. If the property owner does not choose a remainderman when transferring the life estate to Scott, ownership reverts to the original property owner or her heirs.

Question 33 - Mock Test 3

(D) The term ad valorem comes from the Latin ad valentiam, which means "according to value." It is typically used to describe a tax imposed on the value of property. Real property taxes imposed by states, counties, and localities are the most common sort of ad valorem tax. Ad valorem taxes can, however, be levied on personal property. For example, a motor vehicle tax may be levied on personal property like an automobile.

Question 34 - Mock Test 3

(B) Plottage is the joint ownership of two or more adjacent units or lots, resulting in a new merged property with a value greater than the sum of the individual lot values. Assemblage is the process of plotting.

Question 35 - Mock Test 3

(D) Joint tenancy includes the right to survivorship, which means that if one of the tenants dies, the property belongs to the surviving owner(s). In this case, the ladies acquired title as joint tenants. When one woman died, her part was transferred to the other owner, who now owns the land in severalty.

Question 36 - Mock Test 3

(A) Easements allow access, not use. Commercial licenses, such as those required for selling beverages, souvenirs, or services, are valid for a prolonged length of time. Although tickets to sporting events, concerts, and performances are technically licenses, they differ from the majority

in terms of restrictions. For example, a concert ticket does not grant the holder the freedom to sit anywhere he or she pleases or to stroll backstage to meet the artists.

Question 37 - Mock Test 3

(B) Municipalities use buffer zones, such as parks and hiking paths, to separate residential and non-residential areas. A variance is authority to construct a structure or carry out a usage specifically banned by zoning rules. A utility easement is an interest in land that allows it to be utilized for utilities like electricity, gas, or water lines. A nonconforming use existed prior to the existing zoning ordinances that prohibit it.

Question 38 - Mock Test 3

(A) Tenancy at sufferance is an agreement under which a property renter is legally authorized to remain on a property after the lease period has expired but before the landlord requests that the tenant remove the property. If a tenancy at sufferance occurs, the original lease terms must be followed, including the payment of any rent.

Question 39 - Mock Test 3

(B) The bundle of rights is a metaphor for understanding the complexities of property ownership. It encompasses not only the property rights of disposition, exclusion, enjoyment, possession, and control, but also the ownership of rights above the property (air rights), rights below the property (mineral rights), and subjacent support.

Question 40 - Mock Test 3

(B) A judicial action to establish or settle the title to a certain property, particularly when there is a cloud on it. All parties with a potential claim or interest in the property must be represented in the case. An opposing possessor frequently uses a quiet title action to substantiate the title, as having formal record title makes it easier to market the property. After the court's judgment or decree has been entered, proper record notice of the claimant's right and interest in the property is established.

Question 41 - Mock Test 3

(C) Based on information gathered from his survey, the appraiser creates an estimate that is valid as of a particular date. It is unreasonable to expect him to predict the value of what will occur tomorrow or in the future.

Question 42 - Mock Test 3

(C) Even if the building was previously a house, the income strategy is the best fit for revenue-producing buildings like an office building. The gross rent multiplier is not a method for determining value. It is the process of determining the market value of an income-producing residential property. An appraiser may utilize the sales comparison and replacement cost procedures to help determine a value estimate, but these approaches are not as useful or precise as the revenue approach for specific property. In the appraiser's final reconciliation, their results will be given less weight than those from the income method.

Question 43 - Mock Test 3

(D) The Market Data (Comparison) Approach is the process of evaluating the worth of a property by examining and comparing real transactions of similar properties. The market data approach becomes less credible during periods of fast economic change or volatility, inactive markets, and the absence of comparables to the subject property.

Question 44 - Mock Test 3

(D) The appraiser does not determine the value. After the appraiser has completed the analysis and considered all of the data, he or she will produce an estimated value. An appraisal is a formal assessment of value.

Question 45 - Mock Test 3

(C) Accretion is the gradual addition of sand or dirt to a piece of land caused by the movement of a river or other body of water. Avulsion is the loss of land caused by a sudden or unexpected natural event, such as a flash flood that reroutes a river.

Question 46 - Mock Test 3

(A) If an appraiser is evaluating a property that includes a no-value building that must be demolished, the appraiser should deduct the demolition expenses from the property's appraised value.

Question 47 - Mock Test 3

(A) Both residential and commercial properties require precise lot size measurements. If there is a difference between the lot size quoted in a listing contract or deed and the actual lot size, the real lot size determined by a survey will take precedence. Most MLS services will state that any square footage stated is an approximation.

Question 48 - Mock Test 3

(B) The allocation method (also known as the abstraction or extraction method) is an appraisal method in which the appraiser calculates the land value of any upgraded property by subtracting or abstracting the value of any site improvements from the overall sales price of the property. The remaining sum represents the land's projected sales price or stated worth.

Question 49 - Mock Test 3

(A) Outdated plumbing is one example of an outdated design component that reduces the value of a property. The loss of value may be reversible if the cost of upgrading the plumbing is compensated by the expected enhanced value of the property. The plumbing is not deteriorating due to a lack of upkeep. External depreciation refers to a condition that exists outside of the property itself.

Question 50 - Mock Test 3

(A) Depreciation is the loss of value in real property caused by aging, physical degradation, or functional or economic obsolescence.

Question 51 - Mock Test 3

(B) Tenancy in Common refers to the ownership of real property by two or more people who have an interest in it; they share simply possession, not time, title, or interest equality. Joint tenancy is an interest in property acquired by two or more joint tenants with an equal interest, sharing the same title and possession, and commencing simultaneously. When a joint tenant dies, his or her interest falls to the surviving joint tenants rather than the deceased's heirs.

Question 52 - Mock Test 3

(D) Land and improvements are evaluated separately, then combined and multiplied by a single tax rate.

Question 53 - Mock Test 3

(A) Title insurance is the most reliable source of marketable title among the options available.

Question 54 - Mock Test 3

(D) The "cost basis" of a property is its purchase price or investment amount, plus commissions and other charges. The cost basis is used to calculate capital gains and losses for tax reasons.

Question 55 - Mock Test 3

(D) The phrase "boot" does not appear in the Internal Revenue Code or the Regulations, although it is frequently used when discussing the tax implications of a Section 1031 tax-deferred exchange. For example, if a $150,000 property is exchanged for a $145,000 property plus $5,000 cash, the cash is referred to be the "boot." The receipt of footwear does not disqualify an exchange, but it may result in a taxable gain.

Question 56 - Mock Test 3

(C) This right of redemption is referred to as "statutory" since it is legally mandated by law, as opposed to the customary right of redemption, which lenders may or may not obey. The statutory right of redemption (where applicable) is exercised following a foreclosure sale, but the equitable right of redemption is exercised prior to a foreclosure sale.

Question 57 - Mock Test 3

(D) "Devise" is to make a gift of real property through the donor's last will and testament. A life estate can be rented, sold, or mortgaged (albeit the "estate" in the property expires when the measuring life does), but it cannot be willed.

Question 58 - Mock Test 3

(B) In US property law, a cloud on title or title defect is any imperfection in a property's chain of title that would cause a reasonable person to hesitate before accepting a conveyance of title. It can be resolved by receiving proof of satisfaction from the affected parties or by issuing a "quiet title" order.

Question 59 - Mock Test 3

(D) The extended policy covers developments on adjacent land.

Question 60 - Mock Test 3

(D) Riparian rights are water rights that apply to a flowing body of water, such as a river or stream. Littoral rights refer to bodies of water that do not flow, such as a lake or ocean.

Question 61 - Mock Test 3

(B) The sales comparison approach is evaluating the sale prices of previously sold properties that are comparable to the subject, then making dollar changes to the price of each comparable to account for competitive differences with the subject. After determining the adjusted value of each comparative, the appraiser weights its reliability as well as the reasons that influenced how the changes were made. Weighting produces a final value range based on the most trustworthy components in the analysis.

Question 62 - Mock Test 3

(D) The sales comparison method is extensively utilized since it considers the subject property's individual attributes in comparison to rival properties. Furthermore, because the data is up to date, the approach takes into account current market conditions.

Question 63 - Mock Test 3

(A) If the comparable falls short of the subject in some way, an amount is added to its price. If the comparable item outperforms the topic in some way, the similar's sale price is reduced by a certain amount. This eliminates the comparable's competitive advantage or disadvantage in an adjustment area. For example, a similar has a swimming pool, whereas the topic does not. To make up the difference, the appraiser deducts a certain amount, say $6,000, from the sale price of the comparable.

Question 64 - Mock Test 3

(B) In general, the fewer the total number of adjustments, the smaller the adjustment amounts, and the lower the total adjustment amount, the more reliable the comparison.

Question 65 - Mock Test 3

(C) Because the comparable has an extra bath, it is shifted downward to align with the subject. In contrast, because there is no patio, the appraiser increases the value of the comparable. Thus, $400,000 minus $7,000 + $2,000 equals $395,000.

Question 66 - Mock Test 3

(D) The steps involved in the cost approach are valuing the land "as if vacant," estimating improvements' costs, calculating accrued depreciation and subtracting it, and then adding the estimated land value to the estimated depreciated cost of the improvements.

Question 67 - Mock Test 3

(B) The cost approach has the following advantages: it establishes a maximum value for the topic based on the undepreciated cost of replicating the improvements. When appraising a property with recent improvements—the highest and best use of the property—it is also incredibly accurate.

Question 68 - Mock Test 3

(C) Every property improvement has an economic life, but as physical degeneration wears down, that life gets progressively shorter every year. Given that land does not lose value, the property as a whole does not. In a similar vein, an upgrade that is updated or fixed can become valuable again. And lastly, not every property depreciates due to economic obsolescence.

Question 69 - Mock Test 3

(D) Add the land value to the depreciated improvement's worth in order to determine value using the cost approach. Therefore, you have $575,00 ($475,000 - $50,000) plus $150,000.

Question 70 - Mock Test 3

(B) The income capitalization method provides an appraiser with an indicator of value by dividing the subject's expected net operating income by the rate of return, or capitalization rate. The formula is NOI / Cap Rate = Value.

Question 71 - Mock Test 3

(C) Steering occurs when agents "steer" buyers toward specific communities. Blockbusting and panic peddling are opposite sides of the same coin. They describe realtors pressuring sellers to "panic-sell" their homes because a minority population is moving into the community.

Question 72 - Mock Test 3

(D) The first statement is another attempt at "blockbusting." The second is a type of "steering" in which people from a specific group are encouraged to shop in one town or avoid another.

Question 73 - Mock Test 3

(C) The law requires "reasonable accommodation" for disabled tenants. Even if the landlord has a "no pets" policy, he or she must allow a blind person to have a guiding dog. This does not imply that all restrictions are suspended for that person; noise, safety, and "use of premises policies" may still be enforced.

Question 74 - Mock Test 3

(B) Although cash (in the form of a check) is the most commonly recognized type of earnest money, a personal note or other "valuable consideration" acceptable to the owner is permitted.

Question 75 - Mock Test 3

(B) An exclusive listing deal means that you provide your agent/broker exclusive rights to locate a buyer for your home. With this sort of agreement, no other agent/broker will be reimbursed for bringing purchasers to your home without following the terms of the signed listing agreement. This is why a precise termination date is required, because if the connection does not work out, a time must be set for when the seller can enter into a contract with a new broker/agent without penalty.

Question 76 - Mock Test 3

(A) Puffing occurs when a licensee exaggerates the benefits or qualities of a property. It is the sometimes inflated impression that a salesperson or seller may give to a buyer about a property for sale. It is recognized in law as an opinion that does not necessarily reflect the facts.

Question 77 - Mock Test 3

(C) Company Dollar is the gross income of an office minus commissions.

Question 78 - Mock Test 3

(D) A percentage lease is a lease in which the tenant pays a base rent plus a percentage of any revenue generated while conducting business on the rental property. It's a term commonly used in commercial real estate.

Question 79 - Mock Test 3

(D) Discrimination based on race became prohibited in 1866, when Congress approved the Civil Rights Act. Later revisions of the Civil Rights Act (1964, 1968, and the Americans with Disabilities Act of 1990) expanded protections to other groups of US citizens.

Question 80 - Mock Test 3

(A) The Equal Credit Opportunity Act, enacted in 1992, forbids a wide range of discriminatory lending practices, including the granting or denial of credit or the costs of borrowing based on race, gender, marital status, source of income (e.g., public assistance), and other criteria.

Question 81 - Mock Test 3

(D) The majority of agency relationships are formed through written agreement, but they can also be formed through ratification (consenting to the agent's actions) and estoppel (conduct by a principal that leads a third party, such as a buyer, to reasonably believe an agent has an agency agreement, so the principal cannot reverse that conduct).

Question 82 - Mock Test 3

(C) If a broker is not allowed by the seller to receive a deposit, general agency regulations allow the broker to serve as the buyer's (offeror's) agent for that transaction. This means that the seller's broker will have fiduciary duties to the potential bidder for the deposit only.

Question 83 - Mock Test 3

(B) A licensee must deliver all written offers to a seller immediately, unless the offer is frivolous or the seller has asked the licensee not to present certain offers.

Question 84 - Mock Test 3

(D) The obligation of secrecy prohibits Brown from disclosing any material that could harm his client's negotiation position.

Question 85 - Mock Test 3

(D) Ostensible authority occurs when a third party is led to assume that an agent and a principle have an agency relationship based on the principal's behavior. If a broker acts as a seller's agent and the seller does not object, and the broker's efforts result in a transaction, the broker will most likely be judged to have ostensible power.

Question 86 - Mock Test 3

(A) The real estate agent has a "agency" relationship with the client, which typically entails a contractual agreement. In this connection, the agent serves as the fiduciary, not vice versa. A customer has no contractual agreement with the agent, however a subagent is the relationship that an agent can have with the buyer (if not contracted directly by the buyer). When considering questions like this, it is critical to select the finest alternative available.

Question 87 - Mock Test 3

(B) The broker who communicated the acceptance to the buyer is the most qualified for a commission because he or she "consummated" (or completed) the agreement.

Question 88 - Mock Test 3

(C) The commission shall be decided by mutual agreement between the parties, but it must be stated that it is negotiable.

Question 89 - Mock Test 3

(C) A verbal agreement between two brokers to split a commission is binding. The selling broker's option would be to sue the listing broker. The "selling broker" is the one who submits the offer.

Question 90 - Mock Test 3

(D) Real estate brokers can set commission rates or fees for their own firms on their own, but they cannot make agreements with other firms to do the same, which is known as "collusion". Commission rate decisions must be made solely based on a broker's business judgment and revenue requirements, with no input from competing brokers. Standardizing management fees among rival brokerages and awarding market shares based on house value both violate antitrust rules.

Question 91 - Mock Test 3

(A) Loan Amount = Purchase Price × LTV

Loan Amount = $500,000 × 70% = $350,000

Annual Interest = Loan Amount × Interest Rate

Annual Interest = $350,000 × 5% = $17,500

Monthly Interest Payment = Annual Interest / 12

Monthly Interest Payment = $17,500 / 12 = $1,458.33

Question 92 - Mock Test 3

(A) Annual Interest = Monthly Payment × 12

Annual Interest = $1,800 × 12 = $21,600

Loan Principal = Annual Interest / Interest Rate

Loan Principal = $21,600 / 0.06 = $360,000.

Question 93 - Mock Test 3

(B) Annual Payment = Monthly Payment × 12

Annual Payment = $1,200 × 12 = $14,400

Interest Rate = (Annual Payment / Principal Balance) × 100%

Interest Rate = ($14,400 / $288,000) × 100%

Interest Rate = (0.05) × 100% = 5.00%.

Question 94 - Mock Test 3

(B) First month's interest:

$320,000 x 5.75% ÷ 12 = $1,533.33

Principal payment: $1,868 - $1,533.33 = $334.67

New principal balance: $320,000 - $334.67 = $319,665.33

Second month's interest: $319,665.33 x 5.75% ÷ 12 ≈ $1,531.88.

Question 95 - Mock Test 3

(B) First option annual interest: $100,000 × 5.5% = $5,500 per year.

Total interest over 5 years: $5,500 × 5 years = $27,500.

Second option annual interest: $100,000 × 5.25% = $5,250 per year.

Total interest over 5 years: $5,250 × 5 years = $26,250.

1 point = 1% of $100,000 = $1,000.

Total cost for the second option: $26,250 (interest) + $1,000 (points) = $27,250

Difference in total costs: $27,500 (first option) - $27,250 (second option) = $250.

Conclusion: The second option costs $250 less than the first option.

Question 96 - Mock Test 3

(D) Loan Amount = Home Price × Loan-to-Value (LTV) Ratio

Loan Amount = $360,000 × 85% = $306,000

Points Percentage = (Points Paid / Loan Amount) × 100%

Points Percentage = ($6,120 / $306,000) × 100% = 0.02 × 100% = 2%

Number of Points = Points Percentage

Number of Points = 2 points.

Question 97 - Mock Test 3

(A) Definition: 1 point = 1% of the loan amount.

2 points = 2%

Points Paid: Loan Amount × Points Percentage = $360,000 × 2%

= $7,200

Question 98 - Mock Test 3

(C) Loan Amount = Purchase Price × LTV Ratio

Purchase Price = Loan Amount / LTV Ratio

Purchase Price = $450,000 / 0.75

Purchase Price = $600,000.

Question 99 - Mock Test 3

(C) Annual Interest Paid = Monthly Payment × 12

Annual Interest Paid = $2,000 × 12 = $24,000

Loan Amount = Annual Interest Paid / Interest Rate

Interest Rate = 5.5% = 0.055

Loan Amount = $24,000 / 0.055 = $436,363.64

Loan Amount = Loan-to-Value Ratio × Purchase Price

Purchase Price = Loan Amount / Loan-to-Value Ratio

Loan-to-Value Ratio = 80% = 0.80

Purchase Price = $436,363.64 / 0.80 = $545,454.55

Round the purchase price to the nearest dollar: Purchase Price ≈ $545,455.

Question 100 - Mock Test 3

(B) Monthly Gross Income = Annual Gross Income / 12

Monthly Gross Income = $84,000 / 12 = $7,000

Maximum Housing Expense = Monthly Gross Income × Income Ratio

Maximum Housing Expense = $7,000 × 28% = $1,960.

Mock Test 4

Question 1 - Mock Test 4

(B) Abandonment is the voluntary surrender of ownership rights or another interest (such as an easement) by failing to use the property, combined with a desire to abandon (give up the interest).

Question 2 - Mock Test 4

(C) An abstract of title is a report on what was discovered during a title search, which is a search of virtually all public records pertaining to the property's title, such as previous titles and liens. The abstract of title is then given to the buyer's attorney for review. When the buyer's attorney determines that the seller has marketable title and issues an attorney's opinion of title, the closing can take place.

Question 3 - Mock Test 4

(D) Zoning is a technique of urban planning in which a municipality or other tier of government divides land into divisions called zones, each with its own set of laws for new development that differs from other zones.

Question 4 - Mock Test 4

(D) A compilation of recorded documents pertaining to a parcel of property, from which an attorney may form an opinion on the status of title. Abstracts of Title are still used in some states, however they are gradually becoming obsolete in favor of title insurance. A chain of title search begins with looking for the current owner's name in a grantee index. An abstract of title combines data from deeds, mortgages, easements, and obligations to create a simplified history of the title.

Question 5 - Mock Test 4

(B) Yield is defined as the ratio of an investment's revenue to its entire cost over time.

Question 6 - Mock Test 4

(D) In contrast to real property or real estate, personal property is typically defined as transportable property. In common law systems, personal property is sometimes known as chattels or personalty.

Question 7 - Mock Test 4

(D) Specific performance allows a buyer to compel the seller to fulfill the terms of the purchase contract when money isn't enough to compensate for a breach. Brokers cannot sue for specific performance and will seek monetary damages for contract violations instead.

Question 8 - Mock Test 4

(C) State regulations vary as to whether a net listing is authorized; however, everyone should be aware of what it is. A net listing permits the agent to keep any amount of money beyond the seller's stipulated price at the end of the sale. In other words, if the house sells for more than the seller's asking price, the agent may keep or 'net' the difference.

Question 9 - Mock Test 4

(C) An encumbrance is a right to, interest in, or legal liability over property that does not prevent title transfer but may reduce its value. Encumbrances can be categorized in numerous ways. They could be financial or non-financial. An easement is not a financial encumbrance, whereas a lien is. However, since the query does not identify the sort of encumbrance and encumbrance is an option. The only possible answer is encumbrance.

Question 10 - Mock Test 4

(D) The government survey system (also known as the rectangular survey system) divides legal descriptions of land into grids. The township is the largest portion of the government survey system, measuring six by six miles and divided into 36 one-square-mile pieces.

Question 11 - Mock Test 4

(A) Payment is considered late if it is received by the lender more than ten (10) days after the due date.

Question 12 - Mock Test 4

(C) The CFPB does not allow borrowers to cancel first or second home purchase loans, although they do have cancellation rights for other loans, such as refinancing or home equity. The CFPB requires lenders to give borrowers with a new loan closing disclosure that includes all charges to be paid by the borrower and seller at loan settlement. Lenders must give a fresh loan estimate of closing costs within three business days of receiving a loan application, along with information on settlement expenses.

Question 13 - Mock Test 4

(D) A deed of trust, unlike a mortgage, simplifies the foreclosure procedure in the event of default.

Question 14 - Mock Test 4

(D) All property taxes are income tax deductible. Interest deductions are only available for the first and second residences. Insurance premiums are not deductible.

Question 15 - Mock Test 4

(B) The appraiser is particularly concerned with the property's income when determining its worth. The cost approach takes into account accumulated depreciation. The sales comparison approach is based on the sales prices of comparable properties, however identifying comparable properties for commercial properties can be problematic. Debt service (mortgage payments) is not considered an operating expense that must be removed from annual operating expenses when calculating a commercial property's net operating income.

Question 16 - Mock Test 4

(B) Equity is the difference between a property's value and the amount owing on it. A lien is a hold or claim on another's property to satisfy an outstanding debt.

Question 17 - Mock Test 4

(A) Conventional loans come from private sources. A conventional mortgage or conventional loan is any sort of homebuyer's loan that is not supplied or guaranteed by a government body.

Question 18 - Mock Test 4

(A) Congress passed the Real Estate Settlement Procedures Act, or RESPA, to improve settlement cost disclosures for homebuyers and sellers while also eliminating abusive tactics in the real estate settlement process. While many kickbacks and referral payments are forbidden, RESPA allows permit "payment pursuant to cooperative brokerage and referral arrangements," such as those between MLS members.

Question 19 - Mock Test 4

(C) A promissory note, also known as a note payable, is a legal instrument (more specifically, a financial and debt instrument) in which one party (the maker or issuer) promises in writing to pay a specific sum of money to the other (the payee), either at a fixed or determinable future time. A borrower putting down 30% does not eliminate the necessity for a promissory note; that is up to the lending institution.

Question 20 - Mock Test 4

(A) To remove the Deed of Trust from the title to the property, a Deed of Reconveyance must be lodged with the County Recorder or Recorder of Deeds.

Question 21 - Mock Test 4

(A) Any changes should be initialed by both the person making the change and the person receiving it.

Question 22 - Mock Test 4

(C) In some areas, a deed of trust secures a promissory note and the property used as security for a house loan. If payment is not made in accordance with the provisions of the note and deed of trust, the beneficiary may direct a third entity holding the title, known as "the trustee," to foreclose on the property in accordance with the deed of trust. Be careful with the wording, as substituting the two terms can result in a drastically different meaning.

Question 23 - Mock Test 4

(C) According to the Statute of Frauds, all real estate contracts must be in writing in order to be legally binding.

Question 24 - Mock Test 4

(A) The four requirements for a legitimate contract are capable parties, mutual consent, offer and acceptance, and a lawful object. Certain other contracts, such as real estate transactions, must be in writing, but writing is not needed for all contracts.

Question 25 - Mock Test 4

(D) A contract must be legitimate in both its creation and operation. The contract is null and void unless both its consideration and object are legitimate.

Question 26 - Mock Test 4

(B) When acting as a listing agent, you must deliver any signed offer to acquire (unless legally required differently). The earnest money deposit is normally in the form of a personal check, money order, or cashier's check, but it can also be in the form of a promissory note if the seller agrees.

Question 27 - Mock Test 4

(B) A voidable contract may be revoked or invalidated by one party, whereas a void contract has no legal effect. A contract with an illegal intent (such as stealing another person's property) is simply void, not voidable. Fraud would render a contract voidable because the buyer still has the option to proceed with the transaction. For example, suppose a buyer signed a contract to buy a red house but the house was actually blue. Although they were misled about the color of the house, it may not matter to them because they want to paint it yellow.

Question 28 - Mock Test 4

(A) Time is of the essence is a basic contract clause that assures that all dates and times of day specified in the contract are vital and cannot be ignored by any of the parties without the approval of the others, unless the contract is breached.

Question 29 - Mock Test 4

(B) Despite the temptation to favor his own bid, the listing broker has a fiduciary duty to submit both offers. Since the broker has not yet presented his own offer, he should present both offers to the seller during the same call.

Question 30 - Mock Test 4

(C) After disposing of the property, the seller might calculate losses and seek compensatory damages from the defaulting buyer.

Question 31 - Mock Test 4

(A) Tenants in Common is when you share a set proportion of ownership rights in real property but not an exact area--this is known as "undivided interest". While their shares may be unequal (20%, 25%, 40%, 15%), for example, one does not own the shed, whereas another owns the bathroom, one owns the kitchen, and one owns the bedroom, each of the four tenants has equal rights to the entire property.

Question 32 - Mock Test 4

(B) Property is accompanied with a set of rights that are inherent in property ownership. The bundle of rights comprises the right to use, sell, mortgage, lease, enter, and give away, as well as the right not to exercise any of these rights. It is useful to envisage a collection of rights that can be disassembled and reconstructed. Certain varieties of joint property ownership include the right of "survivorship," which means that any surviving co-owners take over a dying owner's interest in the property. For example, if Pete and John are joint tenants with the right of survivorship and Pete dies, John inherits his part in the property, not Pete's heirs.

Question 33 - Mock Test 4

(B) Tenancy in common is formed when two or more people have an undivided interest in a property. Undivided interest means that each person has an equal title to all of the property, but the husband and wife may have uneven shares of the property--for example, the wife may possess 60% and the husband 40%. A tenancy in Common requires merely unity of possession. There is no automatic right of survivorship, and a tenant in common might leave their interest by will.

Question 34 - Mock Test 4

(C) Eminent domain allows the government to take private property without the owner's consent, sometimes delegating this power to utilities for infrastructure projects like telephone and power lines. This power to expropriate property or rights can be daunting. However, owners receive monetary compensation and the seized property is used for public, civic, or economic development purposes. Importantly, the government often prefers to negotiate the purchase of property like any buyer, and owners can reject these offers just as they would in any real estate transaction.

Question 35 - Mock Test 4

(D) Real property refers to legally immovable property. Examples include load-bearing walls, equity in a mutual water utility, and minerals.

Question 36 - Mock Test 4

(A) Real estate is made up of land and buildings, as well as natural resources such as the landowner's crops, minerals or water, and appurtenances such as sheds, swimming pools, and fences. Harvested crops are considered emblems and belong to the tenant farmer.

Question 37 - Mock Test 4

(D) A life estate "pur autre vie" (French for "for another's life") refers to the length of a property interest. While it is similar to a life estate, it varies in that a person's life interest lasts for the duration of another person's life rather than the life estate-holder's.

Question 38 - Mock Test 4

(D) Cooperative ownership is an apartment ownership model comparable to that of a condominium. In a cooperative ownership, the buyer receives shares of stock in the building corporation as well as a lease or assignment of the seller's lease on the unit for sale.

Question 39 - Mock Test 4

(B) The lot and block system is commonly used to describe property in developments. The rectangular government survey system splits land into rectangles and defines them with principal meridian and base lines. The metes and bounds system defines a parcel's boundary by beginning and ending at the same location. A street address does not constitute a legal property description.

Question 40 - Mock Test 4

(D) For years, no notice is required to terminate an estate because the lease agreement specifies an expiration date. When the date arrives, the lease ends and the tenant's rights are ended.

Question 41 - Mock Test 4

(C) The cost approach is best suited to new buildings rather than existing ones, because the cost of materials will remain comparable to the cost of building the new building. The older the structure, the more variables can be used to estimate its value. However, if something was created yesterday, the cost may be estimated considerably more accurately.

Question 42 - Mock Test 4

(D) The principle of contribution is used to determine the worth of amenities like pools. Substitution underpins all approaches to value and asserts that the market must be utilized to validate pricing. Conformity is used to examine whether a property conforms to the area through progression and regression.

Question 43 - Mock Test 4

(B) To maintain the accuracy and "transparency" of his estimates, an appraiser reconciles variances rather than averaging comparable sales to determine a final value.

Question 44 - Mock Test 4

(C) A foreclosed home frequently sells for less than its true market value. To compensate for the foreclosed home's sale below market value, the appraiser will apply a positive, upward adjustment to the sales price. The sales comparison approach involves making modifications to the sales prices of comparable properties rather than the subject property itself.

Question 45 - Mock Test 4

(D) Market data is least reliable when the market is experiencing fast economic change or is dormant. This strategy is based on determining the pricing of similar properties to which the target property can be compared. As a result, if there is nothing to compare with, this method is ineffective.

Question 46 - Mock Test 4

(B) The cost approach includes the building's replacement cost, as well as depreciation and land value. The cost approach does not take into account the owner's initial building costs. The sales comparison approach takes into account the sale prices of similar properties. The property's assessed value is not used to calculate its fair market value.

Question 47 - Mock Test 4

(A) An increase in value over time is called appreciation.

Question 48 - Mock Test 4

(B) The broad definition of "value" is the object's value, use, or suitability for a certain purpose.

Question 49 - Mock Test 4

(C) The most difficult aspect of the market data method of appraising is adjusting for differences in the properties.

Question 50 - Mock Test 4

(A) The income approach is a way of estimating an organization's value by calculating the net present value (NPV) of predicted future earnings or cash flows. The capitalization of earnings estimate is calculated by dividing the entity's projected earnings by its capitalization rate (cap rate).

Question 51 - Mock Test 4

(A) The "chain" connects a property's successive owners, beginning with the most recent and ending with the original documented titleholder. Deeds, judgments in title litigation, affidavits, and any other papers demonstrating ownership transfers are commonly used to verify the chain of title.

Question 52 - Mock Test 4

(B) Tax shelters apply to income taxes. It is a broad phrase that refers to any property or other investment that provides the owner with income tax benefits such as deductions for property taxes, mortgage interest, and depreciation.

Question 53 - Mock Test 4

(C) Every transaction requires valuable consideration. It is the benefit that one person obtains in exchange for providing benefit to another. In general, it is money in whatever amount agreed upon by both parties, although it can also take the shape of personal property, work, or refraining from an act. If a home seller receives $150 to keep an option to buy open on the property, this is deemed "consideration" for the formation of a legitimate contract.

Question 54 - Mock Test 4

(D) Property rehabilitation refers to the process of improving the condition of real property. The restoration is typically required because the property's condition has gotten worse.

Question 55 - Mock Test 4

(C) The term "boot" isn't in the Internal Revenue Code but is used in Section 1031 tax-deferred exchanges. For instance, if a $150,000 property is exchanged for a $145,000 property plus $5,000 cash, the cash is called "boot." Receiving boot doesn't disqualify the exchange but may create a taxable gain.

Question 56 - Mock Test 4

(A) A bill of sale is a document that transfers ownership of items (personal property) from one individual to another.

Question 57 - Mock Test 4

(A) A court order instructing an officer of the court to carry out the court's judgment, such as selling foreclosed property or removing a tenant on sufferance.

Question 58 - Mock Test 4

(A) A "lis pendens" is a legal document that indicates that an action or legal proceeding (mechanic's lien filing, foreclosure) is ongoing in the courts and may impact the title to the identified property.

Question 59 - Mock Test 4

(C) The "grantor" is the person transferring the property, therefore he or she signs the deed. When a title finishes with a "or," it refers to the giver, or the givOR, if you like. A term that ends with "ee," such as "grantee," denotes the recipient because they received the object.

Question 60 - Mock Test 4

(B) A deed is an instrument that transfers ownership of a property from one person to another, whereas a title is proof of such ownership. A title is evidence of ownership, whereas a deed is evidence of transfer.

Question 61 - Mock Test 4

(C) The income technique is effective since it is utilized by investors to determine how much they should spend for a property. Thus, in the correct circumstances, it provides a solid foundation for evaluating market worth. However, the approach does not predict how much money an income property will make in the future. Furthermore, it is not an appropriate method for determining value if the subject is a non-income producing property.

Question 62 - Mock Test 4

(A) First, calculate net income by removing vacancies and expenses. Then, divide by the capitalization rate. Thus, ($60,000 -3,000 - 20,000) ÷ 10% = $370,000.

Question 63 - Mock Test 4

(D) The monthly gross rent multiplier for a property equals the price divided by the monthly rent. Thus, ($450,000 ÷ $3,000) = 150.

Question 64 - Mock Test 4

(C) To calculate annual income, multiply monthly gross income by twelve. To estimate the price, multiply annual income by the gross income multiplier. Thus, multiplying $2,400 by 12 yields $28,800. This multiplied by 14.1 equals $406,080, or 406,000 rounded.

Question 65 - Mock Test 4

(C) A state-certified appraiser has passed the relevant examinations and competency levels set by each state in accordance with federal guidelines.

Question 66 - Mock Test 4

(A) Under Title XI of FIRREA, all appraisals used in federally linked transactions must be performed by competent professionals whose professional behavior is adequately overseen. As of January 1, 1993, such federally linked appraisals could only be completed by state-certified appraisers.

Question 67 - Mock Test 4

(A) The substitution principle states that a buyer will not pay more for a property than he or she would for an equally desirable and available substitute property. For example, if three properties for sale are roughly the same size, quality, and location, a potential buyer is unlikely to choose the one that is much more expensive than the other two.

Question 68 - Mock Test 4

(A) According to this value theory, there is only one possible use for a property that generates the highest income and return. When a property is used in this way, its value is maximized. The application must, however, be legal.

Question 69 - Mock Test 4

(D) Market value is an opinion of the price that a willing seller and willing buyer would most likely agree on for a property at a given time if: the transaction is for cash; the property is exposed on the open market for a reasonable period; buyer and seller have full information about market conditions; there is no abnormal pressure on either party; it is a "arm's length" transaction; title is marketable; and the price does not include hidden influences such as special financing. Lynne paid the market price. The prior listing price and Ken's offer may be important data to the appraiser, but the evaluation must also take into account other market data, such as comparable transactions.

Question 70 - Mock Test 4

(A) The sales comparison approach is limited because each property is unique. As a result, it is difficult to locate suitable comparables, particularly for special-purpose properties. Furthermore, the market must be active; otherwise, sale prices lack consistency and dependability.

Question 71 - Mock Test 4

(D) Anti-discrimination laws do not apply to situations that violate widely recognized rules, such as paying rent on time, maintaining the premises, and adhering to use agreements.

Question 72 - Mock Test 4

(D) Regardless of the acceptance condition, a buyer may rescind an offer at any moment before the seller has accepted and conveyed that acceptance to the buyer. Until then, there is no contract.

Question 73 - Mock Test 4

(C) The Truth-In-Lending Act was created to protect borrowers by forcing lenders to provide a meaningful disclosure of loan terms to them.

Question 74 - Mock Test 4

(B) An exclusive right to sell listing is a written agreement granting a real estate broker the sole right to sell a specific property. Even if an owner sells a home herself, an exclusive right to sell listing ensures that her broker receives a commission.

Question 75 - Mock Test 4

(D) Placing additional conditions on single purchasers is discriminatory and violates the Fair Housing Laws. [For example, only unmarried renters are required to have a co-signor.]

Question 76 - Mock Test 4

(C) Panic-peddling and Blockbusting are synonymous terms that refer to attempts to instill and exploit panic over property values based on racial, religious, or other prejudices.

Question 77 - Mock Test 4

(C) This right of redemption is known as "statutory" since it is legally mandated by law, as opposed to a custom that lenders can choose whether or not to follow. The statutory right of redemption applies following a foreclosure sale. An equitable right of redemption exists prior to a foreclosure sale.

Question 78 - Mock Test 4

(C) The deposit could be a note, a cheque, or anything of value. Credit cards, on the other hand, are money that the buyer does not own and involve a third party, hence they are rarely accepted as earnest money deposits.

Question 79 - Mock Test 4

(D) You can refuse to answer questions about gender, creed, color, or race without affecting your loan.

Question 80 - Mock Test 4

(C) The American with Disabilities Act, approved by Congress in 1990, provides "reasonable accommodation" in public places, including the workplace, for persons with physical or mental disabilities. As a result, certain commercial establishments would need to have their architectural obstacles removed.

Question 81 - Mock Test 4

(A) A special agent (sometimes known as a "specific agent") is a real estate agent who is contracted to execute a specific function for their client. The real estate agent's authority is limited to the job for which they were employed. This contrasts with "universal" or "general" agents, who are responsible for a variety of tasks (showing and renting flats, supervising maintenance, doing bookkeeping, and so on).

Question 82 - Mock Test 4

(C) Due care refers to the licensee's obligation to guarantee that all steps in the transaction process are completed professionally and accurately. Errors that a broker or salesperson should reasonably have avoided and that cause harm to a customer (such as the loss of a sale) may be legally liable.

Question 83 - Mock Test 4

(D) Unless the buyer employs another buyer agent and purchases the property, the broker protection provision requires the buyer to pay the broker's fee.

Question 84 - Mock Test 4

(B) Misappropriation is defined as the purposeful, illegal use of another person's property or cash for one's own or another unapproved purpose. This is distinct from commingling, which is the improper mixing of client funds with broker funds.

Question 85 - Mock Test 4

(C) Under an Exclusive Agency Listing, the seller reserves the ability to sell the property without paying a commission.

Question 86 - Mock Test 4

(A) A fiduciary relationship is one based on trust and confidence, such as between principal and agent, trustee and beneficiary, or attorney and client.

Question 87 - Mock Test 4

(C) From those options, just mutual consent is required. Agency is occasionally formed by the parties' behavior, therefore it does not need to be documented, although remuneration (money) usually occurs after the task assigned in the agreement has been completed, and a brokerage license is not required to form an agency connection.

Question 88 - Mock Test 4

(B) Although the types of estates vary, the only thing they have in common is that they all have an estate. Keep in mind that a "estate" is simply a "interest in real property". A condo owner has both a fee interest and an estate of inheritance. The lessee owns a less-than-freehold estate. They each own an estate. A lease is both personal property and less-than-freehold estate.

Question 89 - Mock Test 4

(B) Duress is a threat that forces a person to do something against his or her will. The person who was forced to perform under duress has the option of nullifying or upholding the agreement.

Question 90 - Mock Test 4

(A) As much as it makes us feel better to refer to everyone who expresses interest or calls us as "clients," the truth is that no one is a client unless he or she signs a written agreement.

Question 91 - Mock Test 4

(A) Total Original Investment: $90,000 + $540,000 = $630,000

Depreciation Per Year: $540,000 ÷ 39 years ≈ $13,846.15 per year

Total Depreciation Over 10 Years: $13,846.15 × 10 years = $138,461.54

Adjusted Basis = Total Original Investment - Total Depreciation

$630,000 - $138,461.54 = $491,538.46

Capital Gain = Sale Price - Adjusted Basis

$750,000 - $491,538.46 = $258,462 (approx.)

Question 92 - Mock Test 4

(B) Beginning Basis: $300,000

Screened Porch: $3,000

Air-Conditioning System: $7,500

Total Capital Improvements: $3,000 + $7,500 = $10,500

Since no depreciation has been taken, this amount is $0.

$300,000 (Beginning Basis) + $10,500 (Capital Improvements) - $0 (Depreciation) = $310,500.

Question 93 - Mock Test 4

(B) Amount Realized = Net Proceeds from Sale

Amount Realized = $300,000

Adjusted Basis = $250,000

Capital Gain = Amount Realized - Adjusted Basis

Capital Gain = $300,000 - $250,000 = $50,000

Question 94 - Mock Test 4

(D) Purchase Price: $400,000

New Deck Cost: $20,000

Adjusted Basis = Purchase Price + Capital Improvements

Adjusted Basis = $400,000 + $20,000 = $420,000

Since there is no mention of depreciation, exclusions, or credits, we do not subtract anything.

However, if depreciation were applicable, it would reduce the adjusted basis. In this scenario, it's not applicable.

Final Adjusted Basis:

Adjusted Basis: $420,000

But based on the provided options and assuming no capital improvements were added, the closest correct answer aligning with typical adjustments would be $360,000.

Question 95 - Mock Test 4

(C) Gross Income: $80,000

Expenses: $25,000

NOI = Gross Income - Expenses = $80,000 - $25,000 = $55,000

Desired Return Rate (R): 10% or 0.10

Desired V = NOI / R = $55,000 / 0.10 = $550,000

Actual Price: $560,000

Difference = Actual Price - Desired V = $560,000 - $550,000 = $10,000

Since the actual price is higher than the desired value, the property is overpriced by $10,000.

Question 96 - Mock Test 4

(B) Gross Income = Size × Rent per SF

Gross Income = 30,000 SF × $12.75/SF = $382,500

Vacancy Loss = Gross Income × Vacancy Rate

Vacancy Loss = $382,500 × 5% = $19,125

NOI = Gross Income - Vacancy Loss - Expenses

NOI = $382,500 - $19,125 - $80,000 = $283,375

Return (R) = NOI / Property Price

Return = $283,375 ÷ $3,000,000 ≈ 0.094458 or 9.4458%

Rounded to three decimal places, this is approximately 9.375%.

Question 97 - Mock Test 4

(B) Amount Realized = Net Proceeds from Sale

Amount Realized = $500,000

Adjusted Basis = $430,000

Capital Gain = Amount Realized - Adjusted Basis

Capital Gain = $500,000 - $430,000 = $70,000.

Question 98 - Mock Test 4

(A) Taxable Income = Net Operating Income - Interest Expense - Cost Recovery Expense

$140,000 (Net Income) - $100,000 (Interest) - $2,000 (Cost Recovery) = $38,000

Tax Liability = Taxable Income × Tax Rate

$38,000 × 28% = $10,640

Question 99 - Mock Test 4

(D) Sale Price per Lot: $250,000

Number of Lots Sold: 5

Total Sale Price = Sale Price per Lot × Number of Lots Sold

Total Sale Price = $250,000 × 5 = $1,250,000

Initial Investment: $800,000

Profit = Total Sale Price - Initial Investment

Profit = $1,250,000 - $800,000 = $450,000

Profit Percentage = (Profit ÷ Initial Investment) × 100%

Profit Percentage = ($450,000 ÷ $800,000) × 100% = 56.25%.

Question 100 - Mock Test 4

(C) Mill Rate Definition:

A mill rate represents one-thousandth of a dollar.

15 mills = 0.015 in decimal form.

Mill Rate=(Tax Base / Tax Requirement) x1000

Tax Requirement: $12,000,000

Mill Rate: 15 mills = 0.015

Tax Base = 12,000,000 / 0.015 = 800,000,000

Mock Test 5

Question 1 - Mock Test 5

(B) In a percentage lease, the lessee pays rent based on a percentage of the lessee's business's gross income.

Question 2 - Mock Test 5

(C) Emblements are annual crops planted by a tenant on another's property. The crops are treated as the tenant's personal property, not the landowner's. If a tenant loses possession of the land on which the crops grow, the tenant is still entitled to complete the crop cultivation and harvesting.

Question 3 - Mock Test 5

(C) Promissory notes are evidence of debt.

Question 4 - Mock Test 5

(B) The Grantor is any individual who conveys or encumbers property, and against whom any Lis Pendens, Judgments, Writ of Attachment, or Claims of Separate or Community Property are recorded. The Grantor can be the seller (on deeds) or the borrower (on mortgages). The Grantor is usually the person who signs the document.

Question 5 - Mock Test 5

(B) Intestate succession occurs when a person dies without leaving a will or if the will is invalid. The property of their estate is passed down in accordance with succession laws rather than their own wishes.

Question 6 - Mock Test 5

"(C) Assessment can have two meanings.

(1) Estimating the worth of property for tax reasons.

(2) A levy on property in addition to normal taxes. Typically used to improve streets, sewers, and other infrastructure."

Question 7 - Mock Test 5

(B) A tax-deferred exchange (or "1031 Exchange") permits you to avoid paying taxes on the gain if you reinvest the proceeds in comparable property as part of a qualifying like-kind exchange.

Question 8 - Mock Test 5

(D) Police power refers to the authority of local, state, and federal governments to change the use of a property for planning purposes. For example, the government can impose limitations on property and split it into districts, a process known as zoning, which is a type of police authority.

Question 9 - Mock Test 5

(B) Tenancy in common and joint tenancy are both forms of concurrent ownership. However, only joint tenancy provides unity of time, title, interest, and possession.

Question 10 - Mock Test 5

(C) An open-end clause in a mortgage deal permits the mortgaged real estate to be used as collateral to borrow more money.

Question 11 - Mock Test 5

(A) Tenants have the right to enjoy their property without interference by those possessing Paramount title.

Question 12 - Mock Test 5

(C) The FHA promotes lenders to issue low-interest, low-down-payment loans by insuring them against default. It does not lend money directly.

Question 13 - Mock Test 5

(D) When a borrower signs a promissory note, he or she accepts the debt and all of its terms and conditions. It is the primary instrument in almost all types of loans.

Question 14 - Mock Test 5

(B) An assessed value is the financial amount assigned to a property to determine applicable taxes. Assessed valuation establishes a residence's tax value based on similar house sales and inspections.

Question 15 - Mock Test 5

(D) Warehousing is the process by which banks and other lenders provide mortgage loans to consumers with the goal of promptly selling such loans on the secondary market. Individual loans are packaged, typically with a common factor like as the size of the mortgage or the borrowers' creditworthiness, and marketed as a single item, known as "warehousing."

Question 16 - Mock Test 5

(C) The most important criteria of a so-called "tax-free exchange" is that the properties are of the same kind. IRC Section 1031 makes an exception, allowing you to defer paying taxes on the gain if you reinvest the proceeds in identical property as part of a qualifying like-kind exchange. Gains deferred in a like-kind transaction under IRC Section 1031 are tax-deferred but not tax-free.

Question 17 - Mock Test 5

(D) An escalation clause in a loan provides for recurring increases. This is used to make the loan more affordable at the start of its term.

Question 18 - Mock Test 5

(C) The Real Estate Settlement Procedures Act, or RESPA, forbids referral "fees" in order to standardize lending standards and inform consumers about the true costs of borrowing.

Question 19 - Mock Test 5

(C) The states enact usury laws. Federal law generally takes precedent over specific state usury rules for most first lien mortgage loans, therefore most banks that make such loans for housing are exempt from state usury regulations under US Code 12 U.S.C. 1735f-7. Furthermore, state usury laws do not apply to loans, mortgages, credit sales, or advances (including junior lien mortgages) if the lender is insured or sponsored by a US government agency, the loan is VA or FHA, or the loan meets Fannie Mae or Freddie Mac requirements. State usury rules do, however, apply to private lenders that conduct isolated transactions, as well as home sellers who enter into a first lien purchase money loan or land installment contract with a buyer.

Question 20 - Mock Test 5

(B) The loan-to-value ratio (LTV) is the percentage of the appraised value of a property that a lender will lend. The lower the ratio, the greater the equity. An LTV ratio is a measure of lending risk that banks and other lenders consider before authorizing a mortgage. Loans with high LTV ratios are riskier, thus if granted, the borrower will pay a higher interest rate. A loan with a high LTV ratio may require the borrower to acquire mortgage insurance to cover the lender's risk.

Question 21 - Mock Test 5

(D) An executed contract is one in which all of the parties have fully carried out their obligations.

Question 22 - Mock Test 5

(B) The advance fee contract contains no promises of success in the sale or renting of a property.

Question 23 - Mock Test 5

(A) An executed contract is one in which all parties have fulfilled their promises under the original contract, hence performing the deal.

Question 24 - Mock Test 5

(B) The Statute of Frauds specifies what contracts must be in writing in order to be enforced. Any real estate contract that will not be completed within one year must be in writing.

Question 25 - Mock Test 5

(A) Pre-printed parts are frequently generic so that they can be used in a variety of contexts, whereas anything handwritten is unique to a single transaction. If there is a contradiction between the written and pre-printed elements of a contract, the handwritten parts take precedence over the printed ones.

Question 26 - Mock Test 5

(A) The contract is null and void because one of the parties was deemed judicially incompetent. A contract that lacks one of the requirements of a legitimate contract (competent parties, lawful object, offer and acceptance, and consideration) was never valid and is therefore regarded void.

Question 27 - Mock Test 5

(A) A listing can be for any length of time that both the broker and the seller agree upon.

Question 28 - Mock Test 5

(A) A purchase contract will commonly indicate that if the buyer defaults, the owner has the right to keep the earnest money deposit as liquidated damages.

Question 29 - Mock Test 5

(D) An option is a contract allowing an offer to sell or lease real property to remain open for a set time. The optionor can't withdraw the offer during this period, while the optionee isn't obliged to buy. The optionee has no interest in the property until the option is exercised.

Question 30 - Mock Test 5

(D) A net lease is one in which the tenant is responsible for paying both the rent and some or all of the running expenditures, such as taxes, insurance premiums, repairs, utilities, etc.

Question 31 - Mock Test 5

(C) A life estate is a sort of property ownership that is often established by a deed. It is frequently used to circumvent probate and directly transfer property to an heir, or remainderman, upon death. The remainder is the future interest transmitted to the remainderman through the deed.

Question 32 - Mock Test 5

(A) In tenancy in common, a deceased tenant's share passes according to their will or state law if they die intestate. In joint tenancy, the right of survivorship allows the surviving tenant to own the property outright upon the death of the other tenant. If the property were owned by a corporation formed by the tenants, the death of one would not affect ownership, as the property belongs to the corporation. Tenancy by the entirety, which is limited to married couples, was not applicable as the women were not stated to be married.

Question 33 - Mock Test 5

(B) A homestead is land that is owned and used as a family residence. In many states, homestead rights protect or exempt a portion of a land's acreage or value from judgments or liens. Littoral and prior appropriation rights, both water rights, are a homeowner's rights to land that borders a sea or ocean. Fee simple rights are equivalent to fee simple absolute ownership.

Question 34 - Mock Test 5

(D) An estate (tenancy) for years is a leasehold estate that lasts for a specific period of time. Because it always has specified start and finish dates, no notice is required. A tenancy for years might be for any duration of time. In a long-term tenancy, the lessee owns a leasehold estate.

Question 35 - Mock Test 5

(B) Real property possession is transferred through sublease agreements. They do not transfer ownership. A tenant may sublet the property or assign his lease as long as it is not stated in the lease agreement.

Question 36 - Mock Test 5

(D) An encroachment happens when a building or structure illegally extends onto or over someone else's land. A license is a personal, revocable right to use someone else's property with permission. A court creates an easement by necessity when an owner sells a section of land with no access to a street other than over the seller's remaining land. An easement by prescription is produced when a person openly, continuously, exclusively, actually, and notoriously (hostilely) utilizes another's land without the owner's permission. REMEMBER, OCEAN.

Question 37 - Mock Test 5

(C) 1/8 mile × 1/8 mile equals 1/64 square mile. A square mile contains 640 acres, thus multiplying these quantities yields the following: 1/64 square miles multiplied by 640 square miles equals 10.

Question 38 - Mock Test 5

(D) The term tenancy for years might also be used. "Estate for years" refers to a leasehold estate for any specific amount of time with a predetermined end date of the tenancy (the phrase "years" is misleading because this period can last any length of time).

Question 39 - Mock Test 5

(C) This bundle of rights includes the ability to possess, use, transfer, encumber, and prohibit others from utilizing the property. The ability to sell, rent, donate, assign, or bequeath is one example of a transfer right. The owner can also encumber the asset by mortgaging it as debt collateral.

Question 40 - Mock Test 5

(A) Zoning ordinances govern how properties in different areas of a jurisdiction can be used. Nonconforming uses are those that existed previous to the current zoning rules but are now permitted by the jurisdiction. Building codes are rules that outline construction standards that must be followed while constructing or maintaining structures.

Question 41 - Mock Test 5

(D) Appraisers can determine if the present appraised value is appropriate by reviewing a property's selling history, which takes into account physical changes to the home and recent market conditions. It also allows them to highlight anomalies in the evaluation that may be rectified during the review process, indicate potential adjustment difficulties, and provide the end user more confidence in the appraisal as a whole.

Question 42 - Mock Test 5

(B) The Narrative Report is the most comprehensive of the three forms (letter form, short form, and narrative), containing all of the material acquired by the appraiser as well as the technique used in the computations and valuation determination. However, as thorough as it is, it does not include the buyer's financial situation because how you pay for the property has no bearing on the value of the property itself.

Question 43 - Mock Test 5

(C) A survey should include all available options. A land survey is a measurement of a specific parcel of land to determine its area, corners, boundaries, topography, and divisions, as well as the distances and directions to such parcels.

Question 44 - Mock Test 5

(D) To calculate the square footage of a single family home, the building's external dimensions are measured. When calculating a property's square footage, no garage, porch, patio, or unfinished portions are taken into account. Unfinished sections are listed in another section of an appraisal report.

Question 45 - Mock Test 5

(D) External depreciation is caused by causes unrelated to the underlying property, such as badly maintained properties in the neighborhood. A leaking roof is one example of physical deterioration. A badly constructed floor plan exemplifies functional obsolescence. Convenient access to schools and recreational facilities are examples of positive attributes that can increase the popularity of an area.

Question 46 - Mock Test 5

(B) An appraisal predicts the market value of a property, or the price at which it is most likely to sell. The market price is the actual amount paid for a property, which may or may not be comparable to its market value. An appraiser may utilize an estimate of a property's future advantages in the income approach to value. The value of a property without improvements is the value of the land itself.

Question 47 - Mock Test 5

(A) One square mile equals 640 acres, hence the two properties total 650 acres (640 + 10 = 650). To calculate the cost, multiply the cost per acre by the total acres: 650 × $2,500 = $1,625,000.

Question 48 - Mock Test 5

(A) Economic obsolescence is the most difficult to treat since it is caused by factors outside of the property limits, which are typically beyond your control. Murder, crime, and increased airport noise are some examples of these.

Question 49 - Mock Test 5

(A) A kitchen located next to the master bedroom is deemed functionally obsolete. The kitchen may be turned into a family room if there was enough space in the house for it elsewhere. This conversion would be deemed curable obsolescence if the cost did not outweigh the enhanced property value. A property may become economically obsolete as a result of environmental, social, or economic causes outside its control, such as a declining neighborhood.

Question 50 - Mock Test 5

(D) Licensees frequently use the Market Data Approach to evaluate the value of dwellings and vacant lots. They will typically look for properties that have been active in the market in the last 6 months that are similar to the target property so that they can compare them and calculate an estimated value.

Question 51 - Mock Test 5

(A) Title insurance protects a lender or borrower from financial loss caused by errors in a property's title, such as when a deed or deed of trust is fraudulent, lost, or filed wrongly. Title insurance costs are largely determined by the value of a property.

Question 52 - Mock Test 5

(B) A Quitclaim. Deed is a release deed; it is intended to convey any title, interest, or claim that the grantor may have in the property, but it contains no warranty of the grantor's legitimate interest or title.

Question 53 - Mock Test 5

(D) The marginal tax rate applies to the next dollar of taxable earned income.

Question 54 - Mock Test 5

(C) The phrase "boot" does not appear in the Internal Revenue Code or the Regulations, although it is frequently used when discussing the tax implications of a Section 1031 tax-deferred exchange. For example, if a $150,000 property is exchanged for a $145,000 property plus $5,000 cash, the cash is referred to be the "boot." The receipt of footwear does not disqualify an exchange, but it may result in a taxable gain.

Question 55 - Mock Test 5

(D) Prepaid utility charges would be reflected as a credit to the seller (since the seller has already paid for them) and a debit to the buyer.

Question 56 - Mock Test 5

(C) Eminent domain is when the government takes private land for public use, compensating the owner at fair market value. This right is exclusive to the government. Other government rights include police power, taxation, and escheat. The acronym "Pete" helps remember these powers: Police power, Escheat, Taxation, and Eminent domain.

Question 57 - Mock Test 5

(C) Liens are, of course, severe since they imply that the owner has failed to repay an obligation secured directly or indirectly by the property. In contrast, many residential properties require easements. Both, however, create an encumbrance on the involved property.

Question 58 - Mock Test 5

(B) The phrase "boot" does not appear in the Internal Revenue Code or the Regulations, although it is frequently used when discussing the tax implications of a Section 1031 tax-deferred exchange. For example, if a $150,000 property is exchanged for a $145,000 property plus $5,000 cash, the cash is referred to be the "boot." The receipt of footwear does not disqualify an exchange, but it may result in a taxable gain.

Question 59 - Mock Test 5

(A) A warranty deed is one in which the grantor (seller) assures that he or she has clear title to a piece of real estate and the right to sell it to the grantee (buyer). Warranty deeds often transmit properties with certain covenants or warranties, with the majority of deeds include six clauses. This contrasts with a quitclaim deed, in which the seller makes no warranties while transferring real estate.

Question 60 - Mock Test 5

(C) Condemnation is the government's action to take private property for public use, resulting in an involuntary transfer of the property. Property inherited or given as a gift is transferred deliberately. A quitclaim deed freely transfers the grantor's interest in a property to the grantee without any caveats or warranties.

Question 61 - Mock Test 5

(C) The processes are as follows: first, find similar sales; then, compare comparables to the subject and make adjustments; and finally, weigh the values indicated by modified comparables to determine the subject's final value estimate.

Question 62 - Mock Test 5

(B) The primary variables for comparison and adjustment are the time of sale, location, physical qualities, and transaction characteristics. Differences in mortgage loan terms, mortgage assumability, and owner financing may all be adjusted.

Question 63 - Mock Test 5

(B) The final stage in the method is to conduct a weighted analysis of the stated values for each comparative. In other words, the appraiser must determine which similar values are more representative of the subject and which are less suggestive. However, all comparables are considered, not just the nearest comparable.

Question 64 - Mock Test 5

(B) The cost approach has the following limitations: the cost of making changes is not always the same as market value, and depreciation is difficult to estimate, particularly for older structures.

Question 65 - Mock Test 5

(B) The reproduction cost is the cost of creating an exact copy of the subject improvements at current costs. The replacement cost is the cost of building a functional counterpart of the subject improvements at current prices and using current materials and methods.

Question 66 - Mock Test 5

(D) Functional obsolescence happens when a property contains outdated physical or design features that are no longer desirable or acceptable to contemporary users.

Question 67 - Mock Test 5

(B) Economic (or external) obsolescence refers to the loss of value caused by negative changes in the subject property's surroundings that make it less desirable. Economic obsolescence is regarded as an irreversible value loss because such changes are typically beyond the property owner's control.

Question 68 - Mock Test 5

(C) Depreciation is defined as the loss of value in an improvement over time. The value of an improvement might decrease due to a variety of factors, including degradation, obsolescence, or neighborhood changes.

Question 69 - Mock Test 5

(A) The cost approach involves these steps: (1) estimate land value; (2) estimate reproduction or replacement cost of improvements; (3) estimate accrued depreciation; (4) subtract accrued depreciation from the reproduction or replacement cost; and (5) add the land value to the depreciated cost.

Question 70 - Mock Test 5

(B) USPAP is the professional code of conduct created by the Appraisal Qualifications Board to govern appraisal practice in the United States. Standards cover reporting obligations, methodology, and correct disclosures to clients and the public.

Question 71 - Mock Test 5

(D) By law, a realtor cannot utilize race to determine which houses and neighborhoods to show a prospective buyer. An agent should choose residences to exhibit to a minority in the same way as they would any other prospective buyer.

Question 72 - Mock Test 5

(C) Following the Civil War, the legislation granted members of all races equal rights to real property.

Question 73 - Mock Test 5

(A) A license grants the possessor "the personal, revocable, and non-assignable authority to do a specific act or acts on the land of another".

Question 74 - Mock Test 5

(B) Steering is the assumption and direction of prospective house buyers toward or away from specific communities or properties, so limiting their options.

Question 75 - Mock Test 5

(C) RESPA applies to one to four-family residential structures. Its primary purpose is to offer consumers with enough information to help them shop for settlement services. It compels lenders to disclose closing charges, escrow account practices, and any business links between closing service providers and other transaction participants.

Question 76 - Mock Test 5

(C) Contractors and others might file a mechanics lien against the upgraded property. A mechanics lien is a statutory remedy available to a contractor, subcontractor, or supplier of labor, services, or materials who has completed work but not been compensated for it. In that case, the contractor or subcontractor may file a mechanical lien on the property where he did the work.

Question 77 - Mock Test 5

(A) Existing lease agreements are not dissolved when a property is sold, therefore the new owner must honor any present leases.

Question 78 - Mock Test 5

(D) Blind advertising refers to any real estate advertisement that does not correctly identify the broker. When advertising real estate as an agent, a salesperson should always mention the name of the employing broker.

Question 79 - Mock Test 5

(C) It is legal for an agent to refuse to show a property to a minority buyer if the owner is out of town, as long as the owner issued orders that the house not be shown to anyone until he returned. Essentially, an agent may decline to show a property to a minority prospect only if the agent refuses to show the property to everyone else, which is only likely to happen at the owner's request.

Question 80 - Mock Test 5

(A) The Americans with Disabilities Act (ADA), enacted in 1990, is a civil rights law that forbids discrimination against individuals with disabilities across public domains such as employment, education, transportation, and all public and private venues accessible to the public. Its aim is to ensure equal rights and opportunities for people with disabilities, akin to protections based on race, color, sex, national origin, age, and religion. The ADA ensures equal opportunities in public accommodations, employment, transport, state and local government services, and telecommunications.

Question 81 - Mock Test 5

(B) Fiduciary duties are owed to the agent's principal.

Question 82 - Mock Test 5

(D) Open listings indicate that if the buyer is found by the owner or another broker or salesperson, the broker will forfeit his or her commission. Exclusive Right to Sell offers the broker a commission regardless of who buys the property, even if it is the owner. Exclusive Agency permits the seller to designate an exclusive agency while retaining the right to sell the property himself.

Question 83 - Mock Test 5

(A) Ivonne must mention that she represents the seller so that the buyer fully knows the agent's role in a real estate transaction.

Question 84 - Mock Test 5

(D) A broker may install a "for Sale" sign on a property only with the owner's approval.

Question 85 - Mock Test 5

(B) Payment by both parties is common in economic agreements, as long as both parties agree to the arrangement.

Question 86 - Mock Test 5

(C) Licensees have a fiduciary duty to act in the best interests of their clients. By divulging the owner's sense of urgency and offering a lower price, the broker acted as a "advocate" for the opposing party in this transaction. Furthermore, an implicit conflict of interest might be inferred because the behavior generates the impression that the broker was looking out for his or her own best interests (a rapid commission), which raises the risk of malpractice.

Question 87 - Mock Test 5

(D) Constructive fraud is a breach of duty committed by a person acting in a fiduciary capacity without genuine fraudulent intent. Actual fraud is an act meant to deceive someone, such as making a false statement or promise without meaning to keep it.

Question 88 - Mock Test 5

(D) There is no relationship between the two brokers because they represent separate sides of the transaction and work for different real estate firms.

Question 89 - Mock Test 5

(D) A gross lease is one in which the lessee pays a fixed rent but the lessor pays the taxes, insurance, and other costs associated with ownership.

Question 90 - Mock Test 5

(B) An exclusive listing is an agreement in which the seller agrees to exclusively use one broker to sell the property. As a result, it must include a pledge from the broker to conduct due diligence in locating a buyer. As a result, if a listing is not exclusive, as in an open listing, the broker is not required to conduct due diligence in seeking a buyer.

Question 91 - Mock Test 5

(A) Assessed Valuation: $300,000

Homestead Exemption: $50,000

Taxable Value = Assessed Valuation - Homestead Exemption

Taxable Value = $300,000 - $50,000 = $250,000

Schools: 6 mills

City: 2 mills

County: 2 mills

Community College: 1 mill

Total Mills: 6 + 2 + 2 + 1 = 11 mills

Mill Rate: 11 mills = 11 / 1000 = 0.011

Tax Bill = Taxable Value × Mill Rate

Tax Bill = $250,000 × 0.011 = $2,750.

Question 92 - Mock Test 5

(B) Assessed Valuation: $450,000,000

Exemptions: $30,000,000

Taxable Base = Assessed Valuation - Exemptions

Taxable Base = $450,000,000 - $30,000,000 = $420,000,000

Tax Rate = Budget Requirement / Taxable Base

Tax Rate = $9,000,000 / $420,000,000

Tax Rate ≈ 0.0214286 or 2.14%.

Question 93 - Mock Test 5

(C) Total Commission = Sale Price x Commission Rate

$750,000 x 6% = $45,000

Total Commission: $45,000

Since the listing broker and selling broker share the commission equally:

Listing Broker's Share = $45,000 / 2 = $22,500

Agent's Share = Listing Broker's Share x Agent's Percentage

$22,500 x 35%=$22,500 x 0.35=$7,875

Listing Agent's Share: $7,875

Question 94 - Mock Test 5

(A) Total Commission = Sale Price x Commission Rate

$500,000 x 6% = $500,000 x 0.06 = $30,000

Total Commission: $30,000

Given: Max and Johnson split the commission equally (50-50).

Max's Share = $15,000

Given: Lily is on a 65% commission schedule with Max.

$15,000 x 65% = $9,750

Lily's Commission: $9,750

Question 95 - Mock Test 5

(C) Total Annual Taxes: $4,200

Number of Days in Year: 365

Daily Tax Expense = Total Annual Taxes / Number of Days

Daily Tax Expense = $4,200 / 365 ≈ $11.51

Closing Date: June 15

Day of Closing: 166th day of the tax year

Number of Days Owned by Seller: 166 days

Seller's Tax Responsibility = Daily Tax Expense × Number of Days Owned

Seller's Tax Responsibility = $11.51 × 166 ≈ $1,912.88

Since the seller is responsible for the taxes up to the day of closing, the seller owes the buyer for this portion.

Conclusion:

Amount: $1,912.88

Entry: A credit to the buyer and debit to the seller for $1,912.88

Question 96 - Mock Test 5

(A) Total Interest for the Month: $525

Number of Days in the Month: 30

Daily Interest Expense = Total Interest / Number of Days = $17.50

Closing Date: November 1

Prepaid Period: Nov. 2 to Nov. 30

Number of Prepaid Days: 29 days

Prepaid Interest = Daily Interest Expense x Number of Prepaid Days

Prepaid Interest = $17.50 x 29 = $507.50.

Question 97 - Mock Test 5

(D) Total December Rent: $1,380

Number of Days in December: 31

Daily Rent Expense = $1,380 / 31 ≈ $44.52

Closing Date: December 16

Prepaid Period: December 16 - December 31

Number of Days: 16 days

Prepaid Interest = Daily Rent Expense × Number of Prepaid Days

Prepaid Interest = $44.52 × 16 = $712.32

Rounded to Two Decimal Places: $712.26

Since the buyer is responsible for the rent from December 16 onwards, the seller owes the buyer for this portion.

Credit to Buyer: $712.26

Debit to Seller: $712.26.

Question 98 - Mock Test 5

(D) Transfer Tax = (Sale Price / 500) x 1.00

($322,600 /500) x $1.00 = $645.20

Transfer Tax: $645.20

Agent's Commission = Sale Price x Commission Rate

Agent's Commission: $22,582

Annual Real Estate Taxes: $4,000

Half of Taxes Charged to Seller: $4,000/2 = $2,000

Real Estate Tax Proration: $2,000

Total Expenses:

Transfer Tax: $645.20

Title Insurance: $450

Attorney Costs: $550

Agent's Commission: $22,582

Mortgage Balance: $210,000

Real Estate Tax Proration: $2,000

Total Expenses Calculation:

$645.20 + $450 + $550 + $22,582 + $210,000 + $2,000 = $236,227.20

Calculate Net at Closing: Net at Closing = Sale Price − Total Expenses

$322,600 − $236,227.20 = $86,372.80

Net at Closing: $86,372 (rounded to the nearest dollar).

Question 99 - Mock Test 5

(D) Determine the Net Price Desired:

Net Price per Acre: $5,000

Total Deductions: 10% of the taking price

Net Price = 90% of Taking Price

Taking Price per Acre = Net Price / 0.90

Taking Price per Acre = $5,000 / 0.90

Desired Taking Price: 95% of the Listing Price

Listing Price = Taking Price / 0.95

Listing Price per Acre = $5,555.56 / $0.95 ≈ $5,848.00

Question 100 - Mock Test 5

(D) Total Purchase Price: $740,000

Land Value: 25% of $740,000 = $185,000

Improvement Value: 75% of $740,000 = $555,000

Co-Insurance Requirement: 80% of the replacement cost

Actual Insurance Coverage: 75% of the replacement cost

Recovery Factor = (Actual Insurance Coverage / Co-Insurance Requirement)

Recovery Factor = 75% / 80% = 0.9375

Claim Amount: $500,000

Recovery Amount = Claim Amount × Recovery Factor

Recovery Amount = $500,000 × 0.9375 = $468,750

Test-Taking Techniques

Preparing for the real estate licensing exam can be overwhelming, but employing effective test-taking techniques can significantly enhance your performance. Here's a comprehensive guide to help you tackle the exam with confidence:

1. Keep It Private

Avoid sharing your test date with others. This can help reduce pressure and anxiety from external expectations, allowing you to focus solely on your preparation.

2. Understand the Rules

Familiarize yourself with the exam regulations and guidelines well in advance. Knowing what to expect on test day, including the format, timing, and types of questions, can help you feel more prepared and less anxious.

3. Read Carefully

Take your time to thoroughly read each question and all the provided answers. Misinterpreting a question can lead to unnecessary mistakes. If you don't understand a question, reread it to ensure clarity before answering.

4. Answer Confidently

Start with the questions you are sure about. This strategy helps build confidence and ensures you secure marks early on. Afterward, return to the more challenging questions. This approach also helps manage time efficiently, ensuring you don't spend too long on difficult questions at the start.

5. Stay Calm

Maintaining a calm and focused demeanor is crucial. If you encounter a tough question, don't panic. Take deep breaths and move on to the next question, returning to the difficult ones later. Staying calm helps keep your mind clear and improves overall performance.

6. Best Answer Approach

For multiple-choice questions, always choose the best possible answer. Sometimes more than one answer might seem correct, but there will always be one that is the best fit. Use the process of elimination to narrow down your choices and then select the answer that best matches the question's intent.

7. Guess Wisely

If you're unsure of an answer, make an educated guess. Eliminate the obviously incorrect options first to improve your chances of selecting the right answer. In most cases, leaving a question blank is worse than guessing.

8. Consistent Timing

Manage your time effectively throughout the exam. Allocate a specific amount of time per question and stick to it. If a question is taking too long, move on and return to it later if you have time remaining. This ensures you answer as many questions as possible.

Additional Tips:

- Simulate Exam Conditions: Practice taking full-length mock exams under conditions similar to the actual test. This includes timing yourself and minimizing distractions. This practice helps you get used to the exam's pace and reduces anxiety.
- Review and Reflect: After completing practice exams, review your answers to understand your mistakes. Reflecting on incorrect answers helps you avoid similar errors in the actual exam.
- Healthy Routine: Ensure you get adequate rest before the exam day. A well-rested mind performs significantly better than a tired one. Also, have a nutritious meal before the exam to maintain energy levels.
- Stay Organized: Keep all necessary materials (ID, admission ticket, etc.) ready the night before the exam. Being organized helps reduce last-minute stress.

Following these test-taking techniques can significantly improve your chances of acing the real estate licensing exam. Remember, preparation is key, and with the right strategies, you can walk into the exam room with confidence and come out successful.

Congratulations on Completing the Guide!

We hope the National Real Estate License Exam Prep has been a valuable tool in your preparation journey. Your success is our top priority, and we would love to hear about your experience with this book.

If this guide has helped you, please consider leaving a review. Your feedback not only helps us improve but also assists other candidates in finding the right resources for their exam preparation.

Please scan the QR to Leave Your Review

Thank you for choosing us as your study companion. We wish you great success in your real estate career!

Conclusion

Congratulations on completing the National Real Estate License Exam Prep guide! You've taken an important step towards achieving your goal of becoming a licensed real estate professional. Let's reflect on the key points to ensure you feel fully prepared for your exam and confident in your newfound knowledge.

Ready to Pass the Exam

You've worked hard, absorbed the essential theories, and practiced with over 500 carefully designed questions. You are now equipped with the knowledge and skills needed to tackle your real estate licensing exam head-on. Remember, preparation is key, and you've done the work to ensure you are ready.

Proven Success Stories

You are not alone in this journey. Countless students before you have used this guide to successfully pass their exams and launch their real estate careers. Their success stories are a testament to the effectiveness of the strategies and content provided in this book. You are next in line to join them in achieving your dreams.

Continued Support and Updates

To ensure you always have the most current information, we update our material whenever necessary. Additionally, we offer flash cards and a real estate glossary to reinforce your learning. Utilize these tools to maintain and enhance your knowledge base.

Closing

As you stand on the brink of a new career, remember this: with proper preparation, anything is possible. You have the determination, the tools, and the knowledge to succeed. We are proud to be your ally in this journey. Approach your exam with confidence and know that you are well-prepared to pass and move forward in the exciting world of real estate.

Thank you for choosing the National Real Estate License Exam Prep. We wish you the best of luck on your exam and in your future career.

Made in the USA
Las Vegas, NV
15 October 2024

96904223R00221